Swift
by Tutorials

By the raywenderlich.com Tutorial Team

Colin Eberhardt & Matt Galloway

Swift by Tutorials

Colin Eberhardt, Matt Galloway

Copyright ©2014 Razeware LLC.

Notice of Rights

All rights reserved. No part of this book or corresponding materials (such as text, images, or source code) may be reproduced or distributed by any means without prior written permission of the copyright owner.

Notice of Liability

This book and all corresponding materials (such as source code) are provided on an "as is" basis, without warranty of any kind, express or implied, including but not limited to the warranties of merchantability, fitness for a particular purpose, and noninfringement. In no event shall the authors or copyright holders be liable for any claim, damages or other liability, whether in action of contract, tort or otherwise, arising from, out of or in connec- tion with the software or the use or other dealings in the software.

Trademarks

All trademarks and registered trademarks appearing in this book are the property of their respective owners.

ISBN: 978-0-9896751-8-5

Table of Contents:

Introduction 9
    About this book 9
    What you need 10
    Who this book is for 10
    How to use this book 11
    What's in store 12
    Book source code and forums 13
    PDF Version 13
    License 13
    About the authors 14
    About the editors 15

Chapter 1: Language Basics I 17
    Getting started 17
    Variables, constants and strings 19
    Semicolons 23
    Numeric types and conversion 24
    Booleans 26
    Tuples 27
    String interpolation 29
    Control flow 30
    Where to go from here? 36

Chapter 2: Language Basics II 37
    Optionals 37
    Collections 43
    Where to go from here? 49

Chapter 3: Classes and Structs 51
    Getting started 51

    My first class... 53
    Swift and MapKit... 63
    Polymorphism.. 70
    Adding annotations.. 73
    Sorting an array.. 76
    Equality and operator overload 78
    Access Control 82
    Where to go from here?... 84

Chapter 4: Generics 85
    Introducing generics 85
    Generics in action 87
    Ordered dictionaries 87
    Aside: Assertions & preconditions................................ 96
    Adding image search... 99
    Generic functions and protocols 105
    Where to go from here?... 109

Chapter 5: Functions and Closures................ 111
    Functions.. 111
    Methods.. 127
    Closures 131
    Where to go from here?... 141

Chapter 6: Enums and Switch Statements 143
    Basic enumerations.. 143
    Switch statements.. 147
    Associated values 149
    Enums as types 153
    Optionals are enums 156
    JSON parsing using enums 157
    Where to go from here?... 162

Chapter 7: Functional Programming 163
Simple array filtering 164
Reducing 167
Building an index..172
Partial application and currying 179
Where to go from here? 185

Chapter 8: Swift and Cocoa 187
Getting started 187
Bridging Swift and Objective-C 191
Adding the UI 194
Fetching data 202
Selectors 212
Protocols and delegates 214
Where to go from here? 223

Chapter 9: Swift vs. Objective-C 225
Getting started 226
Modeling the playing board 226
Additional game state 232
Visualizing the board 234
Views within views 235
Adding user interaction 238
Adding the game logic 241
Handling tap gestures..242
Detailed game logic 244
Keeping score 251
Adding UI flair 254
Handling the end-game 256
Adding a computer opponent.................................259
Challenge...264

Chapter 10: Swift Language Quick Reference .. 265
Language basics 266
Basic control structures 267
Tuples 268
Arrays 269
Dictionaries 270
Optionals 271
Implicitly unwrapped optionals 272
Switch 273
Enums 274
Functions 275
Closures 276
Classes and protocols 277

Conclusion 279

Dedications

"To my lovely wife, Susan, and children,
Jessica, Lauren, Abbie and William."

–Colin Eberhardt

"To my family and friends
for all their encouragement and support."

–Matt Galloway

Introduction

By Matt Galloway

At WWDC 2014, Apple introduced the shiny, new Swift language. Swift brings concise syntax, type safety and modern programming language features to Mac and iOS developers. The Apple developer community has responded with great excitement and adoption is growing rapidly.

From OS X to iOS, from Macs to iPhones to watches, and from command-line scripts to playgrounds — Swift is the way of the future for developing on Apple's platforms.

This book focuses on using Swift to write iOS applications. However, the language fundamentals you'll learn are also applicable to development on any other Swift platform.

About this book

There are three main differences between this book and the other Swift books out there:

1. First, this book teaches through **hands-on tutorials**. We believe you learn best by doing things yourself, so we encourage you to type along with the exercises in this book.

    In some chapters, you'll write full-fledged iOS applications. In other chapters, you'll code within playgrounds, which are easy and lightweight environments in which to test code, without the complexity of a complete application.

2. Second, this book has a **real-world, practical focus**. We've done our best to provide real-life use cases for each Swift feature, making it easy to see how you can put what you learn into practice in real apps. In addition, this book goes into topics beyond the

core of the language, such as using Cocoa APIs in Swift, and functional programming techniques.

3. Finally, this book is **short and concise**. This book is for developers who already have some level of programming experience and who want to get up-to-speed with Swift for iOS development quickly.

If you don't have prior programming experience, we recommend that you first read the *iOS Apprentice*, which is our book for complete beginners to iOS development and programming in general—and which is fully up-to-date with Swift!

We hope you enjoy learning Swift with us!

What you need

To follow along with the tutorials in this book, you need the following:

- **A Mac running OS X Mavericks (10.9) or later**, with the latest point release and security patches installed. This is so you can install the latest version of the required development tool: Xcode.

- **Xcode 6 or later**. Xcode is the main development tool for iOS. You need Xcode 6 at a minimum, since that's the first version that supports Swift. You can download the latest version of Xcode for free from the Mac App Store, here: https://itunes.apple.com/app/xcode/id497799835

If you don't have the latest version of Xcode installed, be sure to do that before continuing with the book.

Who this book is for

Swift being a brand new language introduces an exciting opportunity. It's a perfect time to start learning no matter your programming background.

As mentioned earlier, you do need some programming experience to make the most of this book, but you don't necessarily need Objective-C experience.

If you have Objective-C experience, then you'll be more comfortable with the Cocoa aspects of the book. If this is the case for you, then you'll be particularly interested in the chapter, "Swift vs. Objective-C."

If you don't have Objective-C experience, don't worry—you can still complete this book! You may find the Cocoa aspects a bit hazy, but each project is presented in step-by-step format, so you'll be able to follow along and will learn just as much about the Swift language.

How to use this book

There are two paths through this book, and which is best for you depends on how much Swift experience you have already.

If you are completely new to Swift

The first two chapters of this book cover language basics and are essential reading. They introduce important features that you'll use throughout the book.

We recommend you read chapters 3 through 7 in order to make the most of them, but you can skip around if there are topics that are already familiar to you.

You would do best to read Chapters 8 and 9 at the end, as they pull together everything taught in the previous chapters.

Chapter 10 is a language quick reference that will be forever valuable in your Swift programming career. It will come in handy when you need a look at some example code to refresh your memory on syntax or usage.

If you've read Apple's Swift book

If you've read Apple's Swift book or have equivalent knowledge, then you can probably safely skip Chapters 1–3.

If you feel like you need some review, we recommend performing a quick read of Chapters 4–6 covering generics, functions and closures, and enums and switch statements. These chapters go into more detailed examples than the earlier ones and you will likely learn a thing or two along the way.

The most important chapters for you to read are Chapters 7–9 covering functional programming, Swift and Cocoa, and Swift versus Objective-C. These are topics that Apple's Swift book doesn't cover, but that are essential knowledge for practical Swift development.

What's in store

Here's a more detailed look at each chapter in the book.

1. **Chapter 1, Language Basics 1**: Variables, constants, types, equality, strings, control flow and more—get off the ground with the language essentials.

2. **Chapter 2, Language Basics 2**: Optionals and collections: more essentials that you'll use in everyday Swift code.

3. **Chapter 3, Classes & Structs**: Data structures like classes and structs are at the heart of any object-oriented language. This is the first chapter where you'll build a full-featured iOS app.

4. **Chapter 4, Generics**: In C++ it's called templates; in Swift it's called generics: Generic programming allows you to write an algorithm once and reuse it for multiple types. In this chapter, you'll learn about generics by building a Flickr searching app.

5. **Chapter 5, Functions & Closures**: It's hard to write code without using functions! Closures are a related topic. (Spoiler alert—in Swift, they're just unnamed functions!)

6. **Chapter 6, Enums & Switch Statements**: Swift introduces extremely powerful enum types. Switch statements are crucial to unlocking their potential.

7. **Chapter 7, Functional Programming**: Functional programming is a popular topic right now—quite a departure from more traditional, imperative programming. Swift builds this paradigm right into the core of the language.

8. **Chapter 8, Swift & Cocoa**: 90% of iOS development is interfacing with the Cocoa frameworks—this remains true. This chapter illustrates how you will work with Cocoa in Swift; you'll also see how bridging headers work so you can continue to use Objective-C code and libraries in Swift.

9. **Chapter 9, Swift vs. Objective-C**: Existing Objective-C developers will be wondering what's different with Swift, or how to do their favorite things using Swift. In this chapter, you'll re-implement an Objective-C app in Swift to compare and contrast the two languages.

10. **Chapter 10, Language Quick Reference**: As you're coding your own Swift applications, you can refer back to this reference to remind yourself how something works.

Book source code and forums

You can get the source code for the book here:

- http://www.raywenderlich.com/store/swift-by-tutorials/source-code

Some of the chapters also include starter projects or other required resources, and you'll definitely want to have these on hand as you go through the book.

We've set up an official forum for the book at http://www.raywenderlich.com/forums. This is a great place to ask any questions you have about the book or about developing apps with Swift, or to submit any errata you may find.

PDF Version

We also have a PDF version of this book available, which can be handy if you ever want to copy/paste code or search for a specific term through the book as you're developing.

And speaking of the PDF version, we have some good news!

Since you purchased the physical copy of this book, you are eligible to buy the PDF version at a significant discount if you would like (if you don't have it already). For more details, see this page:

- http://www.raywenderlich.com/store/swift-by-tutorials/upgrade

License

By purchasing *Swift by Tutorials*, you have the following license:

- You are allowed to use and/or modify the source code in *Swift by Tutorials* in as many apps as you want, with no attribution required.
- You are allowed to use and/or modify all art, images and designs that are included in *Swift by Tutorials* in as many apps as you want, but must include this attribution line somewhere inside your app: "Artwork/images/designs: from *Swift by Tutorials* book, available at http://www.raywenderlich.com".

- The source code included in *Swift by Tutorials* is for your personal use only. You are NOT allowed to distribute or sell the source code in *Swift by Tutorials* without prior authorization.

All materials provided with this book are provided on an "as is" basis, without warranty of any kind, express or implied, including but not limited to the warranties of merchantability, fitness for a particular purpose and non-infringement. In no event shall the authors or copyright holders be liable for any claim, damages or other liability, whether in an action of contract, tort or otherwise, arising from, out of or in connection with the software or the use or other dealings in the software.

All trademarks and registered trademarks appearing in this guide are the property of their respective owners.

About the authors

Matt Galloway is a software engineer and programming enthusiast who specializes is iOS app development. You'll find him on Twitter as @mattjgalloway. Be sure to check out his book, *Effective Objective-C 2.0* at http://www.effectiveobjc.com/.

Colin Eberhardt has been writing code for many years, covering a wide range of technologies and platforms. He is currently the CTO of ShinobiControls, creators of iOS charts and controls. When not writing code, you'll find him being a big kid with his four children!

About the editors

Erik Kerber is an iOS guy from Minneapolis. He has worked on everything from big company apps to "Made for iPhone" hearing aids and is currently a lead iOS developer at Target.

Outside of coding, he enjoys cramming as much outdoor activity into summer as he can—from running to road cycling to fishing. In the winter, he codes and patiently waits for summer.

Bradley C. Phillips was the first editor to come aboard at raywenderlich.com. He has worked as a journalist and previously directed the intelligence department of an investigative firm in New York City. Right now, Bradley works freelance and pursues his own projects. Contact him if you need a skilled and experienced editor for your blog, books or anything else.

Greg Heo is the newest member of the Razeware team and has been an editor for raywenderlich.com since 2012.

He has been nerding out with computers since the Commodore 64 era in the 80s and continues to this day on the web and on iOS. He likes caffeine, codes with two-space tabs and writes with semicolons.

Chapter 1: Language Basics I

By Colin Eberhardt

When learning any new language—whether spoken or written, human or machine—it helps to look first for those elements and patterns that are familiar to you from languages you already know. Programming languages, after all, share common ideas and influences.

Swift is no different, having been shaped by the likes of Objective-C, Rust, Haskell, C# and JavaScript. This book assumes that you already have some programming experience, and as a result, you will no doubt find the basic structure of Swift quite easy to follow.

The first two chapters of this book cover the basics of the Swift language and do so *swiftly* (pun intended). These two chapters aren't meant to form an exhaustive guide, but instead aim to "orient" you so that you can transition to Swift as quickly as possible.

Special attention is paid to readers who are already familiar with Objective-C, as you are probably in the majority. This chapter will highlight significant differences between the two languages and the benefits of using Swift. Thankfully, there are a great many of these!

It's time to dive in!

Getting started

Readers acquainted with the "by tutorials" style of our previous books know that our signature approach is learning-through-building, with tutorials that focus on creating apps with real-world value.

Because the first few chapters of this book concentrate on the basic elements of the language itself, building an app within each chapter isn't very practical. Fortunately, Apple has introduced a wholly new type of Xcode file ideally suited to this task: **playgrounds**.

Open Xcode, select **File\New Playground…**, select the iOS platform and save the file wherever you like:

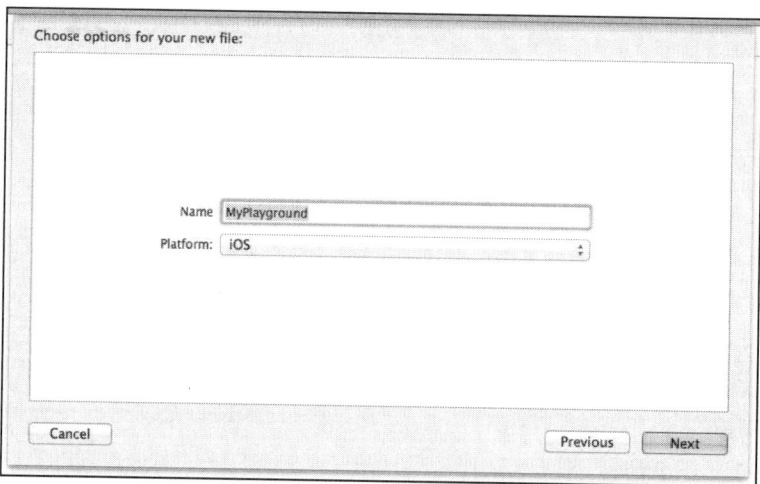

A playground is a single Swift file that the template populates as follows:

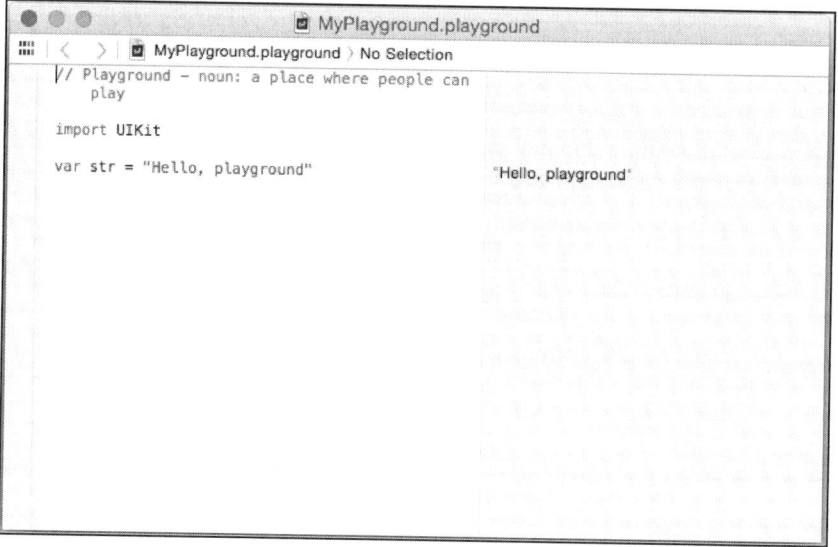

As you enter your Swift code on the left-hand side of the view, the right-hand side automatically displays the value of assignments and other useful hints about the resulting application state. You don't have to explicitly invoke a Build command after making a change. In a playground, Xcode continually builds and executes your code as you type.

Wouldn't a playground be an excellent place to practice your Swift skills?

You'll meet the various features of the playground as you need them. For now, you're ready to start learning Swift.

Variables, constants and strings

Delete the contents of the playground template and replace it with the following:

```
var greeting: String = "Hello"
println(greeting)
```

You should immediately see the "Hello" text in the right-hand pane where the assignment takes place and also for the `println` statement. The right-hand pane is great for short output, but for longer debugging output you would normally look at the Xcode console.

To reveal the console output, select the **View/Assistant Editor/Show Assistant Editor** menu option:

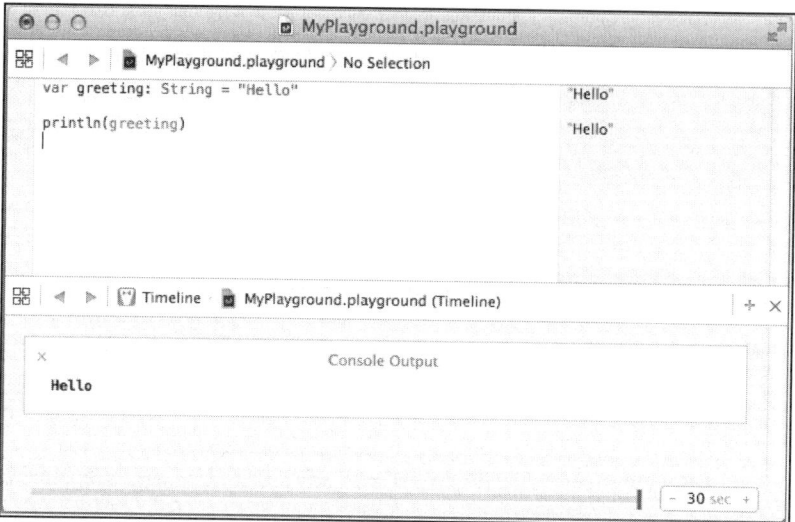

Your current code uses the `var` keyword to define a variable with the name `greeting` of type `String`. You've assigned an initial value of `"Hello"` to this variable.

Update your code as follows:

```
var greeting: String = "Hello"
greeting = "Bonjour"
println(greeting)
```

This changes the console output to `Bonjour` (*bien sûr*), demonstrating that you can assign a new value to a variable, as you might expect.

To see something a bit more exciting, edit the first line of code to remove the type annotation:

```
var greeting = "Hello"
```

You will find the output unchanged.

This is a simple demonstration of **type inference**, where the compiler is able to unambiguously determine the type of the `greeting` variable. Since you're assigning a series of characters inside double quotes, Swift correctly infers the type `String` based on the initial assignment. As a result, you don't need to be explicit about this variable's type and you'll see more of this later with other types.

While it's capable of type inference, Swift is a **statically** typed language with compile-time checking of types. Dynamically typed languages with type inference are much looser with their rules. As a quick demonstration, change your playground code to the following:

```
var greeting = "Hello"
greeting = 23
println(greeting)
```

This causes the compiler to report an error, **type 'String' does not conform to protocol 'IntegerLiteralConvertible'**, at the second line.

Type inference doesn't weaken your application in any way; it simply saves keystrokes by removing the need to specify types that are obvious to the compiler (and hopefully to you). The simple example above shows type inference when assigning literal values, but it will work everywhere within the language—for example, when you create a variable and assign it a value from a function.

> **PRO TIP:** We encourage you to use type inference extensively, as it results in more concise and thus more readable code. However, if there is any instance where you think adding an explicit type to a variable declaration would enhance readability, there is certainly nothing wrong with doing so!

Let's do some simple string manipulation. Update the code as follows:

```
var greeting = "Hello"
greeting = greeting + " World"
println(greeting)
```

The console output is now "Hello World" (surely you didn't need a compiler to tell you that!).

Swift strings are mutable—that is, you can change their values—where the mutations have a much simpler syntax than their `NSMutableString` counterparts. For example, you could change the above to use the more compact `+=` compound assignment operator.

There are many times you want to create a value that does not change. Creating these values as variables is inherently unsafe since accidental assignments can and do happen.

Swift makes it easy to change a variable into a constant. Update the first line of code as follows:

```
let greeting = "Hello"
```

This results in an error at the second line of code: **cannot assign to 'let' value 'greeting'**.

You can control the mutability of the built-in Swift types (e.g., `String`, `Int`, `Dictionary`) by using either the `let` or `var` keywords at the point of declaration. This is in stark contrast to Objective-C and many other languages, where some type implementations are inherently mutable, such as `NSMutableArray`, and some are not, such as `NSArray`.

> **PRO-TIP:** You should define values as constants wherever possible. This not only makes your code more robust, it also allows the compiler to further optimize your code, improving execution times. Thus, you will probably find yourself using `let` far more often than `var`.

The use of `let` in order to make an instance of a type immutable isn't restricted to the built-in Swift types. Any structures (structs) that you define yourself also have this behavior; however there are some subtle differences between constant structures and classes. You can read more on this in Chapter 3, "Classes and Structs".

Change `greeting` back to a variable by changing the `let` to `var`, then add the following line just before the `println` statement:

```
greeting.append(Character("!"))
```

This appends an exclamation mark to the end of the string, with the console outputting the result, "Hello World!".

The Swift `String` type has API methods like the above that allow you to manipulate their values. However, these are quite limited in number. Fortunately, the Swift `String` type is bridged to the Objective-C `NSString` type, providing all the API methods with which you are no doubt familiar if you've used Objective-C.

To introduce these methods, update your playground as follows:

```
import Foundation

var greeting = "hello world".capitalizedString
println(greeting)
```

This results in the output "Hello World".

With the first statement, you import the Foundation framework, which includes `NSString`. This adds `capitalizedString` to Swift's `String`.

Why not experiment with some of the other `NSString` API methods within the playground? You can even append strings using `stringByAppendingString` if you aren't keen on the more compact Swift style!

```
import Foundation
var greeting = "hello".stringByAppendingString(" world")
println(greeting)
```

Finally, the Swift `String` is a **value** type. As a result, when you assign a string to a variable, a constant, or pass it as an argument to a function, its value is copied.

Add the following lines to the end of the playground:

```
var alternateGreeting = greeting
alternateGreeting += " and beyond!"
println(alternateGreeting)
println(greeting)
```

The assignment to `alternateGreeting` creates a new copy of the string "hello world". That means you can change `alternateGreeting` as much as you like, and the original value in `greeting` is unaffected.

Semicolons

Have you spotted something funny about the code you've written so far? Yes, that's right: there are no semicolons.

Remove the `alternateGreeting` code and update the code as follows, adding a semicolon at the end of each line:

```
import Foundation;
var greeting = "hello world".capitalizedString;
println(greeting);
```

The output is exactly the same. Swift, unlike many other languages, doesn't *require* semicolons at the end of every statement!

Now remove all the carriage returns, leaving the semicolons in place:

```
import Foundation; var greeting = "hello world".capitalizedString; println(greeting);
```

Again, you get the same output.

But now what happens if you remove the semicolons? You are greeted with a compiler error:

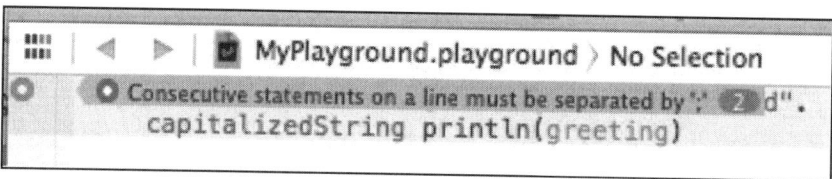

Swift only requires semicolons if you want to write multiple statements on a single line.

> **PRO-TIP:** Dispense with semicolons!
>
> With features such as type inference, Swift is expressive by virtue of being concise. A semicolon is only a single character, but it adds nothing to the understanding of your code, so why not do without it? (However hard it might be to break the habit!)

Numeric types and conversion

Now let's look at some of Swift's other simple types.

Replace your playground code with the following:

```
var radius = 4
let pi = 3.14159
```

This creates two numeric variables: `radius`, of type `Int`, and `pi`, of type `Double`. Again, the Swift compiler is able to infer the types of these two variables based on the literal values you've assigned them.

Swift has a range of integer types of varying size, such as `Int8` (8-bit signed integer) and `UInt16` (16-bit unsigned integer). It also has a `Float` type for lower-precision floating point numbers.

Unless you have some specific requirements, `Int` and `Double` should be your first choices. Those types have a wide useful range for most applications and the compiler will also pick the best size for `Int`—either 32 or 64 bits—to match the machine's word size for the most efficient code.

In Swift, you can use the underscore as a thousands separator. Type the following into your playground:

```
let million = 1_000_000
```

This defines a constant `million` as an integer that is equal to 1,000,000.

You can perform all of the usual arithmetic operations you would expect on your Swift variables. To see something you might not expect, try a simple bit of math by adding this to your Playground:

```
var area = radius * radius * pi
```

In case you've forgotten from math class, this computes the area of a circle. ;]

You might be surprised to see the compiler complain about the second multiplication operation with the error, **cannot invoke '*' with an argument list of type '($T4, Double)**.

What exactly does this mean?

All operations are defined as functions, and the above indicates that the compiler cannot find a multiplication function that takes an `Int` on the left hand side and a `Double` on the right.

This illustrates a very important feature of the Swift language: *all* numeric type conversions must be explicit regardless of whether you want to convert to a type with more or less precision. This is true of integers as well as floating point numbers.

To fix the problem, update the code as follows:

```
var area = Double(radius) * Double(radius) * pi
```

The above reports that your circle has an area of `50.265`.

The solution, as shown, is to convert the radius variable, which is of type `Int`, into a `Double`. You might be tempted to call this a cast, but it isn't! The `Double(radius)` part of the code constructs a new `Double` instance via its initializer. You're going to learn a lot more about initializers in Chapter 3, "Classes and Structs".

> **PRO-TIP:** You can Cmd+Click on any of the Swift types to view a "header" file containing all of Swift's types, functions, protocols and more. You'll find no end of interesting information in there; for example, you can see that the multiplication operation has various overloads, but none that mixes types. Here's one example:
>
> ```
> func *(lhs: Double, rhs: Double) -> Double
> ```

The need for explicit type conversion is one of the many Swift safety features designed to reduce the risk of programming error. Another is bounds checking. Type the following into the playground:

```
var overflow = Int.max + 1
```

You will find that this reports the error, **arithmetic operation '9223372036854775807 + 1' (on type 'Int') results in an overflow**. In other words, Swift is preventing you from storing a number that's larger than the maximum capacity of the `Int` type. In other languages, this overflow will cause the number to "wrap around" to a negative number but Swift treats it as a runtime error.

> **PRO-TIP:** Overflow errors are part of Swift's implementation of arithmetic operators. You can opt out of this safety check and allow overflow/underflow truncation by using what Apple calls overflow operators: &+, &-, &*, &/, &%.
>
> These might be useful when dealing with integers as bitwise fields.

You will encounter more of Swift's safety features throughout this book.

Booleans

Swift has a Boolean type, `Bool`, that holds a value of either `true` or `false`. Once again, you can rely on type inference when creating a variable or constant of this type. Add the following to your playground:

```
let alwaysTrue = true
```

In another of Swift's safety features, control structures that require Boolean values can only use the `Bool` type. In contrast to other languages such as Objective-C, Swift won't treat non-zero integer values as "true". That means you can't use an integer and pretend that it's a Boolean by setting its value to `1` or `0`; you always need to use actual Boolean values to stay within the type system.

Tuples

Tuples are a grouping of multiple values into a single type. Unlike classes and structs, however, you can create a tuple without explicitly defining the type.

Create your first tuple by replacing the playground code with the following:

```
var address = (742, "Evergreen Terrace")
println(address.0)
println(address.1)
```

The first line creates a tuple variable called `address` that is a combination of an integer and a string. The subsequent lines show how you can access these values via indices.

Try accessing a tuple index that's out of bounds. What happens? I'm sure you've guessed already: This is a compile-time error, another Swift safety feature.

You can update the components of a tuple via the index notation, as follows:

```
address.0 = 744
```

The above changes the first component of the tuple to the value `744` (This takes you from the Simpsons' house to the Flanders'!). If you want to make your tuple immutable, simply change the `var` keyword to `let` and the above assignment statement will result in a compilation error.

The compiler is using the literal values you supplied to infer the type of each element in your tuple. If you want to be explicit about the type of each component part, you can use a type alias.

Update your code as follows:

```
var address: (Int, String) = (742, "Evergreen Terrace")
```

You'll find that the `address` variable is exactly the same as before. A tuple's type is expressed as the types of its component parts. In the above code, the type is (`Int`, `String`).

Why not experiment with changing the type of the house number to a double in the above `address` tuple? There are at least three different ways you could achieve this!

Have you figured out the solution? If not, here are the answers:

```
// using a type annotation
var address1: (Double, String) = (742, "Evergreen Terrace")

// by explicit creation of a Double
var address2 = (Double(742), "Evergreen Terrace")

// by using a double literal value
var address3 = (742.0, "Evergreen Terrace")
```

You can also deconstruct tuples into their individual elements. Replace your code with the following:

```
var address = (742, "Evergreen Terrace")
let (house, street) = address
println(house)
println(street)
```

Again, the resulting output is unchanged. The `let` statement above deconstructs the given tuple into the `house` and `street` constants. This approach provides a more human-readable mechanism for accessing each tuple element.

You can also deconstruct a tuple into variables via the `var` keyword. However, mutating one of these variables does not affect the value of the original tuple.

A final way to work with tuples is to name their elements. Replace your code with the following:

```
var address = (number: 742, street: "Evergreen Terrace")
println(address.number)
println(address.street)
```

Even if you name the tuple elements, you can still access them with index notation and by deconstructing them with `let` or `var` as in the previous examples.

Tuples are types, just like any other type in Swift. If you *really* want to, you can create tuples of tuples!

> **PRO-TIP:** As you'll see in later chapters, classes and structs can provide the same functionality as tuples along with a ton of extra features and flexibility. Tuples are a quick and easy way of constructing composite types for very simple uses.

String interpolation

To present your address tuple to the user, you need to format it as a string—a very common task in app development.

Update the code as follows:

```
var address = (742, "Evergreen Terrace")
let (house, street) = address
println("I live at " + String(house) + ", " + street)
```

This outputs the text "I live at 742, Evergreen Terrace" to the console.

The above code combines string concatenation and type conversion from `Double` to `String` (via one of the string initializers) to generate the output you desire. This is certainly more readable than the Objective-C equivalent, but Swift has a few more tricks up its sleeve!

Update the `println` statement in the code above as follows:

```
println("I live at \(house), \(street)")
```

The console output displays the same formatted string as before.

The above makes use of a Swift language feature called **string interpolation** that allows you to embed constants, variables and expressions within string literals.

String interpolation isn't simply a replacement for formatted `NSLog` statements; you can use it wherever you want to construct a string!

Update the code as follows:

```
import Foundation

var address = (742, "Evergreen Terrace")
let (house, street) = address
let str = "I live at \(house + 10), \(street.uppercaseString)"
println(str)
```

The console now reads, "I live at 752, EVERGREEN TERRACE". This demonstrates a more complex interpolation including expressions.

> **NOTE:** If you want to output a backslash character, rather than use it to indicate the start of a placeholder, you need to escape it as follows: \\.

Control flow

For loops

You've made some very basic playground applications using simple variable assignments. Now you're ready to add a few control structures.

Replace your playground with the following code:

```
let greeting = "Swift by Tutorials Rocks!"

for i in 1...5 {
  println("\(i) - \(greeting)")
}
```

The for-in loop iterates over the range 1, through to 5 inclusive, with the constant i containing the current value. Here's the output of the above code:

```
1 - Swift by Tutorials Rocks!
2 - Swift by Tutorials Rocks!
3 - Swift by Tutorials Rocks!
4 - Swift by Tutorials Rocks!
5 - Swift by Tutorials Rocks!
```

The above code demonstrates the for-in loop and the **closed range operator** (...). These are often used together, but they are entirely independent.

> **NOTE:** You don't use `var` when constructing a `for-in` loop because you aren't actually defining a variable. Instead, the `for-in` loop assigns a new constant value on each iteration. You can test this behavior yourself. What happens if you try to mutate `i` within the loop?

Update the code as follows:

```
var range = 1...5
for i in range {
  println("\(i) - \(greeting)")
}
```

Once again, the output is unchanged, demonstrating that the closed range operator and the `for-in` loop are separate constructs.

The `1...5` expression is clearly creating a type of some sort. Perhaps you are wondering just what this type is?

The closed range operator creates a struct of type `Range`. To see this in action, replace the `range` variable creation as follows:

```
var range = Range(start: 1, end: 6)
```

And again, the output is the same.

The above uses an initializer with named parameters to construct the `Range` instance. You'll learn all about these later in this book.

The `x...y` notation is simply the shorthand way to create a `Range`. Incidentally, you can use the shorthand `x..<y` to create a partially-closed range, or one where the final value is y-1. So `1...5` means 1,2,3,4,5 while `1..<5` means 1,2,3,4.

So how does the `for-in` loop know what to do with this range?

There are a number of Swift types that the `for-in` loop can enumerate, with the `Range` type being just one of them. Other types that are clearly enumerable are arrays and dictionaries (which provide key-value pairs), but there are less obvious types you can enumerate, as well.

Have a go at the following:

```
for i in "Swift" {
  println(i)
}
```

This prints each character of the string "Swift" to the console, demonstrating that Swift strings are also enumerable.

> **PRO-TIP:** If you dig a little deeper into the `Range` and `String` type definitions, you'll find that each adopts the `Sequence` protocol that indicates they're enumerable. Types that implement the `Sequence` protocol expose a `generate` method which returns a `Generator`. Generators have a single method that allows you to request their next value.
>
> You'll build your own class that implements `Sequence` and `Generator` in Chapter 4, "Generics".

While loops

Swift supports `while` loops as well as `do-while` loops, where the loop condition is checked at the end of each iteration.

Update your code to use a `while` loop instead:

```
let greeting = "Swift by Tutorials Rocks!"
var i = 0
while i < 5 {
  println("\(i) - \(greeting)")
  i++
}
```

This produces the same result as before. I'll leave you the task of changing this into a `do-while` loop. I'm sure you're up to it!

If statements

Swift supports the standard `if`, `if/else` and `if/else-if/else` constructs. Update your code as follows:

```
import Foundation

let greeting = "Swift by Tutorials Rocks!"

for i in 1...5 {
  if i == 5 {
    println(greeting.uppercaseString)
```

```
    } else {
        println(greeting)
    }
}
```

The output really does assert that *Swift by Tutorials* rocks with its all-caps last line:

```
Swift by Tutorials Rocks!
Swift by Tutorials Rocks!
Swift by Tutorials Rocks!
Swift by Tutorials Rocks!
SWIFT BY TUTORIALS ROCKS!
```

As previously mentioned, the condition that determines the outcome of the `if` statement must be a `Bool`. Thus, you cannot infer true/false from integers or other types.

As another safety feature, Swift's `if` statement *requires* you to use braces even if the resulting code is a single statement. The following isn't valid:

```
for i in 1...5 {
  if i == 5
     println(greeting.uppercaseString)
  else
     println("Inside the else:")
     println(greeting) // uh oh
}
```

Forgetting to add braces and deceptive-looking indentation is a common cause of software bugs! Since braces are required in Swift, this class of bugs will be much more difficult to write.

The `if` statement has another trick having to do with optional values that you'll learn about in the next chapter. Stay tuned, you haven't heard the last of `if`!

Switch statements

Swift supports the standard `switch-case` construct, which compares a value against a number of potential matches and executes the code in the matching block.

Replace your playground code with the following to give `switch` statements a quick try:

```
var direction = "up"

switch direction {
  case "down":
    println("Going Down!")
```

```
  case "up":
     println("Going Up!")
  default:
     println("Going Nowhere")
}
```

The `direction` variable matches the "up" case and as a result, the console displays "Going Up!" Try changing the value of `direction` to something else—you know you want to!

In contrast to Objective-C, Swift `switch` statements can use any type rather than only primitives. Furthermore, the compiler ensures that the type of each case statement matches the variable being "switched" on.

Secondly, there are no break statements in the above code. In Swift, when a variable matches a case statement, the program executes the body of the statement's code and the switch completes. There is no automatic fall-through as with `switch` implementations in many other languages. Again, this is a safety feature; it can be easy to leave out a break statement, with unintended consequences.

Now modify your code to remove the default statement:

```
var direction = "up"

switch direction {
  case "down":
     println("Going Down!")
  case "up":
     println("Going Up!")
}
```

You will receive the error message, **"Switch must be exhaustive, consider adding a default clause"**. Swift is smart enough to know if you've provided matches for every possible value passed into the `switch` statement. Because you could not *possibly* match every possible string value, Swift forces a `default matcher`.

If you are switching on a type where you can provide a match for every type, such as an enum, then you can get away without using `default`!

> **NOTE:** You've probably noticed that Swift is a strict language and has a number of features I've described as safety mechanisms. For a recent lesson about how wrong even a slightly lax language feature can go, I recommend reading about the root cause of Apple's "goto fail" bug, which was a significant and widespread security flaw.
>
> http://nakedsecurity.sophos.com/2014/02/24/anatomy-of-a-goto-fail-apples-ssl-bug-explained-plus-an-unofficial-patch/

The Swift `switch` statement is quite flexible. Update your code as follows:

```
switch direction {
  case "down", "up":
    println("Going Somewhere!")
  default:
    println("Going Nowhere")
}
```

If `direction` is either "up" or "down", the first case matches; any other values result in the default behavior. This demonstrates how you can match multiple values from a single case statement, which is typically the purpose of `switch` fall-throughs.

You can also match ranges of values, as shown below:

```
var score = 570

switch score {
  case 1..<10:
    println("novice")
  case 10..<100:
    println("proficient")
  case 100..<1000:
    println("rock-star")
  default:
    println("awesome")
}
```

This code relies on the partially-closed range operator you used with the `for-in` loops you wrote above.

The Swift `switch` statement has some powerful and flexible variants that allow you to match tuples. You can perform partial matches, value binding (i.e., assign a tuple component to a constant via `let`) and express complex match conditions via `where` statements.

You'll learn a little more about the switch statement in Chapter 6, "Enums and Switch Statement" and the more exotic features are covered in Apple's book *The Swift Programming Language*.

Where to go from here?

In this chapter, you've learned about Swift's core languages features, including variables, constants and the Swift type system. You've also seen some of the interesting options for control flow—I am sure you will find yourself using `for-in` loops extensively in your Swift code!

In the next chapter, you'll encounter optionals, a concept that simplifies the interoperability of Swift and Objective-C code. You'll also learn about Swift's arrays and dictionaries, including the rather curious constant array.

Chapter 2: Language Basics II

By Matt Galloway

In the previous chapter, you learned some of basics of the Swift language, including variables, constants, types, strings and control flow. This chapter takes you one step further.

This chapter still focuses on language basics, but some of the more advanced basics! Just as before, you'll write your code inside a playground so you can see the results right away.

By the end of this chapter, you'll have the Swift language basics in your head and be ready to move beyond playgrounds to a real-life application. For now, I hope you'll agree with me that playgrounds are a fantastically useful way of experimenting with Swift.

Let's get started!

Optionals

If you've programmed in any language, then you're likely familiar with the problems created by the dreaded null pointer. You try to dereference a null pointer, perhaps by calling a method on an object that you haven't yet initialized and, needless to say, find yourself in hot water. In Java, for example, this manifests as a null pointer exception.

In the Objective-C runtime, messaging nil returns nil, which means the null pointer is effectively safe. However, this doesn't particularly help you if you're expecting the reference to be non-nil. The usual way around this is to do an assertion check that the variable is never nil. In debug mode, your app would crash if it encounters nil, so you can find the bug and fix it before releasing the code.

In Swift, things are different.

Open Xcode, select **File\New\Playground…**, call the file **Chapter_2** and select the **iOS** platform. Click **Next** and save the file at your location of choice.

You begin with the sample, which includes just the following line:

```
var str = "Hello, playground"
```

Add the following line underneath it:

```
println(str)
```

As you now know, the first line creates a new variable, called `str`, that the compiler initializes to `"Hello, playground"`. But what if you don't know at this time what `str` should contain? In another language, you might set the variable to nil or NULL to indicate no value.

Remove the assignment in the first line by deleting the equals sign and everything after it. You'll now have an error: **Type annotation missing in pattern**.

This seems to indicate that the compiler doesn't know what type `str` should be.

Of course, the funny thing about type inference is that it needs a value from which to infer the type! So, try explicitly typing the variable to a string:

```
var str: String
```

This results in a different error, this time on the second line: **Variable 'str' used before being initialized**.

Brilliant! Swift isn't letting you use an uninitialized variable at *compile time*. This is a great feature because it means you won't ever have unexpected nil values.

But what if you actually want one? Sometimes, you can't help but have a nil value—for example, an API may return nil in case of error or if there genuinely is nothing to return in some cases.

If you have to initialize the value, try setting it to nil directly:

```
var str: String = nil
```

Another error! This time the compiler complains that **Type 'string' does not conform to protocol 'NilLiteralConvertible'**. Another safety feature of Swift is that if you declare the variable as a `String`, it *must* be a string—and nil is not a String.

When you do need the nil value, you can use an **optional**. Optionals are a way of wrapping up the concept of "has a value" or "may have a value" into a language-wide feature. You may be familiar with other languages, which use sentinel values such as -1 or 0 to indicate "not a value." The null pointer is such a sentinel value. If you think about it, this is why the null pointer is a problem – it's still a valid pointer; it just doesn't happen to point to a valid object.

Declaring optionals

Let's see how to use optionals. Change the first line to this:

```
var str: String?
```

You've simply added a single question mark to the end of the type, designating the string as optional. You can think of the optional as a type in its own right, so `str` can hold either nil or a `String` instance. It is initialized to nil because there is no explicit assignment to a `String` instance.

Notice that your playground no longer has an error and the output shows **nil**. This is because you're printing out an optional that is currently nil.

Next, change the first line to include an assignment, like so:

```
var str: String? = "Hello Swift by Tutorials!"
```

As you may expect, `"Hello Swift by Tutorials!"` is the output. Assigning a value to a `String` with the equal sign looks just like assigning a value to a `String?` – it's magical! During the assignment, Swift wraps the value inside an instance of the optional type and assigns it to `str`.

In the playground sidebar, note that the value of `str` is reported as {Some "Hello Swift by Tutorials!"}. This is what the wrapping looks like – the string value is in there, and the optional type is represented by the curly braces and the "Some".

It sort of looks like a string, but is it? Add the following line to the end of your playground:

```
str = str.uppercaseString
```

This results in **error: 'String?' does not have a member named 'uppercaseString'**.

This error is due to an optional being a type of its own. Until now, `String` and `String?` have been pretty close in usage. Here, you're trying to access the uppercaseString property on an instance of an optional String. That doesn't work because the optional string type doesn't have such a method!

There is, of course, a way to safely access the underlying value of an optional so you can use the underlying value. Swift's emphasis on safety forces you to use an `if` statement while unwrapping an optional type.

Replace the last line of your playground with the following:

```
if let unwrappedStr = str {
  println("Unwrapped! \(unwrappedStr.uppercaseString)")
}
```

With this expression, you unwrap `str` and directly assign it to a new constant named `unwrappedStr`, solely for use within the `if` statement. If `str` is currently wrapping an instance of a string, then `unwrappedStr` becomes a variable of type `String` and the `if` statement passes.

Change the first line of your playground to remove the assignment by deleting the equals sign and everything after it. Also add an `else` to the `if` statement, as follows:

```
} else {
  println("Was nil")
}
```

Notice how if the optional `str` is currently wrapping nil, then the `if` condition fails.

This is perfect. Swift gives you safety where you need it by forcing you to check a value before using it!

Forced unwrapping

If you already know that a particular optional contains a value, then you can use what is known as **forced unwrapping**. This means you don't need the `if` statement to check if the optional contains a value.

Replace the first line of the playground with the assignment:

```
var str: String? = "Hello Swift by Tutorials!"
```

Then, add the following line to the end of the playground:

```
println("Force unwrapped! \(str!.uppercaseString)")
```

The exclamation mark after the variable name signifies the forced unwrapping. You access the `uppercaseString` property on whatever `str` happens to hold. In the current case, it holds a string instance and therefore, everything runs smoothly.

Once again, remove the assignment from the first line of the playground by deleting the equals sign and everything after it.

You will now see **fatal error: unexpectedly found nil while unwrapping an Optional value**.

This is a run time error, which would crash the app. You can tell this because above the error is the console output up until the code that forcibly unwraps `str`. That is, the code ran until the forced unwrap.

> **PRO-TIP:** While forced unwrapping can be useful, it destroys the safety provided by optionals. Use it only when absolutely necessary and when you're sure the optional cannot contain nil during that code's execution.

Implicit unwrapping

It's also possible to use the power of optionals without having to do the manual unwrapping dance of forced unwrapping with `!` or `let`.

Change the first line of your playground to this:

```
var str: String! = "Hello Swift by Tutorials!"
```

If you're observant, you'll notice the change (apart from adding back the assignment!). If you're not sure what I mean, look at the end of the type. Instead of a question mark, it's now an exclamation mark. This tells the compiler that you want to **implicitly unwrap** this variable.

Now you can use the variable just as you would any other variable. For example, add the following to the end of your playground:

```
str = str.lowercaseString
println(str)
```

It's as though the variable isn't an optional!

For a final time, remove the assignment on the first line of the playground by deleting the equals sign and everything after it.

Just as with the forced unwrapping, you get **fatal error: unexpectedly found nil while unwrapping an Optional value**.

This is exactly the same error as before, both in message and under the hood. The only difference is in the syntax.

You might now have a hard time seeing the use of implicit unwrapping. But remember the theme running throughout this discussion on optionals: They are types in and of themselves and are there to solve the sentinel value problem. This means that even implicitly unwrapped optionals are useful.

You can check any optional type using an `if` statement. Wrap the last two lines you added to the playground in an `if` statement, like so:

```
if str != nil {
  str = str.lowercaseString
  println(str)
}
```

Your code now runs without error. You're checking the optional in just the same way as you once might have done in Objective-C. In Objective-C, you were relying on nil evaluating to false; in Swift, on the other hand, you're relying on `nil` truly representing the "not a value" state.

> **PRO-TIP:** You should treat implicit unwrapping with just as much caution as forced unwrapping, if not more. Aside from where they're declared, implicitly unwrapped variables look just like regular variables so use them carefully!

Optional chaining

Optional chaining is a concise way to work with optionals quickly without using `if/let` and a conditional block each time.

If you come from an Objective-C background, then you're no doubt familiar with the delegate pattern, where one object delegates responsibility for certain actions to another object. It's common for the delegate to be optional. If the delegate isn't set, then the object doing the delegation simply doesn't try to call its delegate. This is a great case for optionals!

We don't want to go into classes and delegates right now (you'll see more on that in Chapter 3, "Classes and Structs" and Chapter 8, "Swift and Cocoa"), so the following example uses a `String`. However, the same principles apply.

Add the following lines to the end of your playground:

```
var maybeString: String? = "Hello Swift by Tutorials!"
let uppercase = maybeString?.uppercaseString
```

The first line declares the `maybeString` variable as an optional string. In the second line, the question mark after the variable begins **optional chaining**. At run time, it will check the contents of the `maybeString` optional. If it contains an instance, then continue execution of the `uppercaseString` expression. If it contains nil, then return nil.

In this way, `uppercase` is an optional itself since it's possible that `maybeString` is also nil. This behavior is similar to Objective-C's nil messaging behavior—that is, messaging nil returns nil.

Collections

All languages need collections such as arrays, dictionaries and sets. In Objective-C, the Foundation framework provides quite a few different collection types, the most common of which are `NSArray` and `NSDictionary`. Both of these benefited from becoming much leaner in syntax when Apple introduced literal syntax. Maybe Apple was testing the waters for Swift?

It turns out that in Swift, there are only two primitive collection types: arrays and dictionaries. Both are built-in and provided by the Swift standard library. They work in ways similar to their namesakes in other languages with a few subtle differences.

Arrays

As you might expect, an array in Swift is an ordered collection of elements. Create one by adding the following code to the end of your playground:

```
var array = [1, 2, 3, 4, 5]
```

This creates an array with five elements.

You can access an array using the subscript syntax. Add the following line to the end of the playground:

```
println(array[2])
```

Swift arrays are zero-indexed, so this accesses the third element in the array and prints out the value, 3.

You can append to an array by using `append()`. Add the following code after the line you just added:

```
array.append(6)
println(array)
```

Notice that your array now has six elements.

You can even extend an array by adding a sequence to it, such as a range. Add the following code before the `println` you added above:

```
array.extend(7...10)
```

Your array now contains ten elements!

> **Challenge:** Find the method to remove objects from an array and remove every other element.

Now to mix things up a bit, add the following line at the end of your playground:

```
array.append("11")
```

You see an error. That may surprise you if you come from an Objective-C background. In Objective-C, `NSArray` can contain any sort of object, but in Swift, arrays are strongly typed and can only hold a certain type. In this example, Swift inferred `array` to be an array of integers, because that's what you assigned to it initially.

Remove the last line you added and change the `array` variable declaration to the following:

```
var array: [Int] = [1, 2, 3, 4, 5]
```

This is how you declare the type of the elements of an array in Swift: simply the type, enclosed by []. You could also use the slightly longer "generic" syntax, `Array<Int>` (an array with an `Int` type constraint), but the shorter syntax is better. We'll go over what the longer syntax means in Chapter 4, "Generics".

It's possible to create an array that behaves in the same way as an `NSArray`. You simply need to specify the type as an array of `AnyObject` instances. But you should generally create arrays with a specific type, because that affords you the type safety that is so ingrained in Swift.

> **Challenge:** Create an array to hold `AnyObject` types and add a few integers, strings and anything else you like!

Dictionaries

Arrays provide an ordered list of elements; dictionaries provide a list of mappings between keys and values.

Add the following code to the end of your playground:

```
var dictionary = [1: "Dog", 2: "Cat"]
```

This creates a dictionary with two key-value pairs. The syntax is similar to that of arrays, but instead of a comma-separated list of objects, you use a comma-separated list of pairs, each joined by a colon. Objective-C developers will recognize the `NSDictionary` literal syntax, but with square brackets instead of curly ones.

Just as with arrays, dictionaries are strongly typed. In this example, `dictionary` is of type `Dictionary<Int, String>` so its keys are of type `Int` and the values are of type `String`.

Replace the last line you added to the playground with the following:

```
var dictionary: [Int:String] = [1: "Dog", 2: "Cat"]
```

This is the shorthand form for dictionaries. It's similar to the shorthand form for arrays.

You can access the items in a dictionary using subscript syntax. Add the following line to the end of your playground:

```
println(dictionary[1])
```

This accesses the dictionary by key value, and in this case, it prints out the value for key 1.

You can alter a dictionary after you've created it by using subscripts. Add the following code right after the variable declaration you just added:

```
dictionary[3] = "Mouse"
println(dictionary)
```

The dictionary now contains three values. If you're familiar with Objective-C, or a lot of other languages for that matter, then this syntax should be familiar. The square brackets after the variable indicate to use the subscript on the dictionary. In this case, a value is being set using the syntax because it's being assigned to.

> **Challenge:** Use a subscript to change the value of the 2 key to "Elephant".

It's also possible to remove values from a dictionary. Add the following line before `println(dictionary)`:

```
dictionary[3] = nil
```

In this case, the subscript does exactly what it says: It sets the value for the given key to nil – i.e. it removes it.

Subscripts can also be used to read the value for a given key. Add the following to the playground:

```
println(dictionary[1])
```

You'll see the playground sidebar shows `"Optional("Dog")"`, meaning it's an optional value. This makes sense since you could try to read a key that doesn't exist, and the function needs the option to return `nil`.

To pull it all together, you can combine reading a value with safe unwrapping that you learned about earlier. Add the following code to the end of your playground:

```
if let value = dictionary[1] {
  println("Value is \(value)")
}
```

This is a great example of Swift's "safe by default" nature. It really forces you to think about when values might be nil. Usually it's something you want to know about.

References and copies

Arrays and dictionaries in Swift exhibit a mix of reference-type and value-type behavior. Programming languages and runtimes have their own ways of dealing with this, so it's important to understand how things work in Swift.

First, let's take a look at dictionaries, which as you'll see, are a bit simpler than arrays.

Add the following lines to the end of your playground:

```
var dictionaryA = [1: 1, 2: 4, 3: 9, 4: 16]
var dictionaryB = dictionaryA
println(dictionaryA)
println(dictionaryB)
```

This does what you would expect. The two dictionaries contain the same keys and key values.

Now add the following lines after the ones you just added:

```
dictionaryB[4] = nil
println(dictionaryA)
println(dictionaryB)
```

Now `dictionaryB` contains one fewer value than `dictionaryA`. Similarly, if you update a key value for a certain dictionary instead of removing it, then you will only alter that dictionary.

This is an important point to remember: dictionaries are **copied** when you assign them to new variables and constants, or when you pass them as parameters to functions.

Let's now do the same thing with arrays.

Add the following code to the end of your playground:

```
var arrayA = [1, 2, 3, 4, 5]
var arrayB = arrayA
println(arrayA)
println(arrayB)

arrayB.removeAtIndex(0)
println(arrayA)
println(arrayB)
```

This should come as no surprise. When you remove an object from `arrayB`, only `arrayB` loses an object. The contents of `arrayA` are unchanged.

Now change the `removeAtIndex()` line by replacing it with the following:

```
arrayB[0] = 10
```

Once again, no surprises; only `arrayB` is changed. This is because arrays can be said to have "value semantics". This means that they are copied during assignment.

This is in contrast to references, which you may be more familiar with from other languages such as Objective-C. When a pointer to an `NSArray` is assigned to another variable, it still points to the same `NSArray` instance.

Constant collections

As you saw in Chapter 1, Swift has both constants and variables. So far, you've only used arrays and dictionaries declared with `var`, which creates variables. You can also declare arrays and dictionaries as constants by using `let`, but the semantics are a little different from what you might expect.

Add the following line to the end of your playground:

```
let constantArray = [1, 2, 3, 4, 5]
```

This declares an array in just the same way as before, except that it's a *constant* array. A constant array cannot have elements added to or removed from it.

Let's confirm that. Add the following to the end of your playground:

```
constantArray.append(6)
constantArray.removeAtIndex(0)
```

You'll see two errors:

1. **immutable value of type '[Int]' only has mutating members named 'append'**

2. **immutable value of type '[Int]' only has mutating members named 'removeAtIndex'**

This is the vigilance of Swift in action once again. You cannot accidentally alter an immutable array.

A constant dictionary behaves in just the same way.

> **Challenge:** Create a constant dictionary and confirm that you cannot add to, remove from or change values in it.

Where to go from here?

Over the last two chapters, you've learned the basics of the Swift language by playing with variables, constants, the type system, optional types, collections and more.

What to do now? Take this knowledge and apply it to a real-life application! That's exactly where the next chapter begins.

Grab yourself a well-earned break and come back refreshed and ready for a more serious challenge!

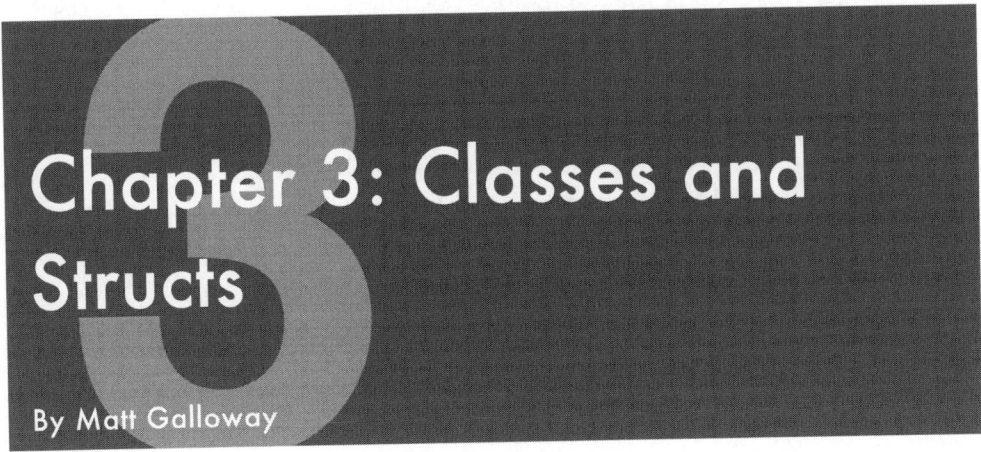

Chapter 3: Classes and Structs

By Matt Galloway

The integers, strings, arrays and dictionaries you've used up until now represent values, but they don't *do* anything themselves. Swift, like any other object-oriented programming language, also provides the ability to define classes that hold data as well as methods for acting upon that data. If you're familiar with Objective-C, Java, C#, C++ or many other object-oriented languages, then you've probably worked with classes before.

Swift also lets you define custom structures, or "structs" for short. Unlike structs in languages such as C, structs in Swift can hold data *and* methods just like classes!

What, then, is the difference between a class and a struct? This is a great question to ask and a very important concept to understand! In this chapter, you'll build an app that makes use of both classes and structs and learn how to create and deploy both in the process.

The app you're going to build will take your users on a "treasure hunt" in locations all around Silicon Valley. Maybe next time you attend WWDC, you can use the app to find these treasures yourself!

Onward, ho!

Getting started

To get you up and running quickly, I've created a starter project for you. This chapter is about classes and structs, so you don't want to spend time writing boilerplate code before you dive into the actual topic!

You'll find the starter project in the book resources for this chapter in the **TreasureHunt-Starter** folder. Open the Xcode project and have a look around. Notice there's not much to it right now: It's simply a storyboard with a navigation controller pointing to a single view controller with an MKMapView.

Build and run the app. You'll see something like this, though the location of the map will depend upon your position on Earth:

The class concept

If you're coming from an Objective-C background or have written code in any other object-oriented language, then you're familiar with classes. Even so, on the way to highlighting the differences between a class and struct, let's revisit the concept of a class.

In object-oriented programming, you build programs mainly through the use of class instances, or objects. Objects have associated data as well as methods to manipulate that data. An object's data may be in the form of primitive types such as numbers or strings, or the data may even be in the form of references to other objects.

A series of objects can often be modeled into a hierarchy. A classic illustration of this involves biological taxonomy. For example, cats, frogs, turtles and owls are all animals (specifically, tetrapod vertebrates). They share some data in common (age, weight, species) but also have their *own* data (cats have fur of a certain color and pattern; owls have a wingspan).

You could represent these relationships in an object-oriented language by using a class hierarchy. There could be a base class called Animal that owns the common animal attributes. Various subclasses could then inherit from `Animal`, such as `Cat`, `Frog`, `Turtle` and `Owl`. Each `Animal` subclass would then exhibit the behavior of its parent, inheriting many of `Animal`'s data and methods.

So what about structs? In Swift, classes and structs both help you model data. They both can store data and have methods to act on that data, but each has distinct characteristics. You'll find out in this chapter how they differ and when you should use a class versus a struct.

My first class

Your app as it stands doesn't do much. It shows you a map centered roughly where you are on Earth, but you want it to do more than that—like show treasure!

Your app is going to have a number of treasures to find around Silicon Valley. Each treasure falls into one of the following categories:

- **History treasures** are historical sites and include a **year**.
- **Fact treasures** are sites with an associated **fact**.
- **HQ treasures** are the current **headquarters** of Silicon Valley-based companies.

Each of these treasures has a location and an associated message. If you're looking at this and thinking, "class hierarchy!", then congratulations, you're on the right track!

You can fit the objects mentioned above into a class hierarchy, like so:

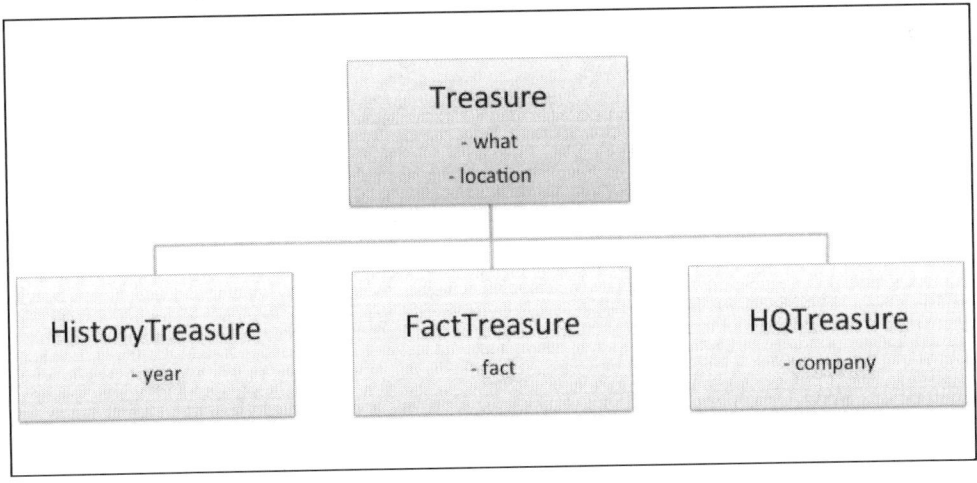

The diagram above shows the intended class hierarchy, with each class as a rectangular box containing its name and its associated data. In this way, all treasures have a "what" (the message associated with that treasure) and a "location" (the geo-point of the treasure).

Now let's put this plan into action!

Creating the class

Add a new file to the project by clicking **File\New\File…**, selecting **iOS\Source\Swift File** and then clicking **Next**. Call the file **Treasure** and click **Create**.

You now have a blank Swift file in front of you. If you've come from Objective-C, it might strike you that there is only a single **.swift** file! In Swift, you won't be writing separate header and implementation files. You also don't have to import header files into your code. This might seem a bit strange at first, but it will make life a lot easier in the long run.

Import statements give you access to classes, structs, functions and so forth that are defined in other libraries. The single import statement in the new file therefore imports the entire Foundation framework for you.

> **PRO TIP:** You may remember that a year before Swift, Apple added `@import` to Objective-C to import entire "modules." No longer did you have to import framework headers and then update the build settings to link those same frameworks. `import` in Swift behaves exactly the same way!

You'll be very familiar with the Foundation framework if you are an existing Objective-C developer. The framework includes many useful objects, including the base `NSObject`.

Swift provides its own implementations of some of the classes found in the Foundation framework, such as the strings, arrays and dictionaries covered in the previous chapters. However, Foundation remains extremely important for Swift developers, as you'll see in this chapter and throughout the book.

Let's add some code! Add the following at the bottom of the file:

```swift
class Treasure {
  let what: String
  let latitude: Double
```

```
    let longitude: Double
}
```

This is a basic example of how to declare a class: follow the `class` keyword with the name of the class you want to define and then, place the class definition inside braces. You can declare properties in your class using either `var` or `let`, just as you do for function local variables. The difference between `var` and `let` is exactly the same in this context: variable or constant.

You need to define the types of the properties because the compiler has nothing from which to infer them. If you want to set an initial value, then you can do so after the declaration just as you would for any other variable.

> **PRO TIP:** If you set an initial value, then you don't need to declare the type explicitly, because the compiler now has a type from which it can infer. However, it's good practice to do so for properties so that you can quickly see the types of all properties at a glance.

The astute reader will realize that these variables are constants, but they're not defined! How can that be?

The even more astute reader will notice Xcode is giving the following error:

```
11  class Treasure {          ⊙ Class 'Treasure' has no initializers
12      let what: String
13      let latitude: Double
```

This error is telling you that there needs to be an initializer defined for this class, because it has constants without initial values. Remember, non-optional types must be initialized with valid values.

Add the following code after the three property definitions but before the closing brace:

```
init(what: String, latitude: Double, longitude: Double) {
  self.what = what
  self.latitude = latitude
  self.longitude = longitude
}
```

This bit of code is what is known as an **initializer** in Swift. It's similar to the `init` family of methods in Objective-C or constructors in C++ and Java.

This is also probably the first function you've written in Swift. Congratulations! :]

Swift is very consistent in its syntax; functions in Swift have arguments with names and types that you declare just as you would all other variables. Notice that you must declare the type, because there's no way the compiler can infer the type without a value.

Initializers have a single job: to initialize everything inside the class that is necessary to get the instance up and running. In the case of `Treasure`, this means setting the values of the three variables. All are passed into the initializer, so the user of the class must know all three values at initialization time. This is another important safety and design feature of Swift. What's the use of a treasure without a latitude value, for example? It needs to have all three values to exist.

That's almost it for this class, but there's room for improvement.

A struct-ural improvement

So far, so good, but latitude and longitude go together. They're a unit of information that happens to be made up of two values, much like a "treasure" is a unit of information made up of a "what" and a "location." It would be nice to wrap up the location in its own encapsulation type rather than store two doubles.

This is where the struct comes in handy. A struct can contain data, just like a class. A struct can have methods, just like a class. But structs are for objects that can be thought of as *values*. Values don't do anything but hold data.

Add a new file to the project by clicking **File\New\File…**, selecting **iOS\Source\Swift File** and clicking **Next**. Call the file **GeoLocation** and click **Create**.

Once again, you have an empty Swift file. Add the following code to it:

```
struct GeoLocation {
  var latitude: Double
  var longitude: Double
}
```

This should remind you of your class definition. There's only one difference: the keyword `struct` instead of `class`. And that's how you make a struct in Swift!

The struct you've defined here wraps up latitude and longitude values and stores them together. It's usual to define the members of a struct as variable rather than constant, but you can choose either, as you wish.

Now deploy this new struct in your `Treasure` class. Open **Treasure.swift** and replace the latitude and longitude property definitions with the following:

```
let location: GeoLocation
```

Notice that you haven't had to import `GeoLocation` in any way. This is because in Swift, every file in your app is automatically imported for use in every other file in that app. The same holds true if you're writing a static library or framework.

This makes life much simpler! Objective-C developers are well aware of the number of imports that can stack up in an Objective-C code file.

Also notice that there are now compiler errors in the initializer. This is because your code still references the `latitude` and `longitude` properties you just removed. Fix this by changing the initializer to the following:

```
init(what: String, location: GeoLocation) {
    self.what = what
    self.location = location
}
```

Everything's working again! And you have a location as a nice, succinct unit rather than as two doubles.

Reference types vs. value types

Structs and classes, as you've seen, are very similar in the way you define them. Recall the idea that structs store *values*. That isn't just abstraction: classes are reference types whereas structs are value types. This means whenever you pass around a class, Swift is passing the object's reference. When you pass around a struct, on the other hand, Swift is copying and passing the object's values, as you'll demonstrate below.

Objective-C developers may recognize this as the same behavior exhibited by classes and structs in Objective-C.

Consider the following code and its output (you may want to try this for yourself in a playground):

```
struct MyStruct {
   var foo: Double = 0.0
}

class MyClass {
   var foo: Double = 0.0
}

var structA = MyStruct()                {foo 0.0}
var structB = structA                   {foo 0.0}
structB.foo = 1.0                       {foo 1.0}
structA.foo                             0.0
structB.foo                             1.0

var classA = MyClass()                  {foo 0.0}
var classB = classA                     {foo 0.0}
classB.foo = 1.0                        {foo 1.0}
classA.foo                              1.0
classB.foo                              1.0
```

This defines a struct and a class, both of which have a single variable. The code creates one of each, stores it in one variable and then assigns it to a second variable. Finally, the code alters the property of the second variable.

Notice that with the struct, only the second variable's `foo` changes, whereas with the class, the values of both variables change. This is reference versus value in action. When you assign `classA` to `classB`, Swift uses the same reference and so the two variables actually point to the same instance. But when you assign `structA` to `structB`, Swift makes a copy and there are now two structs in existence.

> **PRO TIP**: Under the hood, Swift has copy-on-write semantics and is smart about copying the struct's value only when absolutely necessary. That means `structB = structA` won't create an immediate copy since the values are identical to start off; once you start changing values, the runtime will do the copy.

To further illustrate what's going on, this diagram depicts the struct's copied value versus the class's copied reference:

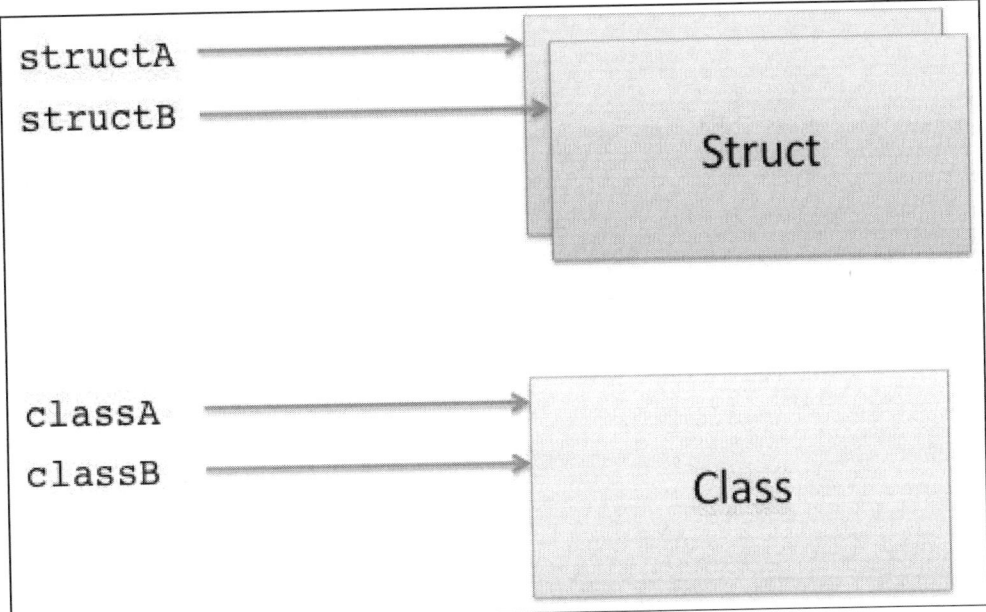

There is also another subtle, yet important, difference between classes and structs, relating to how they behave when constructed as a constant.

Recall from Chapter 1 that the `var` and `let` keywords define variables and constants respectively. When instantiated as variables, classes and structs share the same behavior; you can both mutate (i.e. change) their properties and reassign them to a new value. When instantiated as a constant, classes and structs have a slightly different behavior as follows:

- With constant classes you can mutate the properties of the class, but cannot re-assign the constant to a different or new class instance.
- With constant structs you cannot mutate their properties or re-assign to a new value.

This behavior is demonstrated below (you might want to experiment a little with this for yourself):

```swift
struct MyStruct {
  var foo: Double = 0.0
}
class MyClass {
  var foo: Double = 0.0
}

var classA = MyClass()
let classB = MyClass()
classA.foo = 1.0
classB.foo = 1.0
classB = classA

var structA = MyStruct()           {foo 0.0}
let structB = MyStruct()           {foo 0.0}
structA.foo = 1.0                  {foo 1.0}
structB.foo = 1.0
structB = structA
```

With Swift constant structs are entirely immutable! This feature is one of the reasons why arrays and dictionaries are structs rather than classes.

Convenience initializers

Sometimes it's nice to initialize an object in a simpler way. In the case of `Treasure`, it would be nice to provide an initializer that takes a latitude and longitude so that the user of the class doesn't need to bother with `GeoLocation` instances.

Open **Treasure.swift** and add the following code under the initializer:

```swift
convenience init(what: String,
                 latitude: Double, longitude: Double)
{
  let location = GeoLocation(latitude: latitude,
                             longitude: longitude)
  self.init(what: what, location: location)
}
```

This is what's known as a **convenience initializer**. The `convenience` keyword indicates that it doesn't do the full initialization itself, but rather defers to one of the non-convenience initializers, otherwise known as **designated initializers**.

Objective-C developers will be familiar with the concept of a designated initializer, as it was an Objective-C convention for a long time. Swift formalizes the concept and enforces it at compile time. If you didn't call through to a designated initializer in this convenience initializer, then Swift would throw a compile-time error.

You may be surprised that this method also creates a `GeoLocation`, because you didn't declare an initializer on the `GeoLocation` struct. Structs don't need explicit initializers. Swift creates them for you, with the parameters being each property in the order you define them. This makes struct initializers incredibly simple to read, since they directly describe the data encapsulated within the struct.

Class inheritance

Let's take a look at inheritance. Recall that the `Treasure` class is supposed to have three children: `HistoryTreasure`, `FactTreasure` and `HQTreasure`.

Open **Treasure.swift** and add the following at the bottom of the file:

```swift
// 1
class HistoryTreasure: Treasure {
  let year: Int

  // 2
  init(what: String, year: Int,
       latitude: Double, longitude: Double)
  {
    self.year = year
    let location = GeoLocation(latitude: latitude,
                               longitude: longitude)
    super.init(what: what, location: location)
  }
}

// 3
class FactTreasure: Treasure {
  let fact: String

  init(what: String, fact: String,
       latitude: Double, longitude: Double)
  {
    self.fact = fact
    let location = GeoLocation(latitude: latitude,
```

```
                                   longitude: longitude)
    super.init(what: what, location: location)
  }
}

// 4
class HQTreasure: Treasure {
  let company: String

  init(company: String, latitude: Double, longitude: Double) {
    self.company = company
    let location = GeoLocation(latitude: latitude,
                               longitude: longitude)
    super.init(what: company + " headquarters",
               location: location)
  }
}
```

Let's break this down into sections:

1. You can make a class inherit from another class by declaring it. Add the superclass after a colon following the class name. It's as simple as that!

2. `HistoryTreasure` contains an extra field—the year to which the treasure relates. Therefore, you must define a designated initializer to initialize this new value. If you didn't, then Swift could only use the superclass's initializers, which wouldn't initialize the `year` property (at least, not with a supplied value).

   A class's designated initializer must call through to one of the designated initializers of its superclass. It cannot call through to a convenience initializer. This makes things a little awkward because you have to duplicate the work you did to create the `GeoLocation` struct.

   You might find the placement of this call to `super.init()` confusing if you're an Objective-C developer. It's at the end of the method because in Swift, it's the initializer's job to initialize everything declared in this class and then hand off to the super class. The super class cannot overwrite any of this, because it doesn't know about things declared in its subclass(es).

3. and 4. You then declare the `FactTreasure` and `HQTreasure` classes in much the same way. Each has its own relevant data and therefore its own designated initializer.

Phew! You've written a class, a struct and a full hierarchy. You should be proud. Build and run the app just to make sure that everything still works correctly. Nothing will have changed in the app, because you're not making use of your new classes and struct yet. That comes next.

Swift and MapKit

You've written a class to hold treasures and a struct to hold locations on the map. It's about time you add some treasures to the map!

Open **ViewController.swift**. It's mainly an empty class with a single `mapView` variable. There is an Interface Builder outlet (`@IBOutlet`) for the `MKMapView`, but you need to add the rest.

Add the following code inside the `ViewController` class:

```
override func viewDidLoad() {
   super.viewDidLoad()
}
```

This is your first example of overriding a function. View controllers call a method called `viewDidLoad` after the app has loaded the view. This is the point at which you can customize your view.

Notice that in Swift, if the method you're overriding is an existing method on the class, then you must add the `override` keyword. This makes it clear to whoever's reading the code that behavior from the superclass may be overridden.

The `override` keyword also helps the compiler make decisions about the method you're implementing and provide extra checking. For example, if you misspell the overridden method name, then the compiler will throw an error because the method doesn't exist in the superclass. Likewise, if you had no idea there was such thing as `viewDidLoad` and just happened to pick that method name yourself, the compiler would throw an error.

Also notice that you use the `super` keyword to call a method defined by the superclass rather than your own implementation.

Add the following property declaration below the `@IBOutlet`:

```
var treasures: [Treasure] = []
```

This will hold the treasures that you'll show on the map. You're initializing the array of treasures with an empty array to start.

Now add the following code at the bottom of `viewDidLoad`:

```
self.treasures = [
   HistoryTreasure(what: "Google's first office",
                   year: 1999,
                   latitude: 37.44451, longitude: -122.163369),
```

```
    HistoryTreasure(what: "Facebook's first office",
                    year: 2005,
                    latitude: 37.444268, longitude: -122.163271),
    FactTreasure(what: "Stanford University",
                 fact: "Founded in 1885 by Leland Stanford.",
                 latitude: 37.427474, longitude: -122.169719),
    FactTreasure(what: "Moscone West",
                 fact: "Host to WWDC since 2003.",
                 latitude: 37.783083, longitude: -122.404025),
    FactTreasure(what: "Computer History Museum",
                 fact: "Home to a working Babbage Difference Engine.",
                 latitude: 37.414371, longitude: -122.076817),
    HQTreasure(company: "Apple",
               latitude: 37.331741, longitude: -122.030333),
    HQTreasure(company: "Facebook",
               latitude: 37.485955, longitude: -122.148555),
    HQTreasure(company: "Google",
               latitude: 37.422, longitude: -122.084),
]
```

This sets up all of the Silicon Valley treasures in the `treasures` array.

Class extensions and computed properties

Now you need to show these treasures on the map. To do this with `MapKit` (`MKMapView`), you add "annotations" to the map. Annotations must conform to the `MKAnnotation` protocol.

Open **Treasure.swift** and add the following import at the top of the file, just below the Foundation import:

```
import MapKit
```

Then add the following just underneath the declaration of the `Treasure` class:

```
extension Treasure: MKAnnotation {

  var coordinate: CLLocationCoordinate2D {
    return self.location.coordinate
  }

  var title: String {
    return self.what
  }
}
```

This is what's known as a class extension, which allows you to add additional functionality to a class. If you're from an Objective-C background, you probably know class extensions exist in Objective-C as well. In Swift, there are a few extra advantages, notably the ability to add properties and not just methods. Because of this, there's little difference between putting code in an extension versus putting it in the main class definition, but splitting up the class into logical units aids readability.

The logical unit you are implementing here is the conformance to the `MKAnnotation` protocol. This protocol requires you to define two properties: `coordinate` and `title`. You're declaring these properties but they look a little different: although they're defined with the `var` keyword, they're made up of a block of code and a `return` statement just like a function!

These are **computed properties** and not functions. They're different from regular properties since they're computed every time rather than backed by instance variables. Using a computed property is just like using regular properties, except that the computed property has associated code that runs every time the program accesses the property.

At the moment, this code doesn't compile because it's accessing a property on the location called `coordinate` that doesn't exist. Let's implement that now.

Your first struct extension

Open **GeoLocation.swift** and add the following import at the top of the file:

```
import MapKit
```

Then add the following code at the bottom of the file:

```
extension GeoLocation {
  var coordinate: CLLocationCoordinate2D {
    return CLLocationCoordinate2DMake(
            self.latitude, self.longitude)
  }

  var mapPoint: MKMapPoint {
    return MKMapPointForCoordinate(self.coordinate)
  }
}
```

Just like classes, structs can have extensions too. In this case, your extension isn't declaring conformance to any protocol as you just did to make `Treasure` conform to `MKAnnotation`. Instead, this extension is simply a way to separate code. This is good practice: it keeps logical units separate. In this case, you are keeping the `MapKit`-related code of `GeoLocation` separate from the rest.

The two computed properties you declare here are helpers to return the coordinates (latitude and longitude) and `mapPoint` (point in the `MKMapView`'s coordinate space).

Build and run. Ah. An error!

```
27  extension Treasure: MKAnnotation {              Type 'Treasure' does not conform to protocol 'NSObjectProtocol'
```

Inheriting from NSObject

This error tells you that because you have declared conformance to `MKAnnotation`, you must also conform to `NSObjectProtocol`, because `MKAnnotation` inherits from `NSObjectProtocol`.

Objective-C developers will be familiar with `NSObject`. If you are not, `NSObject` is part of the Foundation framework that is the base class of (almost) all objects in Objective-C, including those of Apple frameworks. `NSObject` is also a protocol to which the `NSObject` class conforms. Why it is both a class and a protocol is beyond the scope of this book, but needless to say, you need to make `Treasure` conform to the `NSObjectProtocol`.

The simplest way is to make `Treasure` inherit from `NSObject`. Do so by changing the declaration of the class as follows:

```swift
class Treasure: NSObject
```

If you are interfacing with Objective-C code, as you are when using `MapKit`, then you'll often find yourself making use of `NSObject`. By inheriting from `NSObject`, you can use your Swift class seamlessly from Objective-C. Magic? Yes, pretty much!

Pinning the map

Now that the `Treasure` class conforms to `MKAnnotation`, you can add it to a map view. Open **ViewController.swift** and add the following to the end of `viewDidLoad`:

```swift
self.mapView.delegate = self
self.mapView.addAnnotations(self.treasures)
```

The first line declares that the view controller is the delegate of the map view and the second adds the treasures as annotations on the map. The delegate allows the view controller to tell the map how to display the treasures.

Next, add the following class extension to the bottom of **ViewController.swift**:

```swift
extension ViewController: MKMapViewDelegate {
  func mapView(mapView: MKMapView!,
               viewForAnnotation annotation: MKAnnotation!)
      -> MKAnnotationView!
  {
    // 1
    if let treasure = annotation as? Treasure {
      // 2
      var view =
      mapView.dequeueReusableAnnotationViewWithIdentifier("pin")
        as MKPinAnnotationView!
      if view == nil {
        // 3
        view = MKPinAnnotationView(annotation: annotation,
                          reuseIdentifier: "pin")
        view.canShowCallout = true
        view.animatesDrop = false
        view.calloutOffset = CGPoint(x: -5, y: 5)
        view.rightCalloutAccessoryView =
          UIButton.buttonWithType(.DetailDisclosure) as UIView
      } else {
        // 4
        view.annotation = annotation
      }

      // 5
      return view
    }
    return nil
  }
}
```

This declares an extension that makes the view controller conform to the `MKMapViewDelegate` protocol so that it can be the delegate for the map view. Here's what the code does:

1. It implements `mapView:viewForAnnotation`. Notice in the method signature that the annotation you pass in is of type `MKAnnotation!`. This means it's an optional, so the value could be nil. But it's an implicitly unwrapped optional, meaning you can use it without checking for nil. But if you don't check for nil and it happens to be nil, then your app will crash at runtime. Many Objective-C APIs are wrapped like this because there are no optionals in Objective-C.

Because the annotation could be nil or even something other than a `Treasure` instance, you need to cast it to a `Treasure`. You do this using the **inline downcasting** syntax. You perform the downcast using `as?` and immediately assign it to the local variable `treasure`. Only if the downcast succeeds will the `if` statement pass. This is another example of Swift's concise syntax. A downcast and `if` statement all in one line! It really does help you play safe with types.

2. If the annotation is a treasure, then dequeue a view from the map for the reuse identifier `pin`. This simply means that if the program has created a pin before, but it's no longer onscreen because the user has moved the map away, then the program will reuse the view rather than create a new one. If you're familiar with `UITableViews`, you've probably used the same concept when you dequeue and reuse a `UITableViewCell`. Notice the use of downcast again, this time in the non-optional form `as`, because you know that all "`pin`" annotation views will be `MKPinAnnotationView` instances.

3. If no view could be dequeued, then create a new one and set it up as appropriate.

4. If a view was dequeued, then change its annotation.

5. Finally, return the annotation view.

Thanks for sticking with me there! Build and run your app. Pan and zoom to the San Francisco Bay Area and you will see something like this:

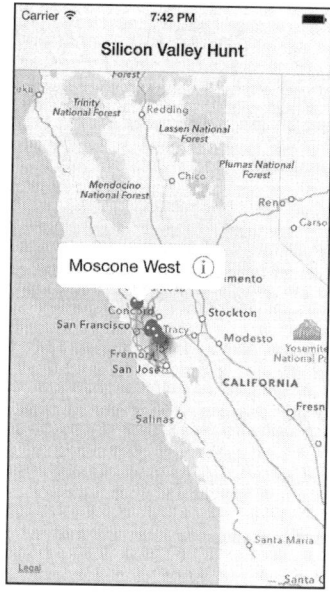

The pins are there! Treasures, ahoy!

The reduce algorithm

You may have felt frustration when the app opened and zoomed to your location instead of taking you directly to Silicon Valley. It's annoying to have to find the place yourself, even before you've begun your treasure hunt!

There's an easy way to solve that, as you'll see now.

Open **ViewController.swift** and add the following code to the end of `viewDidLoad`:

```
// 1
let rectToDisplay = self.treasures.reduce(MKMapRectNull) {
  (mapRect: MKMapRect, treasure: Treasure) -> MKMapRect in
    // 2
    let treasurePointRect =
      MKMapRect(origin: treasure.location.mapPoint,
              size: MKMapSize(width: 0, height: 0))
    // 3
    return MKMapRectUnion(mapRect, treasurePointRect)
}
// 4
self.mapView.setVisibleMapRect(rectToDisplay,
  edgePadding: UIEdgeInsetsMake(74, 10, 10, 10),
  animated: false)
```

Believe it or not, but these five lines of code (excluding comments and after unwrapping to fit in the book!) will make the map zoom to the region enclosing all of the treasures! Here's how it works:

1. This algorithm works by using the `reduce` function of an array. To reduce an array means to run a function over the array that combines each element into a single, final return value. At each step, the next element from the array is passed along with the current value for the reduce. The return value from the function then becomes the current value for the next reduce. Of course, you need to seed the reduce with an initial value. In this case, your seed is `MKMapRectNull`.

2. At each step in the reduce, you calculate a map rectangle enclosing just the single treasure.

3. You then return a rectangle made up of the union of the current overall rectangle and the single treasure rectangle.

4. When the reduce finishes, the map rectangle will be the union of all the map rectangles enclosing each and every treasure point. In other words, it will be a rectangle just large enough to enclose every treasure! What a simple way to find such a useful value!

It then remains to set the map view's visible map rectangle to the calculated rectangle. You use some edge padding to ensure that no pins end up underneath the navigation bar or too close to the edge of the screen.

Build and run the app. This time, you'll see the following immediately:

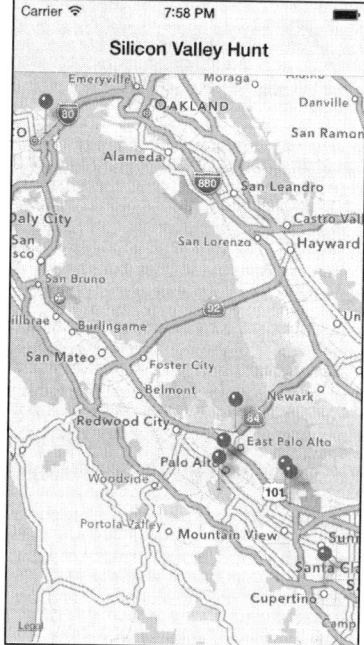

No manual panning and zooming required. W00t!

> **Note**: Reduce is a typical method in functional programming, where the final result is something calculated from iterating through a collection. You'll see this paradigm used quite a lot throughout Swift code, as it is baked into the language. If you're interested in this topic, then be sure to check out Chapter 7, "Functional Programming" later in this book! :]

Polymorphism

Currently all the pins are the same color. It would be nice if each type of treasure could distinguish itself with a different color. This sounds like a job for polymorphism!

Polymorphism, for those non-computer science folk, is the mechanism by which subclasses can each respond differently to the same method. In the case of treasures, you want a method to return the color. Each subclass can then define the color it wants to use.

Open **Treasure.swift** and add the following to the end of the Treasure class implementation:

```
func pinColor() -> MKPinAnnotationColor {
  return MKPinAnnotationColor.Red
}
```

This will be the default implementation. If a subclass doesn't override the method, then it will default to showing a red pin.

Next, add the following override to HistoryTreasure:

```
override func pinColor() -> MKPinAnnotationColor {
  return MKPinAnnotationColor.Purple
}
```

And the following override to HQTreasure:

```
override func pinColor() -> MKPinAnnotationColor {
  return MKPinAnnotationColor.Green
}
```

You are leaving FactTreasure without an override, so it will use the default red color.

Next, open **ViewController.swift** and find the implementation of mapView(_:viewForAnnotation:) that you implemented in the MKMapViewDelegate extension. Add the following just before the return view statement:

```
view.pinColor = treasure.pinColor()
```

This calls pinColor() on the treasure and sets the pin color to the returned value. This will call the correct implementation of pinColor() according to the subclass of each treasure.

Build and run the app. You'll see the following:

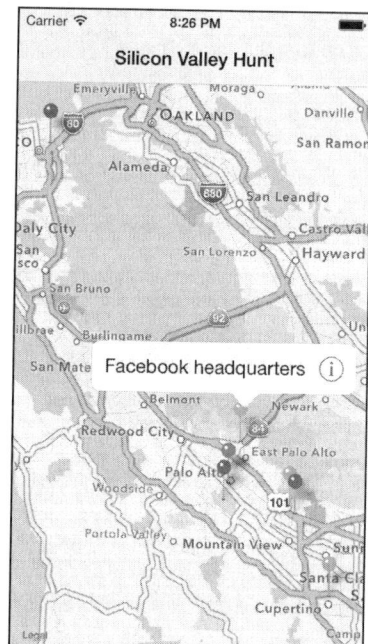

That's better. A bit of spice on the map!

Dynamic dispatch and final classes

Polymorphism requires some way for the code to look up which method implementation to invoke at runtime. In the case of `pinColor()`, it's either the overriding method or the base class method, depending on the subclass of the `Treasure` instance. This behavior is known as **dynamic dispatch**.

Every method call in Objective-C uses dynamic dispatch. The language makes heavy use of it, and it's even possible to add methods or classes at runtime! This makes it impossible for the compiler to do many optimizations ahead of runtime.

Dynamic dispatch still has to exist in Swift to allow polymorphic behavior. Instead of Objective-C-style message-passing dispatch, Swift uses an approach similar to that of C++. It achieves dynamic dispatch through the use of virtual tables or "vtables."

In the example above, when the compiler sees the call to `pinColor()` on a variable of type `Treasure`, it knows it needs to use vtable lookup (and thus dynamic dispatch) because the `Treasure` class has subclasses that implement `pinColor()`.

But what if the type the compiler sees for the variable is one of the subclasses, such as `HQTreasure`? In this case, the compiler still might have to use vtable dynamic dispatch because there might be other classes added somewhere that subclass `HQTreasure`. For this app, there is no subclass of `HQTreasure`. While you the developer know this is the case, the compiler doesn't and will play it safe with dynamic dispatch rather than try to optimize it to a direct function call. But there's a way to give the compiler a hint that there will never be subclasses of `HQTreasure` and alleviate this issue.

To declare that a class cannot have subclasses, you can use the keyword `final`. Any attempt to create a subclass of a final class will result in a compiler error. This can be a useful design feature and also has a notable performance benefit. Once you declare a class final, the compiler knows exactly which implementation of each method it should call for such instances. For example, if you were to mark `HQTreasure` as final and then call `pinColor()` on an instance of `HQTreasure`, the compiler would know to call the `HQTreasure` version of the method.

Let's put this into action. Open **Treasure.swift** and change the class declarations to mark the three subclasses of `Treasure` as final:

```
final class HistoryTreasure: Treasure
final class FactTreasure: Treasure
final class HQTreasure: Treasure
```

It's good practice to mark classes as final when they are logically so. This will allow the compiler to make optimizations and your code will run, ahem, swiftly. ;]

Adding annotations

Right now your users can see the treasure on the map, but they can't do anything with it. There's no way to learn the details behind the treasure, so let's add some annotations.

Open **Treasure.swift** and add the following protocol to the top of the file, above the `Treasure` class:

```
@objc protocol Alertable {
  func alert() -> UIAlertController
}
```

This protocol is going to be what each `Treasure` subclass will conform to. The sole method, `alert`, returns an alert controller that the view controller presents when the user presses the button in the callout box of a tapped pin.

Now add the following extensions to the bottom of the file:

```
extension HistoryTreasure: Alertable {
  func alert() -> UIAlertController {
    let alert = UIAlertController(
      title: "History",
      message: "From \(self.year):\n\(self.what)",
      preferredStyle: UIAlertControllerStyle.Alert)
    return alert
  }
}

extension FactTreasure: Alertable {
  func alert() -> UIAlertController {
    let alert = UIAlertController(
      title: "Fact",
      message: "\(self.what):\n\(self.fact)",
      preferredStyle: UIAlertControllerStyle.Alert)
    return alert
  }
}

extension HQTreasure: Alertable {
  func alert() -> UIAlertController {
    let alert = UIAlertController(
      title: "Headquarters",
      message: "The headquarters of \(self.company)",
      preferredStyle: UIAlertControllerStyle.Alert)
    return alert
  }
}
```

Each of these methods sets the title and message to something that makes sense for that type of treasure. Notice the lovely use of string interpolation!

Now open **ViewController.swift** and add the following to the `MKMapViewDelegate` extension:

```
func mapView(mapView: MKMapView!,
             annotationView view: MKAnnotationView!,
             calloutAccessoryControlTapped control: UIControl!)
{
  if let treasure = view.annotation as? Treasure {
    if let alertable = treasure as? Alertable {
```

```
      let alert = alertable.alert()
      alert.addAction(
        UIAlertAction(
          title: "OK",
          style: UIAlertActionStyle.Default,
          handler: nil))
      self.presentViewController(
        alert, animated: true, completion: nil)
    }
  }
}
```

This delegate method is called when the user taps either the pin or the pin's callout button (the "i" button on the right).

In this method, you downcast the annotation of the view to a `Treasure`, just like before. Then you downcast it again to check if it conforms to `Alertable`, which it needs to for you to be able to get an alert. Then you ask for the alert, add an OK button to it and finally present it.

Build and run the app and tap on a pin. Then tap the callout button on the right side of the callout. Observe the treasure dialog, which looks like this:

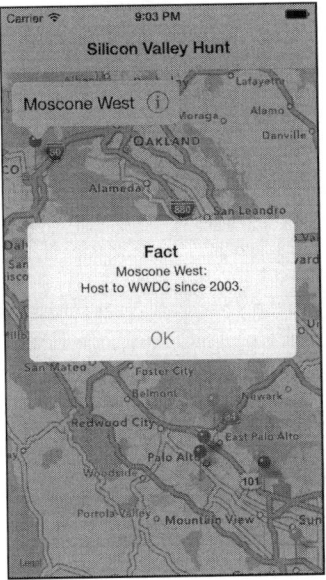

Woo-hoo! There are now treasures to find!

Sorting an array

It would be nice for your user to have an option to find the next nearest treasure once they've found an initial treasure. You can add this both easily and concisely using Swift.

First, open **GeoLocation.swift** and add the following code inside the `GeoLocation` struct definition:

```
func distanceBetween(other: GeoLocation) -> Double {
  let locationA = CLLocation(latitude: self.latitude,
                             longitude: self.longitude)
  let locationB = CLLocation(latitude: other.latitude,
                             longitude: other.longitude)
  return locationA.distanceFromLocation(locationB)
}
```

This adds a method to the `GeoLocation` struct that calculates a distance between itself and another `GeoLocation` instance. It does this with the assistance of Core Location's `CLLocation`, because calculating distance between points on the Earth is really hard!

Notice that structs can have methods just like classes can. This is a useful feature that sets Swift apart from C, in which structs can only have variables. Because C structs can't contain functions, operations to act upon them are often declared as functions at global scope. For example, for you to perform operations on a `CGRect`, you need global functions like `CGRectUnion`, `CGRectDivide` and `CGRectGetMidX`. These functions clutter the global scope and make it difficult to find all the functions that operate on `CGRect`s. It's left up to the developer to be prudent and put all the prototypes together in a header file. But Swift wins again, since related methods can be organized right "inside" a struct!

Now open **ViewController.swift** and find the implementation of `mapView:annotationView:calloutAccessoryControlTapped:` that you just added. Add the following code right before the call to `presentViewController`:

```
alert.addAction(UIAlertAction(
  title: "Find Nearest",
  style: UIAlertActionStyle.Default) { action in
    // 1
    var sortedTreasures = self.treasures
    sortedTreasures.sort {
      // 2
      let distanceA =
        treasure.location.distanceBetween($0.location)
      let distanceB =
```

```
            treasure.location.distanceBetween($1.location)
        return distanceA < distanceB
    }
    // 3
    mapView.deselectAnnotation(treasure, animated: true)
    mapView.selectAnnotation(sortedTreasures[1], animated: true)
})
```

This adds another action to the alert. This new action does the following:

1. You're going to sort the list of treasures, so you create a local variable to hold a copy of the original array. The `sort` method takes a single parameter—a closure that takes two objects—and returns a Boolean indicating whether object one is ordered before object two.

2. Next, you calculate the distance between the current treasure and each of the treasures you're sorting. Notice the use of `$0` and `$1`. This is shorthand syntax for the first and second parameters passed into a closure. There will be more on this in the chapter on closures!

   You check the first distance against the second distance and return `true` if it's smaller. In this way, you sort the array of treasures in order of shortest to longest distance from the current treasure.

3. Finally, you deselect the current treasure and select the new treasure. If you're wondering why the code selects the second element in the sorted array, it's because the first element will always be the current treasure itself!

Build and run the app. Select a treasure pin and then tap on the callout button. Now tap **Find Nearest**. The app finds the next nearest location!

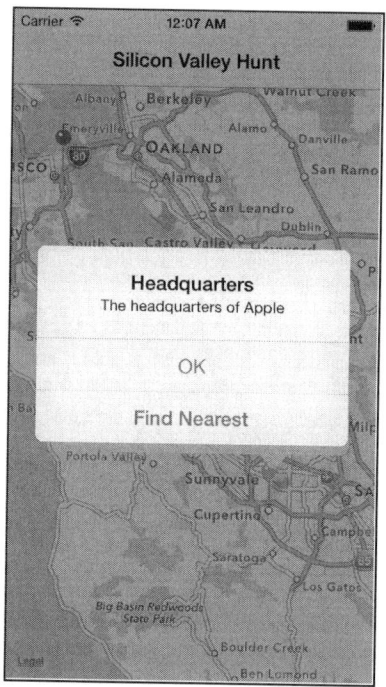

Equality and operator overload

Once the user has found the treasures, there's no record of where they've been. A neat way to create a record would be to show an overlay on the map marking the user's route between the places. If the user tries to claim they've found the same place twice, the app will flash an alert.

Open **ViewController.swift** and add the following properties at the top of the class, just underneath the treasures array property:

```
var foundLocations: [GeoLocation] = []
var polyline: MKPolyline!
```

The first property is going to hold an array of `GeoLocation` structs so that the app can keep track of which treasures the user has found and in what order.

The second property is going to hold an `MKPolyline`, which is an overlay you can add to a map view to show a line with a set of points. The user will see a path joining each of the locations they've found. The type, again, is an implicitly unwrapped optional. This is so it can be nil if necessary, such as before the user has found any treasures.

Next, find the `MKMapViewDelegate` extension at the bottom of the file and add the following method to it:

```
func mapView(mapView: MKMapView!, rendererForOverlay
            overlay: MKOverlay!) -> MKOverlayRenderer!
{
  if let polylineOverlay = overlay as? MKPolyline {
    let renderer = MKPolylineRenderer(polyline: polylineOverlay)
    renderer.strokeColor = UIColor.blueColor()
    return renderer
  }
  return nil
}
```

This method tells the map view how to render a given overlay. The overlay you're using is `MKPolyline`, which has an associated renderer called `MKPolylineRenderer`. Notice the use of optional checking again to downcast the overlay type.

Now find `mapView:annotationView:calloutAccessoryControlTapped:`. It should be right above the function you just added. Add the following action in between the two that are present:

```
alert.addAction(UIAlertAction(
    title: "Found",
    style: UIAlertActionStyle.Default) { action in
      self.markTreasureAsFound(treasure)
})
```

This is what the user will tap when they've found the treasure. Add the following method to the main body of the view controller's class:

```
func markTreasureAsFound(treasure: Treasure) {
  // 1
  if let index = find(self.foundLocations, treasure.location) {
    // 2
    let alert = UIAlertController(
        title: "Oops!",
        message: "You've already found this treasure (at step \(index + 1))! Try again!",
        preferredStyle: .Alert)
    alert.addAction(UIAlertAction(title: "OK",
                                  style: .Default,
                                  handler: nil))
    self.presentViewController(alert,
```

```
                                    animated: true,
                                    completion: nil)
    } else {
      // 3
      self.foundLocations.append(treasure.location)

      // 4
      if self.polyline != nil {
        self.mapView.removeOverlay(self.polyline)
      }

      // 5
      var coordinates = self.foundLocations.map { $0.coordinate }
      self.polyline = MKPolyline(coordinates: &coordinates,
                                 count: coordinates.count)
      self.mapView.addOverlay(self.polyline)
    }
  }
}
```

Here's what this method does:

1. First of all, you check if the location already exists in the found locations array using the global `find()` function, which takes a collection and an element to find in the collection. The function returns either the index into the collection where the element is found, or nil. This is a great use of optionals, and as you can see, the code is easy to read.

2. If the location does already exist in the found locations array, then you display an alert showing at which step the user found the treasure.

3. If the location doesn't exist in the found locations array, then you add it to the array.

4. Then, if a polyline already exists, you remove it from the map. If you didn't do this, then overlays would pile up on the map each time you added a new one.

5. Finally, you create a new `MKPolyline` and add it to the map view. Take note of the use of the `map` function on the array. This function takes each element in the array, converts it using the supplied closure and creates a new array from the results. The code above uses the short syntax for closures where the signature is completely left off because Swift can infer it from the `map` function's signature. Each element in the array is passed into the closure as the `$0` variable.

At this point, you'll see an error on the line that calls `find()`. To understand why, consider what `find()` needs to do: it needs to scan through the array and for each element, see if it's the one you're looking for. It uses the equality operator == to find a match but by default, you cannot equate classes and structs.

For that to happen, they need to conform to the `Equatable` protocol. Therefore, you need to make `GeoLocation` conform to `Equatable`.

This is the protocol definition for `Equatable`:

```
protocol Equatable {
  func ==(lhs: Self, rhs: Self) -> Bool
}
```

You need to implement just one method. But notice that this method is called `==`. That might seem odd. If you're an Objective-C developer, you might have expected to see something like `isEqual`.

This is another fantastic example of a feature that sets Swift apart from Objective-C, one known as **operator overload**. Instead of having a special method to perform equality, Swift lets you overload the `==` operator to perform the equality check.

Open **GeoLocation.swift** and add the following code at the bottom of the file:

```
extension GeoLocation: Equatable {
}

func ==(lhs: GeoLocation, rhs: GeoLocation) -> Bool {
    return lhs.latitude == rhs.latitude &&
           lhs.longitude == rhs.longitude
}
```

The extension is the usual way to declare conformance to a protocol, but notice that the `==` function is not inside the extension. You must declare all operator overloads at global scope because they aren't methods that belong to a class — you can use the `==` operator on its own anywhere. They are only associated with a class in that the type of the two parameters are instances of the class the function is comparing.

The implementation is simple: It checks if both the latitude and the longitude are equal!

Build and run the app. Find a few treasures and build up a trail. You'll see something like this:

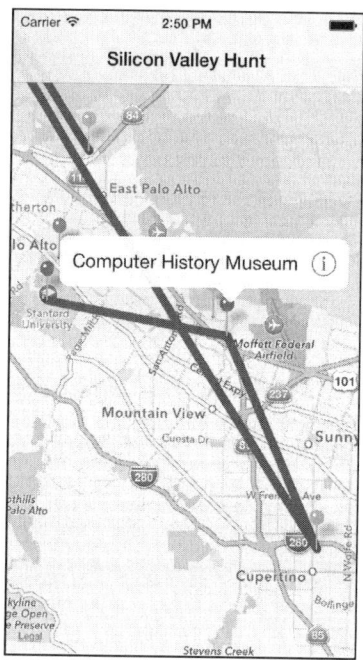 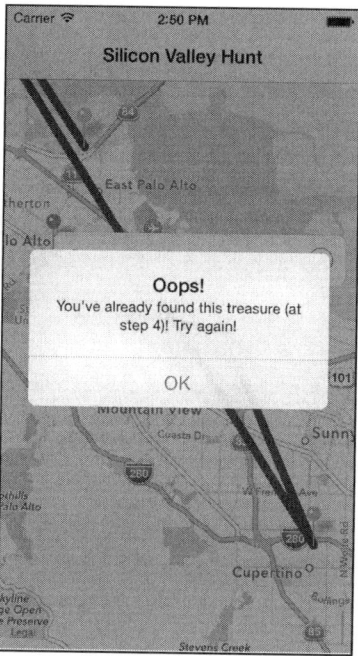

Access Control

Currently, all the methods and variables you have declared on your classes and structs have been public. That means they can be used from anywhere, by any other code. Swift however affords you flexibility over what has access to each property, method, etc. It does so through the use of access control modifiers.

There are three levels of access control as follows:

- **Public**: Everything has access.

- **Internal**: Only other code within the same target (library or app) has access. This is the default access level.

- **Private**: Only the single source file has access.

The use of access control really helps make your code maintainable. For example, you could have many helper methods inside your class, which you don't want to expose publically because they mutate state that should be hidden from the consumer of the class. These could be marked as private to stop consumers from using the methods.

The internal access level is perfect for libraries. Often your classes will have methods that are only to be used by the library itself, because they handle state related to the library. If these methods were exposed to the consumer of the library then they could either see internal data structures that you don't want to expose, or mutate state in such a way as to break the functionality of the library. Since internal is the default, you will want to apply the public modifier to any class, struct, enum, method, etc that should be accessible externally to the library – i.e. users of the library.

For applications, the internal access level is also generally what you want to use (it is handy that it's the default!). The application code won't be used by anything else, so it doesn't need to be accessible by anything other than itself. That said, unit tests mean that public can be useful. Unit tests are usually in a separate target, so anything that needs to be accessed from unit tests will need to be made public.

Objective-C developers will be pleased to learn that in Swift, private methods really are private. There's no runtime inspection and no backdoor way to call private methods that you shouldn't have access to.

Let's see this in action in your app.

Open **ViewController.swift**. Find `markTreasureAsFound`. The view controller uses this method internally to handle the user tapping on the "Found" button in the action sheet. This is a great candidate to become private. You wouldn't want anything outside of the view controller itself setting the state of treasures. Otherwise the user could cheat!

Change the method declaration to the following:

```
private func markTreasureAsFound(treasure: Treasure)
```

Build and run. Everything should work just as it did before. Great! But why stop there?

The view controller also has three properties. These are all to maintain local state and should therefore not be accessible from the outside. Go ahead and change their declarations as follows:

```
private var treasures: [Treasure] = []
private var foundLocations: [GeoLocation] = []
private var polyline: MKPolyline!
```

Once again, build and run. It still works! And now nothing can touch those properties from the outside.

The internal modifier is a little redundant in an app. It only really makes sense when used in a library that is shared between multiple apps. However, imagine you were to create a TreasureHunt library, which packaged up all your code so that another app could display the same treasure hunt. In this case you might mark `Treasure` and `GeoLocation` as `internal`, so that they cannot be used by the other app. Only the `ViewController` class could be used, which in that case might be better renamed to `TreasureHuntViewController`!

Access control modifiers are a great way to declare your intentions. Use `private` wherever possible so that you only expose the core API that is required to use your objects. Doing so will lead to fewer bugs and much more maintainable code. You are free to refactor private methods without breaking the external API, for example.

And that's your app—built! Congratulations and good luck with your treasure hunt!

Where to go from here?

In this chapter, you've learned quite a bit about classes and structs. You've created your own class hierarchy and seen how to extend both classes and structs. You've learned about the differences between classes and structs and when is the right time to use each. You're also learned about how things like dynamic dispatch and equality checks work in Swift.

Moreover, you've built a cool app and perhaps learned something about Silicon Valley. Maybe it's your first iOS app, and if so, give yourself a big pat on the back and feel proud. :]

While this chapter has given you a great basis in these concepts, throughout the rest of this book you will be learning even more about classes and structs. You'll see uses of classes and structs, which will make you aware of real life use cases for each of them. You'll also see how they can be made even more powerful through the use of generic programming.

The experienced Objective-C readers will also be interested to find out how Swift classes can interact with Objective-C directly.

Chapter 4: Generics
By Matt Galloway

By now, you know the basics of Swift and how to write classes and structs. But Swift is more than this—much more. The topic of this chapter is a very powerful Swift feature already popular in several other languages: generics.

With type-safe languages, it's a common problem to want to write code that acts on one type, but is also perfectly valid acting on another type. Imagine, for example, a function to add two integers. A function to add two floats would look very similar—in fact, it would look identical. The only difference would be the type of the variables.

In a strongly-typed language, you would need to define separate functions like `addInts`, `addFloats`, `addDoubles`, etc., where each function had the correct argument and return types.

Many languages implement solutions to this problem. C++, for example, uses templates. Swift, like Java and C#, uses generic programming—hence the topic of this chapter!

Throughout this chapter, you'll tour the existing generics in the language, including some you've seen already. Then, you'll build a Flickr photo search app with a custom generic data structure to keep track of the user's search terms.

Let's get started!

Introducing generics

You might not know it, but you've already seen generics at work while reading this book. Arrays and dictionaries are classic examples of the type safety of generics in action.

Objective-C developers are accustomed to arrays and dictionaries holding objects of many types in the same collection. This provides for great flexibility, but how do you know what an array returned from an API is meant to hold? You can only be sure by looking at documentation or at variable names, another form of documentation. Even with documentation, there is nothing (other than bug-free code!) to prevent something unexpected in the collection at runtime.

Swift, on the other hand, has typed arrays and dictionaries. An array of `Int`s can only hold `Int`s and can never (for example) contain a `String`. This means you can document code by writing code, allowing the compiler to do the type checking for you.

For example, in Objective-C UIKit, the method that handles touches in a custom view is as follows:

```
- (void)touchesBegan:(NSSet *)touches
            withEvent:(UIEvent *)event;
```

The set in this method is known to contain only `UITouch` instances, but only because the documentation says so. Nothing is stopping the objects in there from being anything else, and you generally need to cast the touches in the set as `UITouch` instances to effectively treat them as `UITouch` objects.

Swift doesn't have a set defined in the standard library at this time. However, if you used an array in place of a set, then you could write the above method like this:

```
func touchesBegan(touches: [UITouch]!,
            withEvent event: UIEvent!)
```

This tells you that the `touches` array only contains `UITouch` instances, and the compiler will throw an error if the code calling this method tries to pass anything else. Not only does the compiler control types placed into the `touches` array, but you no longer need to cast elements to instances of `UITouch`!

Overall, generics provide types as a parameter to the class. All arrays act the same way, storing values in a list, but generic arrays parameterize value type. You might find it helpful to think of it like this: The algorithms you'll use on arrays are non-type-specific, so all arrays, with all types of values, can share them.

Now that you have a basic sense of generics and their utility, you're ready to apply them to a concrete scenario.

Generics in action

To put generics to the test, you're going to build an app that searches Flickr for images.

To get you going speedily, there's a starter project in the resources for this chapter. Open it and quickly familiarize yourself with the main classes. The `Flickr` class handles talking to the Flickr API. Notice the API key is located with this class—one has been provided, but you may want to use your own in case you want to expand on the app. You can sign up for one here: https://www.flickr.com/services/apps/by/

Build and run the app. You'll see this:

Not much yet! Never fear, you'll soon have this thing pulling in pictures of cats! (What else?)

Ordered dictionaries

Your app is going to download pictures for each user query. It will display them in a list with the most recent search at the top.

But what if your user searches for the same term twice? It would be nice if the app brought the old results back up to the top of the most recent list and replaced it with new results.

You might use an array for the data structure to back this, but for the purpose of learning generics, you're going to create a new collection: an **ordered dictionary**.

In many languages and frameworks (including Swift) sets and dictionaries do not guarantee any kind of order, in contrast to arrays. An ordered dictionary is like a normal dictionary, but the keys are in a defined order. You'll use this functionality to store search results keyed by search term, making it quick to find results and also to maintain the order for the table view.

If you were being hasty, you might create a custom data structure to handle the ordered dictionary. But you are forward thinking! You want to create something that you can use in apps for years to come! This is a perfect use case for generics.

The initial data structure

Add a new file by clicking **File\New\File…** and selecting **iOS\Source\Swift File**. Click **Next** and call the file **OrderedDictionary**. Finally, click **Create**.

You will have an empty Swift file. Add the following code to it:

```
struct OrderedDictionary {
}
```

So far this should be no surprise. The object is going to be a struct because it should have value semantics (see Chapter 3, "Classes and Structs", for a discussion on the difference).

Now you need to make it generic so it can hold whatever type of values you want. Change the struct definition to the following:

```
struct OrderedDictionary<KeyType, ValueType>
```

The elements inside the angled brackets are the type parameters of the generic. `KeyType` and `ValueType` are not types themselves, but rather become parameters that you can use in place of types within the struct's definition. All will become clear shortly.

The simplest way to implement an ordered dictionary is to maintain both an array and a dictionary. The dictionary will hold the mapping, and the array will hold the order of the keys.

Add the following code inside the struct's definition:

```
typealias ArrayType = [KeyType]
typealias DictionaryType = [KeyType: ValueType]

var array = ArrayType()
var dictionary = DictionaryType()
```

This declares two properties, as described, and also two **type aliases**, which are a way to give a new name to an existing type. Here, you give aliases to the array and dictionary types for the backing array and dictionary, respectively. Type aliases are a great way to take a complex type and give it a much shorter name.

Notice how you can use the type parameters `KeyType` and `ValueType` from the struct definition in place of types. The array is an array of `KeyType`s. Of course, there is no such type as `KeyType`; instead Swift treats it as whatever type the consumer of `OrderedDictionary` passes during instantiation of the generic.

At this point, you'll notice a compiler error:

```
typealias DictionaryType = [KeyType: ValueType]
    Type 'KeyType' does not conform to protocol 'Hashable'
```

This might come as a surprise. Take a look at the implementation of `Dictionary`:

```
struct Dictionary<KeyType: Hashable, ValueType>
```

This is awfully similar to the definition of `OrderedDictionary`, except for one thing— the ": Hashable" after `KeyType`. The `Hashable` after the semicolon declares that the type passed for `KeyType` must conform to the `Hashable` protocol. This is because `Dictionary` needs to be able to hash keys for its implementation.

It's very common to constrain generic type parameters in this way. For example, you might want to constrain the value type to conform to the `Equatable` or `Printable` protocols depending on what your app needs to do with those values.

Open **OrderedDictionary.swift** and replace your struct definition with the following:

```
struct OrderedDictionary<KeyType: Hashable, ValueType>
```

This declares that the `KeyType` for `OrderedDictionary` must conform to `Hashable`. This means that whatever type `KeyType` becomes, it will be acceptable as a key for the underlying dictionary as well.

The file will now compile again without any errors!

Keys, values and all that jazz

What use is a dictionary if you can't add values to it? Open **OrderedDictionary.swift** and add the following function inside your struct definition:

```swift
// 1
mutating func insert(value: ValueType,
                     forKey key: KeyType,
                     atIndex index: Int) -> ValueType?
{
  var adjustedIndex = index

  // 2
  let existingValue = self.dictionary[key]
  if existingValue != nil {
    // 3
    let existingIndex = find(self.array, key)!

    // 4
    if existingIndex < index {
      adjustedIndex--
    }
    self.array.removeAtIndex(existingIndex)
  }

  // 5
  self.array.insert(key, atIndex:adjustedIndex)
  self.dictionary[key] = value

  // 6
  return existingValue
}
```

This introduces a couple of new things. Let's take it step by step:

1. The method to insert a new object, `insert(_:forKey:atIndex)`, needs to take three parameters: the **value** for a particular **key** and the **index** at which to insert the key-value pair. There is a keyword here that you might not have seen before: `mutating`.

   Structs are designed to be immutable by default, meaning you ordinarily can't mutate struct member variables in an instance method. Since that is quite limiting, you can add the `mutating` keyword to tell the compiler that the method is allowed to mutate state in the struct. This helps the compiler make decisions about when to take copies of structs (they are copy-on-write) and also helps document the API.

2. You pass the key to the indexer of the `Dictionary`, which returns the existing value if one already exists for that key. This `insert` method emulates the same behavior as the Dictionary's `updateValue` and therefore saves the existing value for the key.

3. If there is an existing value, then and only then does the method find the index into the array for that key.

4. If the existing key is before the insertion index, then you need to adjust the insertion index because you're about to remove the existing key.

5. You update the array and dictionary, as appropriate.

6. Finally, you return the existing value. Since there might not be an existing value, the function returns an optional value.

Now that you have the ability to add values to the dictionary, what about removing values?

Add the following function to the `OrderedDictionary` struct definition:

```
// 1
mutating func removeAtIndex(index: Int) -> (KeyType, ValueType)
{
    // 2
    precondition(index < self.array.count, "Index out-of-bounds")

    // 3
    let key = self.array.removeAtIndex(index)

    // 4
    let value = self.dictionary.removeValueForKey(key)!

    // 5
    return (key, value)
}
```

Let's take it step by step again:

1. Once more, this is a function that mutates the internal state of the struct, and you therefore mark it as such. The name `removeAtIndex` matches the method on `Array`. It's a good idea to consider mirroring the APIs of the system library when appropriate. It helps make developers using your API feel at home on the platform.

2. First, you check the index to see if it's within the bounds of the array. Trying to remove an out-of-bounds element from the underlying array will trigger a runtime error, so the check here will catch that condition a bit earlier. You may have used assertions in Objective-C with the `assert` function; `assert` is available in Swift too,

but `precondition` is active in release builds so your shipped apps will terminate if the preconditions fails.

3. Next, you obtain the key from the array for the given index while at the same time removing the value from the array.

4. Then, you remove the value for that key from the dictionary, which also returns the value that was present. The dictionary might not contain a value for the given key, so `removeValueForKey` returns an optional. In this case, you know that the dictionary will contain a value for the given key, because the only method that can add to the dictionary is your own `insert(_:forKey:atIndex:)`, which you wrote. Thus you can immediately unwrap the optional with `!` knowing there will be a value there.

5. Finally, you return the key and value in a tuple. This parallels the behavior of `Array removeAtIndex` and `Dictionary removeValueForKey`, which return the existing values.

Accessing values

You can now write to the dictionary but you can't read from it—that's no good for a data structure! You're now going to add the methods that will allow you to retrieve values from the dictionary.

Open **OrderedDictionary.swift** and add the following code to the struct definition, just underneath the `array` and `dictionary` variable declarations:

```
var count: Int {
   return self.array.count
}
```

This is a computed property for the count of the ordered dictionary, a commonly needed piece of information for such a data structure. The count of the array will always match the count of the ordered dictionary, so this is an easy one!

Next, you need a way to access elements of the dictionary. In Swift, you access a dictionary using the subscript syntax, as follows:

```
let dictionary = [1: "one", 2: "two"]
let one = dictionary[1] // Subscript
```

You're familiar with this syntax by now, but have likely only seen it used on arrays and dictionaries. How would you achieve this using your own classes and structs? Swift, fortunately, makes it simple to add subscript behavior to custom classes.

Add the following code to the bottom of the struct definition:

```
// 1
subscript(key: KeyType) -> ValueType? {
    // 2(a)
    get {
        // 3
        return self.dictionary[key]
    }
    // 2(b)
    set {
        // 4
        if let index = find(self.array, key) {
        } else {
            self.array.append(key)
        }

        // 5
        self.dictionary[key] = newValue
    }
}
```

Here's what this code does:

1. This is how you add subscript behavior. Instead of `func` or `var`, you use the `subscript` keyword. The parameter, in this case `key`, defines the object that you expect to appear inside the square brackets.

2. Subscripts can comprise setters and getters, just like computed properties can. Notice that this one has both (a) a `get` and (b) a `set` closure, defining the getter and setter, respectively.

3. The getter is simple: It needs to ask the dictionary for the value for the given key. The dictionary's subscript already returns an optional to allow for indicating that no value exists for that key.

4. The setter is more complex. First, it checks if the key already exists in the ordered dictionary. If it doesn't exist, then you need to add it to the array. It makes sense are for the new key to go at the end of the array, so you add the value to the array using append.

5. Finally, you add the new value to the dictionary for the given key, passing in the new value via the implicitly named variable `newValue`.

Now you can index into the ordered dictionary as if it were a normal dictionary. You can get the value for a certain key, but what about accessing by index, as with an array?

Seeing as how this is an ordered dictionary, it would be useful to access an element by index too.

Classes and structs can have multiple subscript definitions for different argument types. Add the following function to the bottom of your struct definition:

```swift
subscript(index: Int) -> (KeyType, ValueType) {
  // 1
  get {
    // 2
    precondition(index < self.array.count,
              "Index out-of-bounds")

    // 3
    let key = self.array[index]

    // 4
    let value = self.dictionary[key]!

    // 5
    return (key, value)
  }
}
```

This is similar to the subscript you added previously, except that the type of the parameter is now `Int`, because that is what you use to reference the index of an array. This time, however, the return type is a tuple of `key` and `value`, because that is what your `OrderedDictionary` stores at a given index.

Here's what this code does:

1. This subscript only has a getter. You could implement a setter for it as well, first checking that indexes that are within the size range of the ordered dictionary.

2. The index must be within the bounds of the array, which defines the length of the ordered dictionary. You use a precondition to alert programmers who try to access beyond the bounds of the ordered dictionary.

3. You find the key by obtaining it from the array.

4. You find the value by obtaining it from the dictionary for the given key. Notice, again, the use of the unwrapped optional, because you know that the dictionary must contain a value for any key that's in the array.

5. Finally, you return a tuple containing the key and value.

> **Challenge**: Implement a setter for this subscript. Add `set` followed by a closure, just as in your previous subscript definition.
>
> Hint: The type of `newValue` will be a tuple containing the key and value to set at the given index.
>
> Hint: You can extract the values from a tuple using this syntax:
> `let (key, value) = newValue`

At this point, you may wonder what happens if `KeyType` is `Int`. The benefit of generics is to allow any hashable type as the key, including `Int`. In that case, how does the subscript know which subscript code to use?

That's where you would need to give more type information to the compiler to let it know your intentions. Notice that each of the subscripts has a different return type. Therefore, if you tried to set a key-value tuple, the compiler would know that it should use the array-style subscript.

Let's see how that works. Create a new playground by clicking **File\New\File…**, selecting **iOS\Source\Playground** and clicking **Next**. Call it **ODPlayground** and then click **Create**.

Copy and paste the entirety of **OrderedDictionary.swift** into the new playground. You have to do this because, sadly, the playground cannot "see" code in your app module.

Now add the following to the bottom of your playground:

```
var dict = OrderedDictionary<Int, String>()
dict.insert("dog", forKey: 1, atIndex: 0)
dict.insert("cat", forKey: 2, atIndex: 1)
println(dict.array.description
    + " : "
    + dict.dictionary.description)

var byIndex: (Int, String) = dict[0]
println(byIndex)

var byKey: String? = dict[2]
println(byKey)
```

Click **View\Assistant Editor\Show Assistant Editor** to see the output of the `println()`:

```
Console Output
[1, 2] : [1: dog, 2: cat]
(1, dog)
Optional("cat")
```

In this example, the dictionary has an `Int` key, so the compiler will look at the type of the variable being assigned to determine which subscript to use. Since `byIndex` is an `(Int, String)` tuple, the compiler knows to use the array style index version of the subscript which matches the expected return type.

Try removing the type definition from one of the `byIndex` or `byKey` variables. You'll see a compiler error, indicating that the compiler doesn't implicitly know which subscript to use.

> **PRO TIP:** For type inference to work, the compiler requires that the type of an expression be unambiguous. When multiple methods exist with the same argument types but different return types, the caller needs to be specific. Adding a method in Swift can be a build-breaking change, so be aware!

Experiment with the ordered dictionary in the playground to get a feel for how it works. Try adding to it, removing from it and changing the key and value types, before returning to the app.

You can now read and write into your ordered dictionary! That takes care of your data structure. Now you can get cracking with the app!

Aside: Assertions & preconditions

In the previous section you added a couple of precondition statements to the code. They are used in the context here to check that the parameters passed to the method are valid. There's a lot more to assertions and preconditions than that though.

Both assertions and preconditions are used when you want to check a condition to be true before continuing execution. If the condition fails then execution is halted and the app crashes.

The difference between the two is that assertions are compiled out in release builds, whereas preconditions are not. Assertions are designed to catch bugs during development, whereas preconditions are designed to throw fatal errors when a condition that must be true, is not.

An example use of an assertion would be where you have methods that set up your view hierarchy in a view controller. If one method relies on another being executed already, then you would assert that. Like so:

```swift
private func configureTableView() {
    self.tableView = UITableView(frame: CGRectZero)
    self.tableView.delegate = self
    self.tableView.dataSource = self
    self.view.addSubview(self.tableView)
}

private func configureHeader() {
    assert(self.tableView != nil)
    
    let headerView = UIView(frame: CGRectMake(0, 0, 320, 50))
    headerView.backgroundColor = UIColor.clearColor()
    
    let label = UILabel(frame: CGRectZero)
    label.text = "My Table"
    label.sizeToFit()
    label.frame = CGRectMake(0, 0,
                             label.bounds.size.width,
                             label.bounds.size.height)
    headerView.addSubview(label)
    
    self.tableView.tableHeaderView = headerView
}
```

In this case, the `configureHeader()` method requires the table view to have been created, so an assertion that it exists is added before the header for the table view is set up. This would guard against calling these methods in the wrong order during view controller initialization.

This is something that you're going to catch during development. Instead of cursing your computer wondering why the header isn't showing up, you'll be notified of the mistake by the debugger stopping at the assert. There would be no need for this check in release builds because you should catch it during development, but if you don't then you certainly don't want the app to crash just because of this silly mistake.

One interesting thing about asserts is that the compiler is allowed to assume in release builds that the condition is true. With that in mind, consider the following:

```
func foo(value: Int) {
  assert(value > 0)
  if value > 0 {
    println("Yes, it's greater than zero")
  } else {
    println("Nope")
  }
}
```

This might seem a little strange, but it illustrates an interesting point. The assertion will be present in debug builds, so if you pass 0 then the assertion will fail and the app will crash. However in release builds, what happens? Well the compiler is actually allowed to make the function always print "Yes, it's greater than zero"!

The compiler sees the assertion that value is greater than 0 and in release builds is allowed to assume that this is always the case. So the optimizer can, if it likes, ignore the if-statement because it assumes that value is greater than 0. Neat, and clever!

As stated above, preconditions do the same thing as assertions, but are also present in release builds. You might use them when you really do need to ensure that a condition is met. An example of this might be you are going to read into an array and you want to check that the index you've been given is valid. For example:

```
func fetchPeopleBetweenIndexes(start: Int, end: Int) -> [Person]
{
  precondition(start < end)
  precondition(start >= 0)
  precondition(end <= self.people.count)
  return Array(self.people[start..<end])
}
```

In this example, preconditions are used to check that the inputs to the function are valid. Start must be less than end, start must be greater than or equal to zero and end must be less than or equal to the number of people.

These sort of checks make sense to have in for debug and release because the app will crash anyway when the array is read from if the indexes are invalid. Crashing in your own code gives you more signal on what's actually going wrong.

Both assertions and preconditions optionally take a string as its second parameter. This allows you to add a message which will be output when the failure occurs.

As a general rule of thumb, use assertions when execution could continue, but you want to be notified of the failure during development. Use preconditions when it's a hard failure and continuing execution could cause data corruption or other serious problem. Preconditions are also great for when you're developing code for others to use, such as the OrderedDictionary – you *want* the app to crash when that other programmer provides invalid input!

Adding image search

It's time to shift your attention back to the app in hand. Open **MasterViewController.swift** and add the following variable definition, just below the two `@IBOutlet`s:

```
var searches = OrderedDictionary<String, [Flickr.Photo]>()
```

This is going to be the ordered dictionary that holds the searches the user submits to Flickr. As you can see, it maps `String`, the search term, to an array of `Flickr.Photo`, or the photos returned from the Flickr API. Notice you give the key and value in angle brackets just as you would for a normal dictionary. These become the type parameters `KeyType` and `ValueType` in the implementation.

You may wonder why the type `Flickr.Photo` has a period in it. It's because `Photo` is a class defined inside the `Flickr` class. This hierarchy is a rather useful feature of Swift, helping to contain namespace while keeping class names short. Inside the `Flickr` class, you can use `Photo` alone to refer to the photo class, because the context tells the compiler what it is.

Next, find the table view data source method called `tableView(_:numberOfRowsInSection:)` and change it to look like this:

```
func tableView(tableView: UITableView,
            numberOfRowsInSection section: Int) -> Int
{
   return self.searches.count
}
```

This method now uses the ordered dictionary to tell the table view how many rows it has.

Next, find the table view data source method `tableView(_:cellForRowAtIndexPath:)` and change it to look like this:

```swift
func tableView(tableView: UITableView,
        cellForRowAtIndexPath indexPath: NSIndexPath)
        -> UITableViewCell
{
  // 1
  let cell =
    tableView.dequeueReusableCellWithIdentifier("Cell",
      forIndexPath: indexPath) as UITableViewCell

  // 2
  let (term, photos) = self.searches[indexPath.row]

  // 3
  cell.textLabel.text = "\(term) (\(photos.count))"
  return cell
}
```

Here's what you are doing in this method:

1. First, you dequeue a cell from the `UITableView`. You need to cast it directly to a `UITableViewCell` because `dequeueReusableCellWithIdentifier` still returns `AnyObject` (id in Objective-C) and not a `UITableViewCell`. Perhaps in the future, Apple will rewrite its APIs to take advantage of generics as well!

2. Then, you obtain the key and value for the given row, using the subscript by index that you wrote.

3. Finally, you set the cell's text label appropriately and return the cell.

Now for the meat in the pie. Find the `UISearchBarDelegate` extension and change the single method in there to look like this:

```swift
func searchBarSearchButtonClicked(searchBar: UISearchBar!) {
  // 1
  searchBar.resignFirstResponder()

  // 2
  let searchTerm = searchBar.text
  Flickr.search(searchTerm) {
    switch ($0) {
    case .Error:
      // 3
      break
    case .Results(let results):
```

```
        // 4
        self.searches.insert(results,
                           forKey: searchTerm,
                           atIndex: 0)

        // 5
        self.tableView.reloadData()
      }
    }
}
```

This method is called when the user taps on the search button. Here's what you are doing in this method:

1. You resign the search bar as first responder, dismissing the keyboard.

2. Then, you take the search term as the text in the search bar right now, and use the `Flickr` class to search for that term. The `search` method of `Flickr` takes both a search term and a closure to execute on success or failure of the search. The closure takes one parameter: an enumeration of either `Error` or `Results`.

3. In the case of `Error`, nothing happens. You could make it show an alert here if you wanted, but let's keep this simple for now. The code requires a break here to tell Swift's compiler of your intention that the error case do nothing.

4. If the search works, `search` returns the results as the associated value in the `SearchResults` enum type. You add the results to the top of the ordered dictionary, with the search term as the key. If the search term already exists in the dictionary, this will bring the search term to the top of the list and update it with the latest results.

5. Finally, you reload the table view because you now have new data.

Woo! Your app will now search for images!

Build and run the app, and make a couple of searches. You'll see something like this:

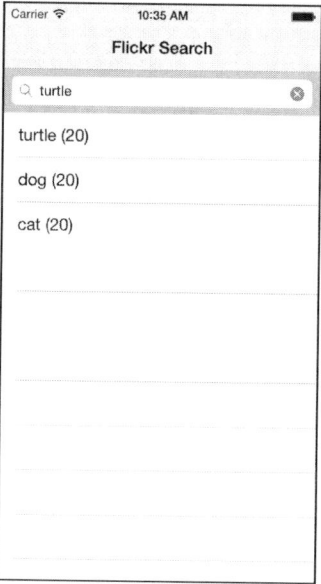

Now repeat one of the searches that's not at the top of the list. You'll see it pop back to the top:

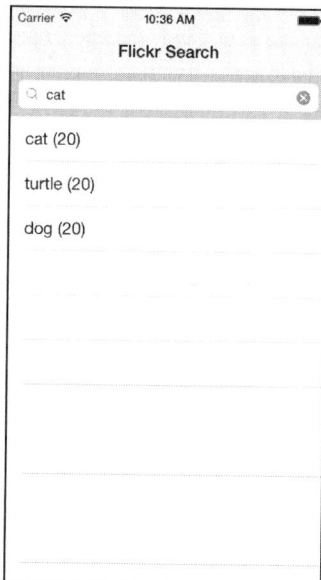

Tap into one of the searches and notice it doesn't show the photos. It's time to fix that!

Show me the photos!

Open **MasterViewController.swift** and find `prepareForSegue`. Change it to look like this:

```
override func prepareForSegue(segue: UIStoryboardSegue,
                              sender: AnyObject?)
{
  if segue.identifier == "showDetail" {
    if let indexPath = self.tableView.indexPathForSelectedRow()
    {
      let (_, photos) = self.searches[indexPath.row]
      (segue.destinationViewController
          as DetailViewController).photos = photos
    }
  }
}
```

This uses the same method of accessing the `searches` ordered dictionary as when creating the cells. It doesn't use the key (search term), though, so you indicate with the underscore that this part of the tuple doesn't need to be bound to a local variable.

Build and run the app, make a search and then tap into it. You'll see something like this:

You can now see the photos! Now as you perform searches, the list will grow and grow. But what about deleting a search after you've finished with it?

Deleting searches

Open **MasterViewController.swift** and add the following to the end of `viewWillAppear`:

```
self.navigationItem.leftBarButtonItem = self.editButtonItem()
```

This will add a button to the navigation bar that toggles the editing state of the view controller.

Next, add the following method underneath `viewWillAppear`:

```
override func setEditing(editing: Bool, animated: Bool) {
  super.setEditing(editing, animated: animated)
  self.tableView.setEditing(editing, animated: animated)
}
```

This passes through the editing state to the table view.

Finally, find `tableView(_:commitEditingStyle:forRowAtIndexPath:)` in the table view delegate extension. Change it to look like this:

```
func tableView(tableView: UITableView,
    commitEditingStyle editingStyle: UITableViewCellEditingStyle,
            forRowAtIndexPath indexPath: NSIndexPath)
{
  if editingStyle == .Delete {
    self.searches.removeAtIndex(indexPath.row)
    tableView.deleteRowsAtIndexPaths(
      [indexPath], withRowAnimation: .Fade)
  }
}
```

You only want to support deletion, so the method checks for that editing style. When the user deletes a row by swiping it to the left, then the method removes the search from the ordered dictionary and updates the table view.

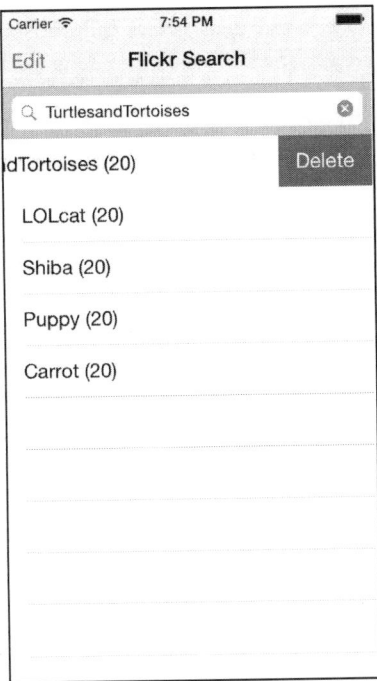

Congratulations, you've finished the app! You now have an ordered dictionary implementation that you could use in any app. What's more, it's generic and therefore can hold any key type (so long as it's hashable!) and any value type.

Generic functions and protocols

You've seen generic structs and classes. You may not know it, but you've also used a generic function. The `find()` function you used in a couple of places is defined like this:

```
func find<C: Collection
          where C.GeneratorType.Element: Equatable>
    (domain: C, value: C.GeneratorType.Element) -> C.IndexType?
```

This is a global function. Notice it has the angle brackets after the function name (just like you used when defining the generic struct), making it a *generic function*. The type provided here defines the type of the `domain` parameter (i.e., the thing being searched). It also indirectly defines the type of the `value` parameter, taking it to be the `Element` type of the `GeneratorType` of `C`, the generic type parameter.

Put simply, the `GeneratorType` is the type of the values in the collection being searched. The return type is also based on the type of the collection being searched.

Open **OrderedDictionary.swift** and find `insert(_:forKey:atIndex:)`. Notice the line that finds the existing index using `find()` does not specify the type in angle brackets.

This is Swift's type inference in play yet again. It can infer the type for the generic by looking at the first parameter (the collection to be searched), the type of which is `C`, the generic type. Neat!

But what is this `GeneratorType`? The `Collection` protocol, to which the first parameter of `find()` must conform, also conforms to the `SequenceType` protocol, which indicates classes and structs that can be considered a sequence. A sequence is anything that has an order to it, such as arrays. The protocol is defined like so:

```
protocol SequenceType {
    typealias GeneratorType : Generator
    func generate() -> GeneratorType
}
```

This says that any `SequenceType` must have a type alias called `GeneratorType` that itself must conform to `Generator`. It must also have a `generate()` function that returns a `GeneratorType`.

The idea behind this is that when the sequence needs to be iterated, it can create a generator by calling `generate()` on the sequence. This generator returned has a method called `next()` that returns the next object in the sequence. The generator starts at the beginning, and you can therefore use it to iterate the sequence from start to finish.

> **PRO TIP:** Generators are very useful when working with large or computationally expensive collections, because they allow you to "generate" each item as needed instead of building them all at once.

What about `OrderedDictionary`, then? You could potentially consider it a sequence (`NSDictionary` does, of course, have `allKeys` and `allValues`). It has an order and therefore, you should make it conform to `SequenceType` so you can iterate over it.

Open **ODPlayground.playground**, the playground you created earlier, and add the following code below the `OrderedDictionary` struct definition:

```
extension OrderedDictionary: SequenceType {
```

```
// 1
typealias GeneratorType = GeneratorOf<(KeyType, ValueType)>

// 2
func generate() -> GeneratorOf<(KeyType, ValueType)> {
  // 3
  var index = 0

  // 4
  return GeneratorOf {
    // 5
    if index < self.array.count {
      let key = self.array[index++]
      return (key, self.dictionary[key]!)
    } else {
      return nil
    }
  }
}
```

This defines the extension that will make `OrderedDictionary` conform to `SequenceType`. Here's how it works:

1. The `GeneratorType` type alias that the `SequenceType` protocol defined must be a type that conforms to `Generator`. You could write your own generator, but the Swift standard library includes a helpful struct called `GeneratorOf` that takes a closure to execute each time `next()` is called. The struct is generic on the type of object that is returned. Therefore, in the case of `OrderedDictionary`, you set the generic type parameter to a tuple of `KeyType` and `ValueType`.

2. You then implement `generate()`, as the final thing you need to conform to `SequenceType`.

3. As mentioned above, `GeneratorOf` will execute a given closure each time you call `next()`. To achieve the desired iteration, you can store the current index in the `index` variable, which starts at zero.

4. Then, you create and return a `GeneratorOf`. While it might not look like it, this is actually a call to the initializer of `GeneratorOf`! It only takes one parameter, the closure to call each time you call `next()`, so you use the shorthand trailing closure syntax to make the code simpler.

5. Inside the generator closure, you check the index to see if it's still in bounds of the array. If it is, then you return the key and value and increment the index for next time

you call `next()`. If the index is outside the bounds of the array (i.e., the iteration has come to an end), then you return nil to signify this fact.

Let's see that in action. Add the following code right at the end of the playground:

```
for (key, value) in dict {
  println("\(key) => \(value)")
}
```

Make sure the assistant editor is open by clicking **View\Assistant Editor\Show Assistant Editor**. You will see the following output:

```
1 => dog
2 => cat
```

It's just as you would expect! The order is correct and the values are correct for each key.

By implementing `SequenceType`, you've made it possible to use `OrderedDictionary` in the `for-in` enumeration technique.

But wait, there's more! Delete the type alias from the `SequenceType` extension on `OrderedDictionary`. Notice the playground still executes correctly. Is that strange?

Well, that's the type inference of Swift in action. It can infer that the type alias should be `GeneratorOf<(KeyType, ValueType)>`, because that's the return type of `generate()`. :]

The `SequenceType` protocol is, if you think about it carefully, a generic protocol. The `GeneratorType` type alias is much the same as the generic type parameters in a generic class, struct or function. But protocols can't use the angle bracket syntax for generics, unlike generic interfaces in Java or C#.

The reason for this is largely syntactical. Protocols are supposed to define an interface to which classes and structs can conform; in a way, they are already a little "generic"! Instead, Swift enforces this separation where protocols define the interface while your classes and structs are concerned with types, generic or otherwise.

This is partly why `GeneratorOf` exists: It is a way to "lift" the `Generator` protocol into a type. Of course, it's just one implementation of such a `Generator`, but one you're likely to use frequently.

Where to go from here?

In this chapter, you've learned how to write a generic struct and use it in an app. You could use the same approach to write a generic class, as well. You can now repurpose your ordered dictionary in other apps requiring you to store different types of keys and values.

You've also learned about subscripts in this chapter. While subscripts make the most sense for collections, they aren't technically limited to such. It would be possible to use a subscript to access internal data of any class or struct. Just make sure you have a good reason and that your implementation is intuitive!

As you continue writing Swift code, think about how generics and the type system make development much easier. You get type safety while maintaining reusability when using generics. Imagine how you might use generics in your own projects and you'll start to see why Swift's type system is beneficial, particularly as compared to that of Objective-C.

Chapter 5: Functions and Closures

By Colin Eberhardt

Functions are one of modern programming's most important building blocks. They allow you to package the logic that performs a specific task within a single unit, encapsulating it for reuse. The encapsulation can also be another abstraction layer, allowing you or other team members to treat it as a standalone "black box" without worrying about its implementation details.

Swift supports both global functions and methods, which are functions associated with classes and other types. Swift also supports closures, expressions that resemble "anonymous" or unnamed functions, which are passed around as first-class objects within your code.

In this chapter, you're going to conduct an in-depth exploration of functions, their syntax and their underlying types. You'll look at in-out parameters and the effects they have on class and structure parameters. You'll also see how Swift's method and function parameter naming conventions have been influenced by Objective-C. Finally, you'll learn about the concise and flexible closure expression syntax, a major reason why Swift is being heralded as a functional language.

Functions

In this section, you're going to explore the immense power and versatility of Swift functions. But before getting carried away, you'll start with something small and simple.

Your first function

Create a new Swift playground and replace its contents with the following:

```
import Foundation

let a = 3.0, b = 4.0
let c = sqrt(a * a + b * b)
println(c)
```

Do you recognize that equation from your math classes in school? That's right, it's the Pythagorean theorem for calculating the lengths of a right-angled triangle!

> **NOTE:** Did you know that U.S. President James Garfield developed an original proof of Pythagoras's theorem? Learn about it here:
>
> https://www.youtube.com/watch?v=EINpkcphsPQ

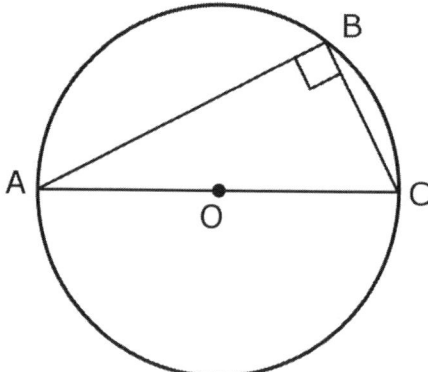

Your playground imports Foundation, which allows you to use `sqrt` later in the code. You define two constants, `a` and `b`, then compute the value `c` using the Pythagorean theorem, outputting the result to the console:

```
5.0
```

Swift doesn't have a built-in function that computes the squares of a number and your playground code performs this task inline. Time to rectify this!

Update your playground as follows:

```swift
import Foundation

func square(number: Double) -> Double {
    return number * number
}

let a = 3.0, b = 4.0
let c = sqrt(square(a) + square(b))
println(c)
```

At this point, the playground output will still be `5.0`.

The above code defines a function named `square` that takes a single input parameter of type `Double` and returns a `Double`.

In Swift, you define a function using the `func` keyword, followed by the function name. Functions can take a number of typed input parameters and return a single typed value. Swift functions are all defined in the global scope, as opposed to a method, which is defined in the scope of a type declaration (e.g. a class or struct).

Apart from differences in syntax, Swift functions are similar to those found in most other modern languages, including Objective-C. Let's try something new!

Functions are first-class

Update your playground as follows:

```swift
func square(number: Double) -> Double {
    return number * number
}

let operation = square

let a = 3.0, b = 4.0
let c = sqrt(operation(a) + operation(b))
println(c)
```

Again, the playground output is still `5.0`. Feel free to change the numbers if you would like a change of pace!

You'll no doubt have noticed that something interesting is going on in the code above. You've defined a new constant `operation` and assigned to it the value of `square`. The code that follows now uses `operation` instead of `square`.

This is an important and fundamental feature of the Swift language. Functions are first-class, which means you can assign them to variables or constants and pass them to or return them from other functions. You can use this very powerful language feature to employ functional programming techniques, as described in-depth in Chapter 7, Functional Programming.

You'll remember that Swift is a strongly typed language, with every variable and constant having a type, and functions are no different. The following line you wrote lacks a type annotation for the `operation` constant, so the compiler must be inferring the type:

```
let operation = square
```

But just what type is `square`, and by inference, `operation`?

Update the assignment as follows:

```
let operation:(Double) -> Double = square
```

Does your playground still output `5.0`, or if you changed the numbers, whatever it was outputting before you made this change? Great! ;]

The type of both `square` and `operation` is `(Double) -> Double`. The type of a function describes its input parameters (both the number of parameters and their types) and the return type. This is often termed the signature of a function, and any function that shares the same signature is considered to have the same type.

> **PRO TIP:** Function types can become quite hard to decipher when functions are used as parameters for other functions. Consider the following example:
>
> ```
> func doMath(operation:(Double) -> Double) -> Double { … }
> ```
>
> If you find yourself drowning in a sea of type information, consider using a `typealias`, which allows you to assign a simple name to a more complex type:
>
> ```
> typealias OperationType = (Double) -> Double
> ```
>
> ```
> func doMath(operation:OperationType) -> Double { … }
> ```

Function syntax

As you've already seen, Swift's syntax for functions is quite straightforward. It's comprised of the `func` keyword followed by the function name, the input parameters in parenthesis, the return arrow and finally, the return type.

Here are a few more quick examples:

You can define functions with no input parameters. For example, you could create a random number generation function as follows:

```
func generateRandomNumber() -> Double { ... }
```

Functions that take multiple parameters use a comma-separated list of typed parameters. For example, you could create a function that pads a string to a given length as follows:

```
func padString(string: String, length: Int) -> String { ... }
```

> **Quick challenge:** Implement the two functions above.

Functions with no return value, or void functions, are a little more interesting. Add the following to the end of your playground:

```
func logDouble(number:Double) -> Void {
    println(String(format: "%.2f", number))
}
logDouble(c)
```

This creates a `logDouble` function that takes a single double value and outputs its value to the console formatted to two decimal places. Passing in the result `c` (from the `sqrt` function) produces the following output:

```
5.00
```

> **NOTE:** This code makes use of the `NSString` initializer `initWithFormat`, which is bridged to Swift as an initializer for the `String` type.

You may notice that `Void` is not a keyword like it is in Objective-C, but another type itself! If you look at the Swift header, you'll find that `Void` is a `typealias` for a shorthand equivalent:

```
typealias Void = ()
```

This is the same syntax you would use for a tuple with no elements, which is of course a type itself, although not one of much use.

> **PRO TIP:** You can view the definition of any Swift type in Xcode by holding the command key and clicking on a type in the editor. This will jump to the definition of that Swift type.

For fun, change the function signature to the more compact form, like this:

```
func logDouble(number:Double) -> () {
  println(String(format: "%.2f", number))
}
```

Does it still compile? Do you still see the same output? Great! You can even assign the return value to a constant or variable, although the compiler will kindly give you a warning that the value stored isn't very useful.

There is an even more concise alternative. You can drop the return arrow and void type altogether. Update your playground as follows:

```
func logDouble(number:Double) {
  println(String(format: "%.2f", number))
}
```

Apple designed Swift to be compact and concise by allowing you to drop unnecessary structure and syntax. :]

However, a quick word of caution about the shorthand for void functions: While you can drop the return arrow and type from the function declaration, `logDouble`'s type is still `(Double) -> ()`.

To verify this, update your code to assign the function to a variable with an explicit type annotation:

```
func logDouble(number:Double) {
  println(String(format: "%.2f", number))
}
```

```
}
var logger: (Double) -> () = logDouble
logger(c)
```

The above code will compile just fine, giving the expected output of **5.00**. However, if you omit the return type, like so:

```
var logger: (Double) = logDouble
```

You'll find the compiler raises an error that indicates the assignment requires a type conversion. This is because `(Double)` is actually a tuple rather than a function!

Now that you know the basics of functions, it's time to discover some of the new and exciting features. It's time for generics!

Overloading and generics

Create a new playground and replace its contents with the following:

```
func checkAreEqual(value: Int, expected: Int, message: String) {
  if expected != value {
    println(message)
  }
}
```

The above function checks that a given integer is equal to another expected integer. If the two are not equal, the function writes a message to the console. You could use this as a form of verification or precondition check.

Put this function to the test by adding the following code:

```
var input = 3
checkAreEqual(input, 2, "An input value of '2' was expected")

input = 47
checkAreEqual(input, 47, "An input value of '47' was expected")
```

The first check fails while the second passes, resulting in the following output:

```
An input value of '2' was expected
```

The current function is a little restrictive in that it only allows you to check whether an integer matches an expected value. What if you also want to check strings? Or doubles? Or any other type?

Fortunately, Swift lets you create **overloaded functions**. These are functions that share the same name, but differ in either the number or types of their input parameters.

Add the following to your playground:

```
func checkAreEqual(value: String, expected: String,
    message: String) {
  if expected != value {
    println(message)
  }
}

var inString = "cat"
checkAreEqual(inString, "dog",
  "An input value of 'dog' was expected")
```

The new checks fails, resulting in the following console output:

```
An input value of 'dog' was expected
```

By overloading `checkAreEqual`, you're able to perform the check on strings as well as integers.

This isn't a terribly scalable solution to the problem, with a separate function required for each new type. Fortunately, there's a much better solution.

Remove both of your `checkAreEqual` implementations, replacing them with the following:

```
func checkAreEqual<T: Equatable>(value: T, expected: T,
    message: String) {
  if expected != value {
    println(message)
  }
}
```

As you might expect, your playground's output is unchanged.

Your newly added `checkAreEqual` function is **generic**, where the first two parameters have a type designated by the placeholder T. Whenever this function is invoked, the type of T is inferred. Furthermore, the compiler also checks the constraints, which in this case are:

1. The first and second arguments passed to the function must be of the same type, because T is used for both.

2. The type must adopt the `Equatable` protocol. This constraint is a requirement of your implementation of `checkAreEqual`, which leverages the `!=` operator.

Verify the above points by first trying to call the function with mixed argument types, and then by trying to drop the `Equatable` constraint. What type of compiler error occurs?

For more about generics and their use with classes and structs, see Chapter 4, "Generics".

> **PRO TIP:** Swift's type inference can be surprisingly clever. If you assign the literal values `47` and `48.67` to a couple of constants and allow the compiler to infer the type, it will choose `Int` and `Double`, respectively. With that in mind, you might be surprised that the following compiles without error:
>
> `checkAreEqual(47, 48.67, "'48.67' was expected")`
>
> In this instance, the Swift compiler is smart enough to infer that `T` should be a `Double` and that the literal `47`, which could be interpreted as an `Int`, a `Double` or several other types, should also be a `Double`.
>
> Clever stuff!

In-out variables

All the functions you've written so far have taken a number of input parameters and returned a value without affecting the state of any of the parameters. But what if you want to modify one of the arguments passed to a function? This is called a **side effect** of a function and is behavior you have to explicitly declare. Time for an example!

Open a new playground and replace the default template code with the following:

```swift
import Foundation

func square(number: Double) {
    number = number * number
}

var a = 2.0
square(a)
println(a)
```

The above code defines a simple function, `square`, which squares the `Double` that is passed to it.

Or at least, that's what it's supposed to do!

You'll find that this code fails, with the following error within the body of the `square` function:

```
Cannot assign to 'let' value number.
```

This error message is telling you something very important about the parameters of a function—by default, they are constants. In other words, they behave in the same way as constants defined with the `let` keyword.

The compiler error clearly indicates that this is prohibited.

> **PRO TIP:** Many other mainstream languages (Objective-C, Java, C#, JavaScript) allow you to mutate a function's parameters within the body of the function. However, these changes only apply to the function's local copy of the parameter value, not the actual variable passed in by the caller.
>
> Swift's stance, which prohibits the mutation of function parameters, is only possible because it has a first-class concept of constants. The net result is less room for unexpected behavior.

You can make the compiler happy by changing the default behavior of constant parameters and defining a variable function parameter. Update your code as follows:

```
func square(var number: Double) {
    number = number * number
}
```

The introduction of the `var` keyword ensures that the argument passed to the function is assigned to a variable parameter. As a result, you'll find the compiler error disappears and the console output is as follows:

```
2.0
```

That clearly is not correct! Two squared is four, not two!

Moving to a variable parameter keeps the compiler happy, but it doesn't produce the desired output. The `number` variable is just a copy of the value passed in and doesn't affect anything outside the function call.

What you really need is for the number parameter within the body of the function to refer to the same variable that is passed in as an argument when the function is invoked.

Let's give this one last try. Change `square`'s implementation, replacing `var` with `inout`:

```
func square(inout number: Double) {
  number = number * number
}
```

Also update the code that invokes this function, prefixing the argument with an ampersand:

```
square(&a)
```

Finally, you'll see the correct result:

```
4.0
```

As in many other languages, including Objective-C, using & before a parameter indicates that you're passing the value by reference and that the function can modify the value.

Although your playground code has an in-out parameter of type `Double`, you can designate parameters of any type as in-out, including classes and structures.

> **PRO TIP:** Use in-out and variable parameters sparingly. The effects of both of these techniques are not immediately obvious to the caller, which can cause confusion.

Classes and structures as function parameters

In the previous section, you saw how value types such as `Int`, `Double` and `String` are copied when they are passed as an argument to a function and how you can modify this behavior via the `var` or `inout` keywords.

Swift handles classes a little differently. Let's look at a little example.

Create a new playground, remove the boilerplate code and replace it with the following:

```
class Person {
```

```
    var age = 34, name = "Colin"

    func growOlder() {
      self.age++
    }
  }

  func celebrateBirthday(cumpleañero: Person) {
    println("Happy Birthday \(cumpleañero.name)")
    cumpleañero.growOlder()
  }

  let person = Person()
  celebrateBirthday(person)
  println(person.age)
```

> **PRO TIP:** To type the ñ character, an important letter in languages such as Spanish, press and hold **option** while typing **n**, and then release both keys and press **n** again. ¡Ya está!

This playground defines a `Person` class, which has `name` and `age` properties and a function that increments the age. `celebrateBirthday` is a useful function that prints a celebratory message, then increments the age of the cumpleañero, which is Spanish for person-who-is-celebrating-their-birthday. Unfortunately, English doesn't have an equivalent noun!

The console output of this playground is as follows:

```
Happy Birthday Colin
35
```

You can see that invoking `celebrateBirthday` has successfully incremented this person's age—on the screen, at least. How does this work?

When you pass an instance of a class as an argument to a function, Swift passes a reference to that class. In your playground code, both `person` and `cumpleañero` are constants that hold references to the same `Person` instance.

Changing the parameter of `celebrateBirthday` to make it a variable parameter will not impact the playground's output. However, making a variable does allow you to re-assign it:

```
func celebrateBirthday(var cumpleañero: Person) {
```

```
cumpleañero = Person()
println("Happy Birthday \(cumpleañero.name)")
cumpleañero.growOlder()
}
```

In this context, that's not very useful. And as you might expect, if you remove the `var` keyword, the above will result in the familiar compilation error, "`cannot assign to 'let' value`".

So how would this code behave if `Person` were defined as a structure?

Within your playground, update the `Person` type, changing it to a structure:

```
struct Person {
  var age = 34, name = "Colin"

  mutating func growOlder() {
    self.age++
  }
}
```

Notice that as well as changing from `class` to `struct`, you mark `growOlder` as `mutating`. Any method that changes the state of a structure is a mutating method and requires this keyword.

Update `celebrateBirthday` as follows:

```
func celebrateBirthday(inout cumpleañero: Person) {
  println("Happy Birthday \(cumpleañero.name)")
  cumpleañero.growOlder()
}
```

Structures are passed by value, just like `Int`, `Double`, `String` and so forth. For this function to mutate the age via `growOlder`, the parameter needs to be marked as in-out.

Finally, change the use of this function to the following:

```
var person = Person()
celebrateBirthday(&person)
println(person.age)
```

You've made a couple of changes here. First, `person` is now a variable rather than a constant. This is because you can mutate the properties of a class that is assigned to a constant, but not the properties of a constant structure, because they are value types. Second, as before, you use an ampersand when passing `person` as an argument to `celebrateBirthday`.

With all of these changes in place, your playground's output is as expected:

```
Happy Birthday Colin
35
```

As you've seen, functions handle classes and structs in very different ways.

> **NOTE:** Recall that arrays and dictionaries are structs, which are passed by value. If you want to mutate their contents when passing them as function arguments, you'll have to mark them as in-out parameters.

Variadics

In this section, you're going to learn about **variadic parameters**, which you can use to pass a variable number of arguments to a function.

You indicate that a parameter is variadic by following the type with three period characters (**...**). Here's an example of a function with a single variadic parameter:

```swift
func longestWord(words: String...) -> String?
```

This function takes a list of strings and returns the longest string, or `nil` if no strings were passed. It's time to create another playground, because you're going to implement this function!

Add the following function to your playground:

```swift
func longestWord(words: String...) -> String? {
  var currentLongest: String?
  for word in words {
    if currentLongest != nil {
      if countElements(word) > countElements(currentLongest!) {
        currentLongest = word
      }
    } else {
      currentLongest = word
    }
  }
  return currentLongest
}
```

The variadic parameter `words` becomes a constant array within the body of the function, allowing you to use the `for-in` control structure to iterate over its contents. The implementation of this simple algorithm is quite straightforward: The function iterates over each word, comparing it to the word that is currently the longest.

Exercise this function by adding the following code:

```
let long = longestWord("chick", "fish", "cat", "elephant")
println(long)
```

This yields the following console output:

```
Optional("elephant")
```

The output indicates that the `long` constant is an optional type containing the value "elephant". Try varying the number of string arguments to `longestWord` to exercise this function a little further.

Have you read Chapter 7, "Functional Programming" yet? If so, you might be interested in a functional equivalent to your current `longestWord` function that uses `reduce`:

```
func longestWord(words: String...) -> String? {
  return words.reduce(String?()) {
    (longest, word) in
    longest == nil || countElements(word) > countElements(longest!)
        ? word : longest
  }
}
```

That's much more concise. :]

You may not often use variadics, but when the need arises, it's an elegant solution.

External parameter names

The functions you've written so far take a number of input arguments in order, like this:

```
checkAreEqual("cat", "dog", "Incorrect input")
```

There are times when it can be hard to determine the purpose of each argument from the context of its usage. With the code above, it's not so easy to tell which of the first two arguments is the expected value.

External parameter names help resolve this ambiguity. Create a new playground and add the following implementation of `checkAreEqual`:

```swift
func checkAreEqual(value val: String, expected exp: String,
    message msg: String) {
  if exp != val {
    println(msg)
  }
}
```

This is similar to your earlier implementations of this function, but this time, each parameter has two names—for example, the first parameter has the names `value` and `val`. For each parameter, the first name is the external name used by the caller, and the second is the internal name used within the function body.

To see the external names in action, add the following code to invoke `checkAreEqual`:

```swift
checkAreEqual(value: "cat", expected: "dog",
  message: "Incorrect input")
```

By supplying external parameter names when defining `checkAreEqual`, you enforce the use of these names when calling the function. You can see the advantage of this approach—it removes any ambiguity regarding the purpose of each argument.

When using named parameters, you still have to provide the function arguments in the correct order. Despite the following code being unambiguous, it will not compile:

```swift
checkAreEqual(expected: "dog", value: "cat",
  message: "Incorrect input")
```

You won't commonly need different internal and external parameter names—hence the contrived use of `value` and `val` in your current code. Because of this, Swift provides shorthand for sharing one name as both internal and external; you simply prefix the parameter name with a hash.

Update your code as follows:

```swift
func checkAreEqual(#value: String, #expected: String,
    #message: String) {
  if expected != value {
    println(message)
  }
}

checkAreEqual(value: "dog", expected: "cat",
  message:"Incorrect input")
```

Confirm that your playground's output is unchanged.

To keep your code clean and concise, I recommend using external parameter names sparingly; only employ them when they help resolve ambiguity. Here are a few brief examples to illustrate:

The following function converts a string into a date:

```
dateFromString("2014-03-14")
```

The purpose of the single parameter that this function accepts is entirely obvious, so the addition of an external parameter name would just add noise.

In contrast, the following function performs some form of operation on a cell at a given location:

```
convertCellAt(42, 13)
```

One of the input arguments is the cell's row and one is the column, but which is which? You could clearly resolve this ambiguity using external parameter names:

```
convertCellAt(column: 42, row: 13)
```

Methods

Swift is an object-oriented language and as a result, you write most of your application logic within methods as opposed to global functions. A method is a special type of function that is associated with a type, such as a class, structure or enumeration. In this section, you'll discover some of the special behavior associated with methods in Swift and how Objective-C has influenced the Swift syntax.

Instance methods

Instance methods associate a function with an instance of a specific type. You can define instance methods on classes, structures and enumerations using exactly the same syntax that you use for global functions.

Create a new playground and replace its contents with the following:

```
class Cell: Printable {
  private(set) var row = 0
  private(set) var column = 0
```

```
func move(x: Int, y: Int) {
  row += y
  column += x
}

func moveByX(x: Int) {
  column += x
}

func moveByY(y: Int) {
  row += y
}

var description: String {
  get {
    return "Cell [row=\(row), col=\(column)]"
  }
}
}
```

This defines a simple `Cell` class type that has `row` and `column` properties, a few mutation methods and a `description` property, as defined by the `Printable` protocol.

To exercise this class, add the following to your playground:

```
var cell = Cell()
cell.moveByX(4)
println(cell.description)
```

This instantiates a `Cell` instance, uses `moveByX` to modify its location and then prints the result to the console:

```
Cell [row=0, col=4]
```

That's nothing unexpected!

Now, update your code to make use of `move` to adjust the row and column:

```
var cell = Cell()
cell.moveByX(4)
cell.move(4, y: 7)
println(cell.description)
```

Notice in the above code that when using `move`, you include a name for the second argument. If you remove the `y:` argument prefix, you'll get a compilation error.

Swift methods share the same concept of internal and external parameter names as do functions. However, their default behavior is subtly different. All the parameters of a function lack external names unless you supply them explicitly. With methods, the first parameter lacks an external name, yet subsequent parameters have local and default external names by default.

You are free to adjust the parameter naming of a method by adding your own external names, exactly the same way you would for a function. Furthermore, you can add an underscore to remove the default external name for parameters.

Give this a try by modifying move to opt out of the default external name for the second parameter:

```swift
func move(x: Int, _ y: Int) {
    row += y
    column += x
}
```

You'll find that you can now invoke move without naming the second argument:

```swift
cell.move(4, 7)
```

While you *can* change the default parameter naming behavior for methods, I would advise against it. The Apple APIs adopt this standard from Objective-C, where the first parameter is named in the method name itself such as moveByX and moveByY.

Another cool feature of functions and methods is the ability to provide default argument values. Update move to adopt a default value of 0 for both the x and y parameters:

```swift
func move(x: Int = 0, y: Int = 0) {
    row += y
    column += x
}
```

And update the use of this method accordingly:

```swift
cell.move(x: 4, y: 7)
cell.move(x: 2)
cell.move(y: 3)
```

Normally the first parameter doesn't have an external name but since it has a default value and could be left off, you need to name it.

If you're familiar with default argument values in other languages, they usually only allow defaults for arguments at the end of the list. Here, notice that with just one method definition you can call `move` in three different ways: with both x and y, with x only, and with y only!

> **NOTE:** The parameter naming convention for Swift methods has its roots in Objective-C. If you are coming to Swift from a language other than Objective-C, you might find this convention a little confusing. For guidance on how to select suitable method names, have a look at the Cocoa documentation:
>
> https://developer.apple.com/library/mac/documentation/Cocoa/Conceptual/CodingGuidelines/Articles/NamingMethods.html

Methods are first-class, too

In an earlier section, you discovered that functions in Swift are first-class, allowing you to assign them to variables or constants and pass them to other functions. Methods are also first-class.

To see this in action, replace the `Cell` usage code underneath the `Cell` class with the following:

```
var cell = Cell()
var instanceFunc = cell.moveByY
instanceFunc(34)
println(cell.description)
```

The above creates a `Cell` instance, assigns the `moveByY` instance method to a variable, then invokes the method via the variable reference, providing the following output:

```
Cell [row=0, col=34]
```

But you've already covered this concept with functions. With instance methods, there is another feature you should find quite interesting.

Replace the code you added previously with the following:

```
var cell = Cell()
var moveFunc = Cell.moveByY
moveFunc(cell)(34)
println(cell.description)
```

This time, you obtain a reference to `moveByY` via a class method on `Cell` rather than via an instance method.

This returns a curried function where the first invocation binds to a particular `Cell` instance, returning a function that is equivalent to `instanceFunc` in your earlier code.

If a "curried function" sounds like gibberish or makes you hungry, have a read of Chapter 7, "Functional Programming," then come back and re-read this section. :]

Closures

Closures, like functions and methods, are blocks of code that you can invoke and pass around. But unlike functions and methods, closures are "anonymous" and have the unique ability to "capture" values that exist in the scope in which they are defined. Over the next few sections, you'll learn about these features and how powerful and expressive they can be.

Closure expressions as anonymous functions

A number of functions and methods within the Swift APIs make use of the first-class nature of functions. An example of this `sorted`, defined on `Array`:

```
func sorted(isOrderedBefore: (T, T) -> Bool) -> [T]
```

This method has a single parameter: `isOrderedBefore`. This parameter is itself a function that takes two parameters of type `T` (the type of item held by this array) and returns a Boolean indicating the relative order of these two items. `sorted` uses this function to build a sorted array, returning the result.

Let's see this method in action. Create a new playground and replace its contents with the following:

```
let animals = ["fish", "cat", "chicken", "dog"]

func isBefore(one: String, two: String) -> Bool {
  return one > two
}

let sortedStrings = animals.sorted(isBefore)
println(sortedStrings)
```

This creates a constant array, `animals`, and a function, `isBefore`, that determines the relative sort order of two strings. Swift defines a greater-than operator for comparing strings, making the implementation of `isBefore` quite trivial.

Following the function definition, you invoke `sorted`, passing a reference to `isBefore`, which results in the creation of a sorted array:

```
[fish, dog, chicken, cat]
```

In brief, your playground tells `sorted` that it should sort the array based on whether one item is "greater than" another. The only thing `sorted` really needs to know is the following:

```
one > two
```

In this case, declaring a separate `isBefore` function just to pass it in to `sorted` is just extra boilerplate. In the next few steps, you're gong to strip away the unnecessary structure to create a much more concise implementation.

First-class functions are fantastic, and the code in your playground certainly benefits from this language feature, but there are improvements to be made. Let's get rid of that function.

Update your playground as follows:

```
let animals = ["fish", "cat", "chicken", "dog"]
let sortedStrings = animals.sorted({
    (one: String, two: String) -> Bool in
    return one > two
})
println(sortedStrings)
```

This yields the same output, a sorted array of strings.

Instead of passing a function reference to `sorted`, you use a closure expression. In this context, you can think of the closure you've created as an anonymous function. It performs exactly the same logic as `isBefore` from earlier, but there is no extra function declaration; the code that was in `isBefore` is passed directly into `sorted`.

The syntax of your current closure expression is very similar to the equivalent function syntax: a list of parameters, a return arrow (->) and return type, the `in` keyword followed by the closure implementation.

However, this is where things start to get interesting. You've already seen how the compiler is able to infer constant and variable types from their context. The compiler can perform similar tricks with closures.

Over the next few examples, you're going to gradually remove code from your closure expression until it's in its most minimal form. With each step, your playground's output will be the same as before.

First, those parameter types annotations can go. Remove them:

```
let sortedStrings = animals.sorted({
    (one, two) -> Bool in
    return one > two
})
```

The compiler is able to infer the type of `one` and `two` from the signature of `sorted`.

The expression only has one statement, and as a result, the `return` keyword is a little redundant, so remove it, as well:

```
let sortedStrings = animals.sorted({
    (one, two) -> Bool in
    one > two
})
```

The return type of the closure can also be inferred from the signature of `sorted`, so drop that, also:

```
let sortedStrings = animals.sorted({
    (one, two) in
    one > two
})
```

While they only occupy a couple of characters, the parentheses around the closure parameters don't add much. Make them disappear:

```
let sortedStrings = animals.sorted({
    one, two in
    one > two
})
```

That's almost 50% of the non-white-space characters removed already, but you've only just started!

The next step gets a bit unusual. You can remove the closure parameter declaration altogether by assigning the input parameters to shorthand local constants:

```
let sortedStrings = animals.sorted({ $0 > $1 })
```

As you can see, Swift provides these numbered local constants if you don't name the parameters. This is great for very short closures such as this one with a simple set of parameters.

If a closure is passed as the last argument to a function or method, you can place the closure outside of the parentheses, using what is termed a **trailing closure**:

```
let sortedStrings = animals.sorted() { $0 > $1 }
```

Finally, you can remove the empty parentheses, giving the most compact form:

```
let sortedStrings = animals.sorted { $0 > $1 }
```

By my calculations, your closure expression is now 300% more compact!

This is the most compact closure possible in this context, but not the most compact form of the code. `sorted` takes a parameter of type `(String, String) -> Bool`. The greater-than operator has exactly that signature, so it can be passed directly:

```
let sortedStrings = animals.sorted(>)
```

Remember how you defined `isBefore` as a function at the beginning of this section? As a final corollary, you could also assign a closure expression directly to a variable:

```
var isBefore = {
  (one: String, two: String) -> Bool in
  return one > two
}
let sortedStrings = animals.sorted(isBefore)
```

Here, the compiler infers the type of `isBefore` from the closure expression. As a result, you cannot shorten the closure by removing the parameter type annotations. If you did, the compiler would be unable to infer the type of the `isBefore` variable. The following cannot be compiled:

```
var isBefore = {
  (one, two) -> Bool in
  return one > two
}
let sortedStrings = animals.sorted(isBefore)
```

The compiler can't look ahead to the way you use the `isBefore` variable to infer its type! That shows the value of passing the closure directly to `sorted`: the sort operation is right inline, and the compiler can do more type inference.

Capturing values

One of the most powerful features of closures is their ability to "capture" constants and variables from their surrounding context. A closure can use these values even after the original context has been destroyed!

The easiest way to understand this concept is via an example. That's right, it's time to create a new playground.

Replace the contents of your new playground with the following:

```
typealias StateMachineType = () -> Int
```

This `typealias` defines `StateMachineType`, a function type that returns an integer on each invocation. States are represented as integers, and a state machine cycles through its permitted states on each invocation. For example, a state machine with three states cycles as follows:

```
0, 1, 2, 0, 1, 2, 0, 1, 2, …
```

Next, add a function that creates a state machine based on the number of states it cycles through.

```
func makeStateMachine(maxState: Int) -> StateMachineType {
  var currentState: Int = 0
  return {
    currentState++
    if currentState > maxState {
      currentState = 0
    }
    return currentState
  }
}
```

Before diving into the details of this function, check that it works properly. Add the following to create a state machine that occupies three states:

```
let tristate = makeStateMachine(2)
println(tristate())
println(tristate())
println(tristate())
println(tristate())
println(tristate())
```

This produces the following output:

```
1
2
0
1
2
```

Looking good! Now, add the code below to get a state machine with two states:

```
let bistate = makeStateMachine(1)
println(bistate());
println(bistate());
println(bistate());
println(bistate());
```

This toggles between a state of 0 and 1, as expected:

```
1
0
1
0
```

You've confirmed this function creates a state machine of the required cardinality, so it's time to look at the implementation in a bit more detail. Here it is again:

```
func makeStateMachine(maxState: Int) -> StateMachineType {
  var currentState: Int = 0
  return {
    currentState++
    if currentState > maxState {
      currentState = 0
    }
    return currentState
  }
}
```

The first line of `makeStateMachine` defines a local variable, `currentState`, that stores the current state of the machine under construction. The second line returns a closure expression that is the state machine itself. Note that you omit the signature for this closure expression, `() -> Int`, because the compiler is able to infer this type from the signature of the enclosing function. Type inference is really, *really* smart!

Looking at the closure expression in more detail, it makes use of the `currentState` variable that is local to the enclosing `makeStateMachine` function. This is where things get interesting!

`currentState` is local to `makeStateMachine`, and you would expect it to be destroyed when the function returns:

```
let tristate = makeStateMachine(2)
// currentState variable is destroyed at this point?!
println(tristate())
```

However, for the state machine to work, `currentValue` must still exist and be available to the closure expression that is returned from `makeStateMachine`.

Your current playground code is a nice and simple demonstration of value capture in practice. Because the closure expression makes use of the `currentValue` variable, it captures `currentValue` so it can be used beyond the lifecycle of its defining context.

Furthermore, you don't have to worry about memory management of captured values. Swift automatically determines what should be captured and disposes of those "captives" when it disposes of the closure.

Many of the existing Cocoa APIs use delegates for executing code asynchronously. For example, `CLLocationManager` notifies of location changes via the `CLLocationManagerDelegate` protocol. The expressivity of closures will no doubt result in Apple introducing more closure-based APIs, where you supply a closure that is invoked asynchronously rather than a delegate object. When this happens, you will find that value capture becomes vital to the functioning of your code!

Memory leaks and capture lists

I'm sure by now you're convinced that closures are quite awesome and that you'll be unleashing their power throughout your code! Before you do that, though, there is one more important lesson you need to learn: how to avoid letting your closures turn into memory leaks. Let's look at a simple example.

Swift playgrounds are not the best place to learn about memory management. The code within a playground is run repeatedly, and as a result, object de-allocation isn't entirely predictable. For this final section, you need to create a fully-fledged app.

Within Xcode, select **File/New/Project…** and create a **Single View Application** named **MemoryLeakTest**. Within this project, add a new Swift file named **Person.swift** and add the following code to it:

```
class Person {
  let name: String
  private let actionClosure: (() -> ())!
```

```swift
init(name: String) {
  self.name = name

  actionClosure = {
    println("I am \(self.name)")
  }
}

func performAction() {
  actionClosure()
}

deinit {
  println("\(name) is being deinitialized")
}
}
```

The `Person` class is pretty simple, having a `name` constant property that is set via the initializer. It also has a simple `deinit` implementation that prints a message to the console when an instance of this class is destroyed, freeing the memory it occupies.

The class also has a `performAction` method that prints the person's name to the console. You've implemented this method via the `actionClosure` function property.

It's time to put this class to use.

Open **ViewController.swift**, which Xcode created as part of the application template, and update `viewDidLoad` as follows:

```swift
override func viewDidLoad() {
  super.viewDidLoad()

  let person = Person(name: "bob")
  person.performAction()
}
```

This simply creates a `Person` instance, assigns it to the `person` constant and asks it to perform its action. The `person` constant is local to `viewDidLoad`, and as a result, when this method exits, `person` will be destroyed. As a direct result, you would also expect the `Person` deinitializer to be invoked, signifying the destruction of this instance of `Person`.

Now you can put this theory to the test. Build, run, and keep an eye on the console output. You'll see the following:

```
I am bob
```

This confirms that your `Person` instance was created and is fully functional, but what about the `println` statement within `deinit`? Why wasn't that method called?

The answer is simple: You have a memory leak on your hands! If you want to double-check this, you can profile your application to inspect memory allocations. This will confirm that a `Person` instance remains on the heap after `viewDidLoad` exits.

Closures are reference types, and as a result, the following objects and relationships are constructed within `viewDidLoad`:

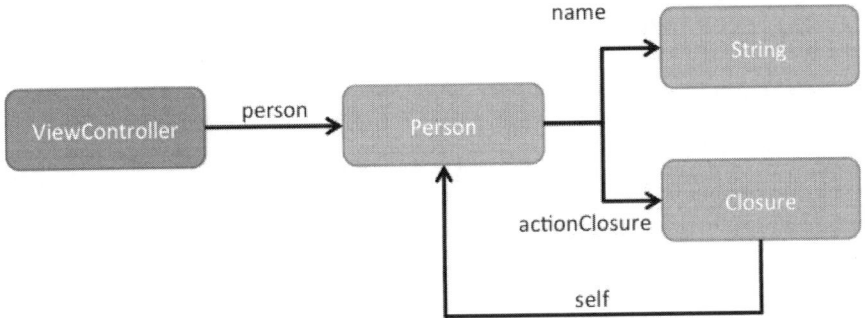

`ViewController` has a reference to a `Person` instance via the local `person` constant. `Person` has a reference to a `String` instance via its `name` constant property, and it also has a reference to the closure that was assigned to the private `actionClosure` constant property. Finally, the closure has a reference back to `Person` via its use of `self` within the interpolated string.

When `viewDidLoad` exits, its local `person` constant is destroyed, removing the link between the `ViewController` and the `Person` instance.

At this point, you would expect the retain count of this `Person` instance to drop to zero and for the object to be destroyed. Unfortunately, that doesn't happen, due to the reference from the closure back to the `Person` instance, as highlighted in red below:

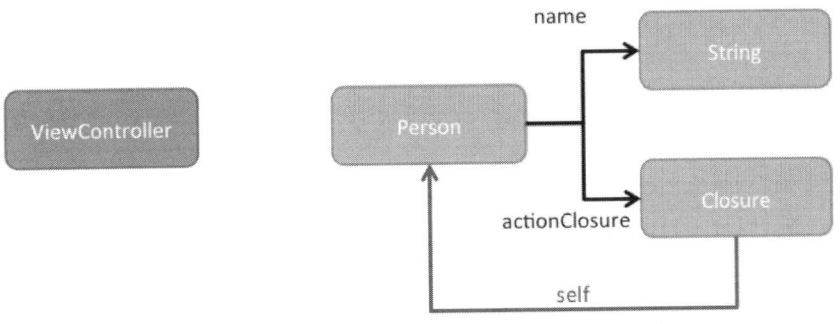

This is a classic **retain cycle**, a circular reference between objects that results in the objects becoming orphaned and lingering in memory.

> **NOTE:** If you're coming to Swift from C#, Java, JavaScript or any other language that employs a garbage collector, you might find this a little surprising. Garbage collectors trace references back to known "roots," removing objects from the heap that are not reachable from a root. As a result of this technique, orphaned circular references are detected and the removed during garbage collection.
>
> Swift uses Automatic Reference Counting, which tracks the usage of objects by incrementing their retain counts. When an object's retain count becomes zero, that object is immediately destroyed. This removes the need to halt an application's main thread to collect "garbage," but it does mean you need to avoid circular references within your code.

This problem is not unique to Swift—it already manifests itself within Objective-C code that uses blocks. The standard solution to this problem, which you are likely familiar with if you are coming from Objective-C, is to create a weak reference to `self`, then create a strong reference based on the weak reference, using this new strong reference within the body of the block, as outlined below:

```
__weak typeof(self)weakSelf = self;
[self.context performBlock:^{
    __strong typeof(weakSelf)strongSelf = weakSelf;
    // do something with strongSelf
}];
```

Yikes! That is both ugly and error-prone!

Thankfully, solving this same retain cycle issue with Swift is much simpler.

Open **Person.swift** and update the creation of `actionClosure` within the class initializer, as follows:

```
actionClosure = {
  [unowned self] () -> () in
  println("I am \(self.name)")
}
```

The above code defines a **capture list** for the closure, detailing the ownership semantics for the variables and constants that the closure captures. The capture list appears before the closure signature, and contains a list of variables inside square brackets.

In this case, `unowned self` indicates that this closure doesn't own the reference to `self` and as a result, there's no longer a retain cycle.

Build and run to confirm that the `Person` instance is now successfully destroyed:

```
I am bob
bob is being deinitialized
```

That was simple, wasn't it?

It is unlikely that you would write a `Person` class that implements its methods via private closures, but you can expect to encounter retain cycles as a result of using closures!

Retain cycles commonly occur within view controllers. You often need to update the UI of a view controller based on asynchronous activity. If you use a closure to perform this update, you can easily reach a situation where you have a retain cycle that ensures your view controller is never destroyed… a very memory-hungry memory leak!

Where to go from here?

In this chapter, you've explored the versatility of Swift's functions and closures, learning about their first-class status, syntax and expressivity.

As a final thought, you've no doubt noticed that in most contexts, you can use functions and closure expressions interchangeably. This is because functions and closures are one and the same; a function is simply a named closure.

Now go forth and use closures creatively and safely!

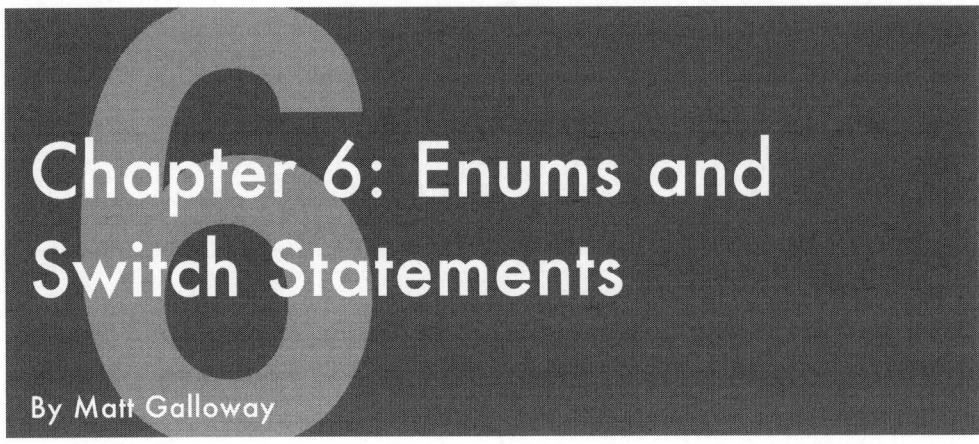

Chapter 6: Enums and Switch Statements
By Matt Galloway

A common feature of many programming languages is a type called an **enumeration**, or **enum**. Enums are data types that group similar values together. For example, when dealing with text alignment in Cocoa you might see enum values such as `NSTextAlignment.Center`. The `NSTextAlignment` enum lets you use friendly and readable names like `Center` or `Left`.

Swift's enum type is more than just an enumeration. It has discrete values like a traditional enum, but behaves like a class or struct. In Swift, enums can have associated methods—even constructors!

Throughout this chapter, you'll use playgrounds to learn and practice the various ways you can put enums and switch statements to work in your apps. Switch statements go hand in hand with enums and are what make enums so powerful. Together, these two form the basis of some very powerful programming techniques, as you're about to see.

Switch on your brain and prepare to enumerate through the rest of this chapter!

Basic enumerations

Enumerations are a building block of many languages, enabling developers to define a set of values that together form a type.

The suits in a pack of cards are a common example. A card game app might use an enumeration to describe the suits, with one value for each suit—hearts, spades, clubs and diamonds. Like so:

```
enum Suit {
   case Heart
   case Club
   case Diamond
   case Spade
}
```

In Swift, you define an enumeration similarly to the way you do in C or Objective-C. Let's take a look at a basic enumeration in Swift.

Before you start, you need a playground in which to stretch your legs. Open Xcode and click **File\New\Playground…**. Call the playground **Enum_1** with the platform set to **iOS**. Click **Next** and then save the playground wherever you wish.

Add the following code to your playground:

```
enum Shape {
   case Rectangle
   case Square
   case Triangle
   case Circle
}
```

This declares an enumeration called `Shape` with four cases, each representing an enumerated value.

Now that you've defined it, you can use this enumeration as a type. Add the following code to the end of your playground:

```
var aShape = Shape.Triangle
```

Notice the syntax you're using to reference the value: `Shape` to name the enum, and then `.Triangle` to name the specific case.

If you declare the type of the variable, then Swift's type inference allows you to drop the enum type name from the value side. For example, change the original declaration of the `aShape` variable to look like this:

```
var aShape: Shape = .Triangle
```

Since you've declared the type as `Shape`, you can drop the type from before the `Triangle`.

Add the following code underneath the line you just added:

```
aShape = .Square
```

No matter how you declare the variable to start, you can drop the `Shape` from any subsequent assignments since you've already established the type.

Raw values

If you're an Objective-C developer, you may know you can assign each enum case a value. Swift gives you this ability, as well, which you'll see is much more powerful than what you may be used to from Objective-C.

Change the `Shape` definition to look like this:

```
enum Shape: Int {
    case Rectangle
    case Square
    case Triangle
    case Circle
}
```

You'd be forgiven for thinking that the type now appears to inherit from `Int`, due to the similar syntax to class and struct inheritance. In the case of an enum, however, this syntax means the enum holds raw values of type `Int`.

Now that the enum has a raw value type, it gains one property, `rawValue`, and one initializer, `init(rawValue:)`. Add the following code to the bottom of your playground:

```
var triangle = Shape.Triangle
triangle.rawValue
```

`rawValue` returns the raw value associated with a given enum case. Look in the playground sidebar, and you'll see `Triangle` has the raw value of 2:

```
31
32    var triangle = Shape.Triangle        (Enum Value)
33    triangle.rawValue                    2
34
```

As you may have deduced, the raw values are zero-indexed—that is, `Rectangle` is 0, `Square` is 1, `Triangle` is 2 and `Circle` is 3.

Conversely, the initializer, `init(rawValue:)` takes a raw value and converts it into the related enum case. Add the following code to the bottom of your playground:

```
var square = Shape(rawValue: 1)
```

You'll notice the sidebar output is a little different: rather than `(Enum Value)` you'll see `{(Enum Value)}` instead. Since not every integer relates to an enum case, `init(rawValue:)` returns an optional. The extra curly braces show that `square` is a wrapped value.

Add the following code to the bottom of the playground:

```
var notAShape = Shape(rawValue: 100)
```

Notice in the playground sidebar that this returns nil:

```
34
35    var square = Shape(rawValue: 1)                {(Enum Value)}
36    var notAShape = Shape(rawValue: 100)           nil
37
```

If you want, you can assign each enum case a specific value, rather than letting Swift assign them automatically. You do this simply by placing an assignment after the case. Change the `Rectangle` case to look like this:

```
case Rectangle = 10
```

The `Triangle` case now has a raw value of 12, which you can see if you look in the sidebar next to the `triangle.rawValue` line. When the enum is an integer, for any case that you haven't assigned a specific value, Swift will assign it the previous case's value incremented by 1.

One of the main reasons to use raw values is to be able to serialize and deserialize enum values. For example, an enum type itself is just a symbol and can't be sent from a server in a JSON response like a number or a string. If you define the value of each case, you can do the same thing on the server. Then the communication between server and app will be in numbers such as 10, and each side will have a defined enumeration to map this back to values like `Rectangle`.

The type of the raw value doesn't have to be `Int`—it can be any number type, such as `Float` or `Double`, or it can be `String`.

> **Challenge:** Change the raw value type of `Shape` to `String`. Right away, you'll notice compiler errors. This is because if the type is not an `Int` (or a literal convertible to an `Int`), then you must supply all the raw values.

> Here's a starter hint:
>
> ```
> enum Shape: String {
>   case Rectangle = "Rectangle"
> ```
>
> You'll need to set a value for each case, as well as change the types in the `init(rawValue:)` method calls.

Add the following to the playground:

```
enum Ratios: Float {
  case pi = 3.141
  case tau = 6.283
  case phi
}
```

You'll notice a compiler error:

```
Enum case must declare a raw value when the preceding raw value
is not an integer.
```

While you can omit specific values for integer enums since they increment by 1 by default, this isn't the case for other types of raw values. When using raw values with non-integer types, you must specify all values.

Switch statements

Enums are powerful when paired with switch statements. Most critically, you can use a switch statement to test the case of an enum value.

In Swift, switch statements behave much the same as in other languages—with a few extra tricks, of course! Let's take a look.

Create a new playground, just as you did before, this time calling it **Enum_2.playground**. Then, replace its contents with the following code:

```
enum Shape {
  case Rectangle
  case Square
  case Triangle
}
```

```
    case Circle
}
```

This is the same simple enum you created earlier. Next, add the following code to the bottom of your playground:

```
var aShape = Shape.Rectangle

switch(aShape) {
case .Rectangle:
  println("This is a rectangle")
}
```

This may be familiar syntax to you if you're an existing Objective-C developer. You declare a switch statement that tests the enum case of the variable.

But there's a problem—your playground has an error. Click **View\Assistant Editor\Show Assistant Editor** and you'll see the following:

```
Playground execution failed: error: <EXPR>:17:1: error: switch
must be exhaustive, consider adding a default clause
```

Switch statements in Swift must be **exhaustive**, meaning you must handle each and every case of the enum. This is a wonderful safety feature, because careless case handling is a common source of bugs, especially when adding enum values! In other languages, you might add an enum value and the entire switch statement would be skipped without a matching case; in Swift, the compiler will throw an error to prevent this from happenening.

Change the entire switch statement to look like this:

```
switch(aShape) {
case .Rectangle:
  println("This is a rectangle")
case .Square:
  println("This is a square")
default:
  break
}
```

This adds a case for `Square`, as well as a default case for any unhandled cases. You'll now see "This is a rectangle" in the sidebar, matching the value of aShape.

The statement is now exhaustive, because it handles the `Rectangle` and `Square` cases independently, while handling the remaining cases through the default case.

If you're familiar with switch statements in other languages, it might catch your eye that there's no `break` statement on the first two cases. You might then think that in the case of `Rectangle`, control will fall through to call both `println` functions. This would be true in languages such as Objective-C due to fall-through logic, whereby without a `break`, each case falls through to the next.

However, Swift doesn't have fall-through. Not having fall-through eliminates an entire class of bugs caused by forgetting a break statement. Thank you, Swift!

The `default` case in the code above requires the `break` because you can't have empty code blocks for a case. This is the only time you need to use a `break`.

The one instance in which you might *mean* to use fall-through is to have one block of code handle multiple cases. Modify the switch statement to look like this:

```
switch(aShape) {
case .Rectangle, .Square:
  println("This is a quadrilateral")
case .Circle:
  println("This is a circle")
default:
  break
}
```

As you can see, Swift has a convention to handle multiple cases at once. Using a comma between enum cases (rather than `case` statements on separate lines) not only reads much cleaner, but also removes forgotten break statements from the list of common bug causes.

You'll see many more switch statements as you go through the rest of this chapter.

Associated values

Even now, you're probably thinking that enums in Swift are mundane and not very different from enums in other languages, such as Objective-C. However, there's more—much more.

Swift lets you assign one or more values to each case, called **associated values**. This is one feature that makes enums in Swift so powerful.

You're going to see an example of this, but first, create a new iOS playground called **Enum_3.playground**.

Next, add the following code to your new playground:

```
enum Shape {
  case Rectangle(Float, Float)
  case Square(Float)
  case Triangle(Float, Float)
  case Circle(Float)
}
```

Just like before, you declare an enum called `Shape`. This time, however, you're declaring associated values attached to each case. The associated values will have the types specified in the parentheses.

In this example, you're using the associated values to hold the dimensions of the shape. The two `float`s indicate width and height in the case of `Rectangle`, side length in the case of `Square`, base and height in the case of `Triangle` and the radius in the case of `Circle`.

Now you can associate values with this enum type when you create one. Add the following code to your playground:

```
var rectangle = Shape.Rectangle(5, 10)
```

This creates a new `Rectangle` value with a width of 5 and a height of 10. Notice, though, that it's hard to tell which parameter is which in this case. Does the width come first or the height? To help, you can name each parameter. Change the enum definition to look like this:

```
enum Shape {
  case Rectangle(width: Float, height: Float)
  case Square(side: Float)
  case Triangle(base: Float, height: Float)
  case Circle(radius: Float)
}
```

Now the associated values have names. This really helps readability to know which order the parameters are in and what they mean. For example with `Circle`, is it the radius or the diameter. Giving it the name of `radius` makes it clear.

As a result of adding the names, you must change the `rectangle` variable definition to include the names:

```
var rectangle = Shape.Rectangle(width: 5, height: 10)
```

These are starting to look an awful lot like structs and classes! At this point, you might be thinking of trying something like `rectangle.width` to access the associated value.

It may come as a surprise, but you can't access associated values directly as you can with properties in a struct or class. Associated values are also different from raw values. Raw values provide a way to represent an enum type with another type, such as using integers to serialize and deserialize the values of an enum. On the other hand, you can only access associated values when testing an enum with a switch statement.

Let's see how that works. Add the following code to the bottom of your playground:

```
switch (rectangle) {
case .Rectangle(let width, let height):
  println("Rectangle: \(width) x \(height)")
default:
  println("Other shape")
}
```

Now click **View\Assistant Editor\Show Assistant Editor**, and you'll see this:

```
Console Output
Rectangle: 5.0 x 10.0
```

The code above looks much like a normal switch statement, except you pull the associated values out of the case by binding them to the local variables `width` and `height`.

But wait—there's more! With associated values, switch statements move beyond a mere way to read values. Change the switch statement to look like this:

```
switch (rectangle) {
case .Rectangle(let width, let height) where width <= 10:
  println("Narrow rectangle: \(width) x \(height)")
case .Rectangle(let width, let height):
  println("Wide rectangle: \(width) x \(height)")
default:
  println("Other shape")
}
```

This switch statement now has two cases for `Rectangle`. Notice the first, however, has an additional `where` clause that will match only certain `Rectangle` values—those where the `width` is less than 10.

Since your rectangle has a width of 5, you'll see it reported as a narrow rectangle in the output.

You can do almost anything you want in the `where` clause. For example, add the following two clauses to the top of the switch statement:

```
case .Rectangle(let width, let height) where width == height:
  println("Square: \(width) x \(height)")
case .Square(let side):
  println("Square: \(side) x \(side)")
```

Here you're using the fact that a rectangle with equal sides is actually a square. Nifty!

Notice, however, that the order of the cases matters. To see why, move the plain `Rectangle` case to the top of the switch statement so that the entire switch statement looks like this:

```
switch (rectangle) {
case .Rectangle(let width, let height):
  println("Wide rectangle: \(width) x \(height)")
case .Rectangle(let width, let height) where width == height:
  println("Square: \(width) x \(height)")
case .Square(let side):
  println("Square: \(side) x \(side)")
case .Rectangle(let width, let height) where width <= 10:
  println("Narrow rectangle: \(width) x \(height)")
default:
  println("Other shape")
}
```

Then, look at the Assistant Editor. You'll see this:

```
Console Output
Wide rectangle: 5.0 x 10.0
```

Is that what you expected? The width is less than 10, so why didn't the other `Rectangle` case, where width is less than 10, also match? It does match, but much like an `if-`

statement, the *order* of the cases in the switch matters. The switch statement will use the first case that matches.

> **Challenge**: Write additional cases to match `Square`, `Triangle` and `Circle` values. Your cases should match the following:
>
> 1. Triangles that are taller than 10.
>
> 2. Triangles whose height is twice their base.
>
> 3. Circles that have a radius smaller than 5.

Enums as types

In Swift, enums are in many ways similar to classes and structs. They have the same value semantics as structs, meaning they are stack-allocated and are passed by value to functions. Enums can also have instance methods, just like classes and structs.

Let's look at an example. Create a new iOS playground called **Enum_4.playground**. Then, add the following code to your new playground:

```
enum Shape {
    case Rectangle(width: Float, height: Float)
    case Square(side: Float)
    case Triangle(base: Float, height: Float)
    case Circle(radius: Float)
}
```

You begin with the same enum from the last section of this chapter.

Next, add the following method inside the enum:

```
func area() -> Float {
    switch(self) {
    case .Rectangle(let width, let height):
        return width * height
    case .Square(let side):
        return side * side
    case .Triangle(let base, let height):
        return 0.5 * base * height
    case .Circle(let radius):
```

```
        return Float(M_PI) * powf(radius, 2)
    }
}
```

Now do you believe me when I say enums are much more powerful in Swift than in Objective-C?

This adds an instance method to the `Shape` enum to obtain the shape's area. It switches on itself to determine the correct formula to use to compute the area.

Add the following code to the bottom of your playground:

```
var circle = Shape.Circle(radius: 5)
circle.area()
```

You'll see the calculated area in the sidebar:

```
24
25  var circle = Shape.Circle(radius: 5)      (Enum Value)
26  circle.area()                              78.5398178100586
27
```

Perfect! You can now calculate the area of any of these shapes. Of course, there are many other types of methods you could add to `Shape`.

> **Challenge**: Add a perimeter method to the `Shape` enum. It should calculate the total length of all the sides of the shape.

You can even add an initializer to an enum. Add the following code to the bottom of the enum:

```
init(_ rect: CGRect) {
    let width = Float(CGRectGetWidth(rect))
    let height = Float(CGRectGetHeight(rect))
    if width == height {
        self = Square(width)
    } else {
        self = Rectangle(width: width, height: height)
    }
}
```

This allows construction of a `Shape` using a `CGRect`. Inside the initializer, you assign to `self`, rather than return a value. In this case, if the sides of the `CGRect` are the same, then the method creates a `Square`, otherwise it creates a `Rectangle`.

Now add the following code to the end of your playground:

```
var shape = Shape(CGRect(x: 0, y: 0, width: 5, height: 10))
shape.area()
```

This uses the new constructor to make a `Shape` with a `CGRect`. Take a look in the sidebar, and you'll see the area calculated as 50.0, as expected.

The initializer of an enum must assign something to `self`. Otherwise, there will be a compiler error. This means you can't do something like this:

```
init(_ string: String) {
  switch(string) {
  case "rectangle":
    self = Rectangle(width: 5, height: 10)
  case "square":
    self = Square(side: 5)
  case "triangle":
    self = Triangle(base: 5, height: 10)
  case "circle":
    self = Circle(radius: 5)
  default:
    break
  }
}
```

Even though the above might be a useful initializer to have, the default case of the switch statement doesn't assign to `self`.

Such an initializer would better serve as a factory method. Add the following method to the end of the enum:

```
static func fromString(string: String) -> Shape? {
  switch(string) {
  case "rectangle":
    return Rectangle(width: 5, height: 10)
  case "square":
    return Square(side: 5)
  case "triangle":
    return Triangle(base: 5, height: 10)
  case "circle":
    return Circle(radius: 5)
  default:
    return nil
  }
}
```

This method is static, meaning it belongs to the type itself rather than to any instance and is called on the type (`Shape`, in this case), rather than on an instance. The method takes a string and returns a relevant `Shape` value. Using an optional return type allows the method to return nil in case the string doesn't match one of the shapes.

Now, add the following code to the end of your playground:

```swift
if let anotherShape = Shape.fromString("rectangle") {
  anotherShape.area()
}
```

This uses the new factory method to create a shape from a string. Since the return type is optional, it needs to be unwrapped. In this case, you unwrap the optional via an `if`-statement that binds it to a local variable.

This brings you nicely to an enum "case study" (pun intended!) that makes use of the fact that enums are full types.

Optionals are enums

It may surprise you to learn this, but Swift's optional type is implemented as an enum. The implementation looks like this (with some detail removed):

```swift
enum Optional<T> : NilLiteralConvertible {
  case None
  case Some(T)

  init()
  init(_ some: T)

  static func convertFromNilLiteral() -> T?
}
```

The first case is `None`, which represents an optional containing nil. The second case is `Some`, which represents an optional containing a value. Notice the use of generics to allow the `Optional` type to contain any type of value. Also notice the use of associated values to hold the value in the non-nil `Some` case.

The `Optional` type also shows that enums can implement protocols, just like other full types like classes and structs.

The `NilLiteralConvertible` protocol allows you to use nil in place of an optional—the compiler automatically converts it to a call to the `convertFromNilLiteral` method on the type.

This illustrates just how powerful enums are in Swift. They really are much more than their namesake in Objective-C.

JSON parsing using enums

This might all sound quite abstract so far. Shapes are interesting, but not many apps have a need to use shapes. Optionals are something you will use with Swift and you've seen how these are enums. They're powerful, but the fact it's an enum is quite hidden from you.

Let's now take a look at another real life example. JSON parsing is something that is extremely common in applications. In Swift, with its type safety, it's relatively tedious to parse a JSON response. You end up with a lot of nesting. Let's see that in action.

Parsing JSON the hard way

Create a new playground called **Enum_5.playground**. Then add the following code to it:

```
let json =
"{\"success\":true,\"data\":{\"numbers\":[1,2,3,4,5],\"animal\":
\"dog\"}}"

if let jsonData =
  (json as NSString).dataUsingEncoding(NSUTF8StringEncoding)
{
  let parsed: AnyObject? =
    NSJSONSerialization.JSONObjectWithData(
      jsonData,
      options: NSJSONReadingOptions(0),
      error: nil)

  // Actual JSON parsing section
  if let parsed = parsed as? [String:AnyObject] {
    if let success = parsed["success"] as? NSNumber {
      if success.boolValue == true {
        if let data = parsed["data"] as? NSDictionary {
          if let numbers = data["numbers"] as? NSArray {
            println(numbers)
```

```
        }
        if let animal = data["animal"] as? NSString {
          println(animal)
        }
      }
    }
   }
  }
 }
}
```

What a mouthful! And this uses `NSDictionary`, `NSArray`, etc which ends up losing some of the safety of Swift. This is by no means the only way to parse JSON in Swift, but it always ends up being quite complex and nested.

Introducing JSON.swift

Instead, you can use enums to make life *much* simpler. In Chapter 4, "Generics", you used JSON parsing without knowing. The Flickr class required parsing the JSON response from the Flickr API. You might have looked into it, but if not, then you're going to see how that worked now.

In the resources for this chapter you will find the file where the magic happens. Open the file called **JSON.swift** and take a look at it. It's an enum! And it makes JSON parsing significantly easier. Let's see how it works.

First of all, the enum definition:

```
enum JSONValue {
    case JSONObject([String:JSONValue])
    case JSONArray([JSONValue])
    case JSONString(String)
    case JSONNumber(NSNumber)
    case JSONBool(Bool)
    case JSONNull
}
```

This is the heart of the solution. Each value in JSON can either be an object, an array, a string, a number, a Boolean, or null. An object is a dictionary from string to other JSON values, and an array is an array of JSON values. This is perfect for describing as an enum with associated values. So, that's what we do!

In this way, you can describe every value in a JSON object by one of the cases of the `JSONValue` enum.

Then comes the interesting part.

Most JSON parsing involves reading into objects by the string key. In the example earlier, the `data` and `success` values were read from the outer object for example. This can be done through the use of a subscript. The following subscript is defined on the enum:

```
subscript(key: String) -> JSONValue? {
  get {
    switch self {
    case .JSONObject(let value):
      return value[key]
    default:
      return nil
    }
  }
}
```

Notice that this subscript returns an *optional* `JSONValue`. This means that if the value doesn't exist then nil is returned. Similarly, if the `JSONValue` is not an object, then nil is also returned. If you examine the **JSON.swift** file then you will also see an integer index subscript. This is similar to this subscript, but for reading into arrays.

That enables you to read more `JSONValues` from objects and arrays, but what about obtaining actual `String`, `Bool`, etc objects from the values? This is achieved through computed properties such as the following:

```
var string: String? {
  switch self {
  case .JSONString(let value):
    return value
  default:
    return nil
  }
}
```

Like the subscripts, these computed properties return optionals. If the `JSONValue` is a `JSONString` case then it can be a string, so the value in the associated value is returned. Otherwise, nil is returned. The same happens for the other cases and their associated computed property accessors.

Finally, there is a method that reads an object into a `JSONValue`. This is used to bring a dictionary, array or any other JSON representable object into the `JSONValue` enum. It looks like this:

```
static func fromObject(object: AnyObject) -> JSONValue? {
  switch object {
```

```swift
    case let value as NSString:
      return JSONValue.JSONString(value)
    case let value as NSNumber:
      return JSONValue.JSONNumber(value)
    case let value as NSNull:
      return JSONValue.JSONNull
    case let value as NSDictionary:
      var jsonObject: [String:JSONValue] = [:]
      for (k: AnyObject, v: AnyObject) in value {
        if let k = k as? NSString {
          if let v = JSONValue.fromObject(v) {
            jsonObject[k] = v
          } else {
            return nil
          }
        }
      }
      return JSONValue.JSONObject(jsonObject)
    case let value as NSArray:
      var jsonArray: [JSONValue] = []
      for v in value {
        if let v = JSONValue.fromObject(v) {
          jsonArray.append(v)
        } else {
          return nil
        }
      }
      return JSONValue.JSONArray(jsonArray)
    default:
      return nil
    }
  }
```

This method is for use with `NSJSONSerialization`, which returns Foundation objects such as `NSArray` and `NSDictionary`. The method checks the objects type and returns a relevant `JSONValue` instance as appropriate.

Putting it into practice

Let's now put this **JSON.swift** file into practice! Copy and paste the entirety of the file into the top of the playground, above the existing code. You have to copy and paste because playgrounds can't reference other files yet.

Now add the following code to the bottom of the playground:

```
if let jsonData =
```

```
    (json as NSString).dataUsingEncoding(NSUTF8StringEncoding)
{
  if let parsed: AnyObject =
    NSJSONSerialization.JSONObjectWithData(
      jsonData,
      options: NSJSONReadingOptions(0),
      error: nil)
  {
    if let jsonParsed = JSONValue.fromObject(parsed) {

      // Actual JSON parsing section
      if jsonParsed["success"]?.bool == true {
        if let numbers = jsonParsed["data"]?["numbers"]?.array {
          println(numbers)
        }
        if let animal = jsonParsed["data"]?["animal"]?.string {
          println(animal)
        }
      }

    }
  }
}
```

There is an extra if-statement at the top because `JSONValue.fromObject()` returns an optional so that needs to be unwrapped. However the actual JSON parsing section has gone down from 5 levels of nested if-statements to just 2 levels.

Notice the use of optional chaining to really unlock the power of this approach. For example, if the "data" key doesn't exist then when parsing `numbers`, the expression will return nil and the "numbers" key won't be touched at all.

Similarly, if the "animal" key exists but is not actually a string then the if-statement reading that value will return nil and the animal will not be printed.

What's more, you maintain the safety of Swift over the previous code.

I think you will agree that enums are extremely powerful, and you should make the most of them when writing your applications. They're perfect when you have a type that can be a pre-defined set of different things, just like JSON.

Where to go from here?

In this chapter, you've created simple enums and used raw and associated values to store additional information on an enum value.

You also used switch statements to check the case of a given enum value. In addition, you've seen the advantages of switch statements in Swift over traditional languages such as Objective-C, such as the exhaustive case checking and advanced pattern matching.

Finally, you've seen how to associate methods and initializers with an enum type, both by doing it yourself and by examining the implementation of the optional type—which is itself an enum!

You'll probably find yourself using enums frequently in Swift, because you can simply do more with them than you can in languages like Objective-C. Put into practice the techniques you've learned here, and harness the full power of enums in your own apps.

Chapter 7: Functional Programming

By Colin Eberhardt

In the preceding chapters, you've learned about generics, classes, enumerations, range operators and a host of other interesting features of the Swift language. Looking at these features collectively, it's evident that Swift is a more expressive and concise language than Objective-C.

When making the transition from Objective-C to Swift, it's logical to map concepts you know in Objective-C onto Swift. You know how to create classes with Objective-C, and now you know the equivalent in Swift. There are, of course, some completely new features, such as generics and range operators, but these are still little more than refinements of what you already know. (OK, perhaps not so little!)

However, Swift does more than provide a better syntax for your applications. With this new language, you have the opportunity to change the way in which you tackle problems and write code. With Swift, **functional programming** techniques become a viable and important part of your programming toolkit.

This book is a practical guide to the Swift language. Functional programming can be a theory-heavy topic, so this chapter will introduce the topic by example. You'll work through a number of programming examples using what will likely be the more familiar, imperative style, and then try your hand at solving the same problems using functional techniques.

Briefly put, functional programming is a programming paradigm that emphasizes calculations via mathematical-style functions, immutability and expressiveness, and minimizes the use of variables and state.

Since there's minimal shared state and each function is like an island in the ocean of your app, it makes things easier to test. Functional programming has also come into popularity because it can make concurrency and parallel processing easier to work with. That's one more thing in your toolbox to improve performance in these days of multi-core devices.

Its time to put the fun- into functional programming!

Simple array filtering

You'll start with something quite easy: a simple bit of math. Your first task is to create a simple Swift script that finds all the even numbers between 1 and 10 (inclusive). A pretty trivial task, but a great introduction to functional programming!

Filtering the old way

Create a new Swift playground file and save it wherever you like. Replace the contents of the newly created file with the following code:

```
var evens = [Int]()
for i in 1...10 {
  if i % 2 == 0 {
    evens.append(i)
  }
}
println(evens)
```

This produces the desired result:

```
[2, 4, 6, 8, 10]
```

(If you can't see the console output, remember that you need to show the Assistant Editor via the **View/Assistant Editor/Show Assistant Editor** menu option.)

This little script is very simple; the key points of the algorithm are as follows:
1. You create an empty (and mutable) array.
2. The `for` loop iterates over the numbers from 1 to 10 (remember "..." is inclusive!).
3. If the condition (that the number must be even) is met, you add it to the array.

The above code is imperative in nature. The instructions tell the computer how to locate the even numbers by giving it explicit instructions that use basic control structures, in this case `if` and `for-in`.

The code works just fine but the important bit—testing whether the number is even—is buried inside the for loop. There's also some tight coupling, where the desired action of adding the number to the array is inside the condition. If you wanted to print each even number somewhere else in your app, there's no good way to reuse code without resorting to copy-and-paste.

It's *fun*-ctional time. (Sorry, I'll stop it with the "fun" puns now!)

Functional filtering

Add the following to the end of your playground:

```
func isEven(number: Int) -> Bool {
   return number % 2 == 0
}
evens = Array(1...10).filter(isEven)
println(evens)
```

You'll see that the above, functional code creates exactly the same result as the imperative version:

```
[2, 4, 6, 8, 10]
```

Let's look more closely at the functional version. It's comprised of two parts:

1. The `Array(1...10)` section is a simple and convenient way to create an array containing the numbers 1 through 10. The range operator `1...10` creates a `Range` you pass to the array's initializer.

2. The `filter` statement is where the functional programming magic takes place. This method, exposed by `Array`, creates and returns a new array that contains only the items for which the given function returns true. In this example, `isEven` is supplied to `filter`.

You're passing in the function `isEven` as a parameter to `filter` but as you've already learned from Chapter 5, "Functions and Closures", functions are just named closures. Try adding the following, more concise version of the code to your playground:

```
evens = Array(1...10).filter { (number) in number % 2 == 0 }
println(evens)
```

Again, verify that the results from all three approaches are identical. The above example demonstrates that the compiler infers the type of the parameter `number` and return types of the closure from its usage context.

If you like your code to be as concise as possible, take it one step further and try the following:

```
evens = Array(1...10).filter { $0 % 2 == 0 }
println(evens)
```

The above uses argument shorthand notation, implicit returns, type inference... the works!

> **Note:** The use of shorthand argument notation is a matter or preference. Personally, I think that for simple examples like the one above, shorthand notation is just fine. However, I'd opt for explicit argument names for anything more complicated. Compilers aren't concerned with variable names, but they can make a world of difference to humans!

The functional version of this code is certainly more concise than the imperative equivalent. This simple example exhibits a few interesting features that are common to all functional languages:

1. **Higher-order functions:** These are functions that you pass as arguments to other functions. In this simple example, `filter` requires that you pass a higher-order function.

2. **First-class functions:** You can treat functions just like any other variable; you can assign them to variables and pass them as arguments to other functions.

3. **Closures:** These are effectively anonymous functions you create in-place.

You may have noticed that Objective-C also exhibits some of these features through the use of blocks. Swift, however, goes further than Objective-C in promoting functional programming with a mix of more concise syntax and built-in functional abilities such as `filter`.

The magic behind filter

Swift arrays have a number of functional methods, such as `map`, `join` and `reduce`. What, exactly, goes on behind the scenes in these methods?

It's time to look behind the magic of filter and add your own implementation.

Within the same playground, add the following function:

```
func myFilter<T>(source: [T], predicate:(T) -> Bool) -> [T] {
  var result = [T]()
  for i in source {
    if predicate(i) {
      result.append(i)
    }
  }
  return result
}
```

The above is a generic function that takes as its inputs a `source`, which is an array of type `T`, and `predicate`, a function that takes an instance of `T` and returns a `Bool`.

The implementation of `myFilter` looks a lot like the imperative version you added at the start. The main difference is that you supply the condition being checked as a function rather than hard-code it.

Try out your newly added filter implementation by adding the following code:

```
evens = myFilter(Array(1...10)) { $0 % 2 == 0 }
println(evens)
```

Once again, the output is the same!

> **Challenge:** The above filter function is global; why not see if you can make it a method on `Array`?
>
> Here are a few hints to get you started:
>
> • You can add `myFilter` to `Array` via a class extension.
>
> • You can extend `Array`, but not `Array<T>`. This means that as you iterate over the items in the array via `self`, you'll have to perform a cast.

Reducing

The previous example was a simple one, making use of a single functional method. In this section, you'll build upon the last, showing how you can implement more complex logic using functional techniques.

Create a new Swift playground and get ready for your next assignment!

Manual reduction

Your task in this section is just a little more complicated: Take the even numbers between 1 and 10 and compute their sum. This calls for what is known as a **reduce** function, which takes a set of inputs and generates a single output.

I'm sure you are more than capable of working this one out yourself, but here it is anyway! Add the following to your playground:

```
var evens = [Int]()
for i in 1...10 {
  if i % 2 == 0 {
    evens.append(i)
  }
}

var evenSum = 0
for i in evens {
  evenSum += i
}

println(evenSum)
```

The Assistant Editor will display the following result:

```
30
```

The imperative code above continues in the same vein as the previous example, adding an additional `for-in` loop.

Let's see what a functional equivalent looks like!

Functional reduce

Add the following to your playground:

```
evenSum = Array(1...10)
    .filter { (number) in number % 2 == 0 }
    .reduce(0) { (total, number) in total + number }

println(evenSum)
```

You'll see exactly the same result:

```
30
```

The previous section covered the array construction and use of `filter`. The net result of these two operations is an array with five numbers, [2, 4, 6, 8, 10]. The new step in the above code uses `reduce`.

`reduce` is a tremendously versatile `Array` method that executes a function once for each element, accumulating the results.

To understand how `reduce` works, it helps to look at its signature:

```
func reduce<U>(initial: U, combine: (U, T) -> U) -> U
```

The first parameter is the initial value, which is of type `U`. In your current code, the initial value is 0 and is of type `Int` (hence `U` is `Int` in this case). The second argument is the `combine` function that is executed once for each element of the array.

`combine` takes two arguments: the first, of type `U`, is the result of the previous invocation of `combine`; the second is the value of the array element that is being combined. The result returned by `reduce` is the value returned by the last `combine` invocation.

There's a lot going on here, so let's break it down step by step.

In your code, the first `reduce` iteration results in the following:

	combine		
iteration	total: U	number: T	result
#1	0	2	2

The inputs to `combine` are the initial value, 0, and the first item in the input array, which is 2. `combine` sums these values, returning 2.

The second iteration is illustrated below:

	combine		
iteration	total: U	number: T	result
#1	0	2	2
#2	2	4	6

On the second iteration, the inputs to `combine` are the result from the previous iteration and the next item from the input array. Combining them results in 2 + 4 = 6.

Continuing this process for all the items in the array gives the following inputs and outputs:

	combine		
iteration	total: U	number: T	result
#1	0	2	2
#2	2	4	6
#3	6	6	12
#4	12	8	20
#5	20	10	30 *

The number highlighted in the bottom-right corner is the overall result.

This is quite a simple example; in practice, you can perform all kinds of interesting and powerful transformations with `reduce`. Below are a few quick examples.

Add the following to your playground:

```
let maxNumber = Array(1...10)
            .reduce(0) { (total, number) in max(total, number) }
println(maxNumber)
```

This code uses `reduce` to find the maximum number in an array of integers. In this case, the result is rather obvious! Remember that here, `total` is really just the result of `max` of the last iteration of `reduce`.

If you're struggling to see how this works, why not create a table like the one above where you compute the inputs and output of `combine` (i.e., the closure) for each iteration?

The examples you've seen so far all reduce arrays of integers into single integer values. Of course, `reduce` has two type parameters, U and T, which can be different and certainly don't have to be integers. This means you can reduce an array of one type into a completely different type.

Add the following to your playground:

```
let numbers = Array(1...10)
```

```
    .reduce("numbers: ") {(total, number) in total + "\(number) "}
println(numbers)
```

This produces the following output:

```
numbers: 1 2 3 4 5 6 7 8 9 10
```

This example reduces an array of integers into the string shown above.

With a bit of practice, you'll find yourself using `reduce` in all kinds of interesting and creative ways! You may remember seeing it crop up elsewhere in this book. For example, in Chapter 4, "Generics", you used it to find the bounding rectangle for an array of points on a map.

> **Challenge**: See if you can use `reduce` to take an array of digits and convert them into an integer. Given the input array:
>
> ```
> let digits = ["3", "1", "4", "1"]
> ```
>
> Your `reduce` method should return an `Int` with the value 3141.
>
> You can find the answer to this challenge in the playground that accompanies this chapter, but have a go at solving it yourself first!

The magic behind reduce

In the previous section, you developed your own implementation of `filter`, which was surprisingly simple. You'll now see that the same is true for `reduce`.

Add the following to your playground:

```
extension Array {
  func myReduce<T, U>(seed:U, combiner:(U, T) -> U) -> U {
    var current = seed
    for item in self {
      current = combiner(current, item as T)
    }
    return current
  }
}
```

The above adds a `myReduce` method to `Array` that mimics the built-in `reduce` function. This method simply iterates over each item in the array, invoking `combiner` at each step.

To test out the above, replace one of the `reduce` methods in your current playground with `myReduce`.

At this point, you might be thinking, "Why would I want to implement `filter` or `reduce` myself?" The answer is, "You probably wouldn't!"

However, you might want to expand your use of the functional paradigm in Swift and implement your own functional methods. It's encouraging (and important!) to see and understand just how easy it is to implement powerful methods like `reduce`.

Building an index

It's time to tackle a more difficult problem, and that means it's time to open a new playground. You know want to!

In this section, you're going to use functional programming techniques to group a list of words into an index based on the first letter of each word.

Within your newly created playground, add the following:

```
import Foundation

let words = ["Cat", "Chicken", "fish", "Dog",
             "Mouse", "Guinea Pig", "monkey"]
```

To accomplish this section's task, you're going to group these words by their first letters (case insensitive!).

In preparation, add the following to the playground:

```
typealias Entry = (Character, [String])

func buildIndex(words: [String]) -> [Entry] {
  return [Entry]()
}
println(buildIndex(words))
```

The `Entry` typealias defines the tuple type for each index entry. Using a typealias in this example makes the code more readable, removing the need to repeatedly specify the tuple type in full. You're going to add your index-building code in `buildIndex`.

Building an index imperatively

Starting with an imperative approach, update `buildIndex` as follows:

```
func buildIndex(words: [String]) -> [Entry] {
  var result = [Entry]()

  var letters = [Character]()
  for word in words {
    let firstLetter = Character(word.substringToIndex(
      advance(word.startIndex, 1)).uppercaseString)

    if !contains(letters, firstLetter) {
      letters.append(firstLetter)
    }
  }

  for letter in letters {
    var wordsForLetter = [String]()
    for word in words {
      let firstLetter = Character(word.substringToIndex(
        advance(word.startIndex, 1)).uppercaseString)

      if firstLetter == letter {
        wordsForLetter.append(word)
      }
    }
    result.append((letter, wordsForLetter))
  }
  return result
}
```

This function has two halves, each with its own `for` loop. The first half iterates over each of the words to build an array of letters; the second iterates over these letters, finding the words that start with the given letter, to build the return array.

With this implementation in place, you'll see the desired output:

```
[(C, [Cat, Chicken]),
 (F, [fish]),
 (D, [Dog]),
 (M, [Mouse, monkey]),
 (G, [Guinea Pig])]
```

(The above is formatted a little for clarity.)

This imperative implementation has quite a few steps and nested loops that can make it difficult to understand. Let's see what a functional equivalent looks like.

Building an index the functional way

Create a new playground file and add the same initial structure:

```swift
import Foundation

let words = ["Cat", "Chicken", "fish", "Dog",
             "Mouse", "Guinea Pig", "monkey"]

typealias Entry = (Character, [String])

func buildIndex(words: [String]) -> [Entry] {
  return [Entry]();
}

println(buildIndex(words))
```

At this point, the `println` statement will output an empty array:

```
[]
```

The first step toward building an index is to transform the words into an array that contains only their first letters. Update `buildIndex` as follows:

```swift
func buildIndex(words: [String]) -> [Entry] {
  let letters = words.map {
    (word) -> Character in
    Character(word.substringToIndex(advance(word.startIndex, 1)
      ).uppercaseString)
  }
  println(letters)

  return [Entry]()
}
```

The playground now outputs an array of uppercase letters, each one corresponding to a word in the input array.

```
[C, C, F, D, M, G, M]
```

In the previous sections, you encountered `filter` and `reduce`. The above code introduces `map`, another functional method that's part of the array API.

`map` creates a new array with the results of calls to the supplied closure for each element in the supplied array. You use `map` to perform transformations; in this case, `map` transforms an array of type `[String]` into an array of type `[Character]`.

The array of letters currently contains duplicates, whereas your desired index has only a single occurrence of each letter. Unfortunately, Swift's array type doesn't have a method that performs de-duplication. It's something you're going to have to write yourself!

In the previous sections, you saw how easy it is to re-implement `reduce` and `filter`. It will come as no surprise that adding a de-duplication method of your own isn't tricky, either.

Add the following function to your playground before `buildIndex`:

```swift
func distinct<T: Equatable>(source: [T]) -> [T] {
  var unique = [T]()
  for item in source {
    if !contains(unique, item) {
      unique.append(item)
    }
  }
  return unique
}
```

`distinct` iterates over all the items in an array, building a new array that contains only the unique items.

Update `buildIndex` to put `distinct` to use:

```swift
func buildIndex(words: [String]) -> [Entry] {
  let letters = words.map {
    (word) -> Character in
    Character(word.substringToIndex(advance(word.startIndex, 1)
      ).uppercaseString)
  }
  let distinctLetters = distinct(letters)
  println(distinctLetters)

  return [Entry]()
}
```

Your playground will now output the unique letters:

```
[C, F, D, M, G]
```

Now that you have an array of distinct letters, the next task in building your index is to convert each letter into an `Entry` instance. Does that sound like a transformation? That'll be another job for `map`!

Update `buildIndex` as follows:

```
func buildIndex(words: [String]) -> [Entry] {
  let letters = words.map {
    (word) -> Character in
    Character(word.substringToIndex(advance(word.startIndex, 1)
      ).uppercaseString)
  }
  let distinctLetters = distinct(letters)

  return distinctLetters.map {
    (letter) -> Entry in
    return (letter, [])
  }
}
```

The second call to `map` takes the array of characters and outputs an array of `Entry` instances:

```
[(C, []),
 (F, []),
 (D, []),
 (M, []),
 (G, [])]
```

(Again, the above is formatted for clarity.)

You're almost done. The final task is to populate each `Entry` instance with the words that begin with the given letter. Update the function to add a nested `filter`, as follows:

```
func buildIndex(words: [String]) -> [Entry] {
  let letters = words.map {
    (word) -> Character in
    Character(word.substringToIndex(advance(word.startIndex, 1)
      ).uppercaseString)
  }
  let distinctLetters = distinct(letters)

  return distinctLetters.map {
    (letter) -> Entry in
    return (letter, words.filter {
      (word) -> Bool in
      Character(word.substringToIndex(advance(word.startIndex, 1)
        ).uppercaseString) == letter
    })
  }
}
```

This provides the desired output:

```
[(C, [Cat, Chicken]),
 (F, [fish]),
 (D, [Dog]),
 (M, [Mouse, monkey]),
 (G, [Guinea Pig])]
```

In the second half of the function, there's now a nested call to `filter` inside `map`. That will filter the list of words for each distinct letter, and thus identifies the words starting with the given letter.

The above implementation is already more concise and clear than its imperative equivalent, but there's still room for improvement: this code extracts and capitalizes a word's first letter multiple times. It would be good to remove this duplication.

If this were Objective-C code, you would have a few different options at your disposal: You could create a utility method that performs this functionality, or perhaps you could add this method directly to `NSString` via a class category. However, if you only ever need to perform this task within `buildIndex`, a utility method lacks semantic clarity and using a class category is overkill.

Fortunately, with Swift, there's a better way!

Update `buildIndex` with the following:

```
func buildIndex(words: [String]) -> [Entry] {
  func firstLetter(str: String) -> Character {
    return Character(str.substringToIndex(
        advance(str.startIndex, 1)).uppercaseString)
  }

  let letters = words.map {
    (word) -> Character in
    firstLetter(word)
  }
  let distinctLetters = distinct(letters)

  return distinctLetters.map {
    (letter) -> Entry in
    return (letter, words.filter {
      (word) -> Bool in
        firstLetter(word) == letter
    })
  }
}
```

You'll see exactly the same output as before.

The above code adds a `firstLetter` function that is nested within `buildIndex` and as a result, is entirely local to the outer function. This takes advantage of Swift's first-class functions that you can treat much like variables, allowing for assignment and scoping.

The new code removes the duplicate logic, but there's even more you can do to clean up `buildIndex`.

The first `map` step that constructs the array of letters takes a closure whose signature is `(String) -> Character`. You may notice this is exactly the same signature as the `firstLetter` function you just added, which means you can pass it directly to `map`.

Making use of this knowledge, you can rewrite the function as follows:

```swift
func buildIndex(words: [String]) -> [Entry] {
  func firstLetter(str: String) -> Character {
    return Character(str.substringToIndex(
        advance(str.startIndex, 1)).uppercaseString)
  }

  return distinct(words.map(firstLetter))
    .map {
      (letter) -> Entry in
      return (letter, words.filter {
        (word) -> Bool in
        firstLetter(word) == letter
      })
    }
}
```

The end result is concise, yet highly expressive.

Perhaps you've noticed an interesting side effect of the functional techniques you have employed so far. While your imperative solutions have relied on variables (as defined using the `var` keyword), you've defined everything in the functional equivalents as constants (via `let`).

You should strive for immutability; immutable types are easier to test and aid concurrency. Functional programming and immutable types tend to go hand in hand. As a result, your code will be more concise as well as less error-prone. And it will look cool and impress your friends!

> **Challenge**: Currently, `buildIndex` returns an unsorted index; the order of the `Entry` instances depends on the order of the words in the input array. Your challenge is to sort the index into alphabetic order. For the example array of strings, this would give the following output:
>
> ```
> [(C, [Cat, Chicken]),
>  (D, [Dog]),
>  (F, [fish]),
>  (G, [Guinea Pig]),
>  (M, [Mouse, monkey])]
> ```
>
> Tip: Swift's Array type has a `sort` method, but this method mutates the array rather than returning a new, sorted instance, and it requires a mutable array on which to operate. In general, it's safer to deal with immutable data, so I would advise against using this method! As an alternative, use the `sorted` method that returns a second sorted array.
>
> Of course, if you happen to get stuck, you can find a solution playground in this chapter's resources.

Partial application and currying

The previous three sections have all concerned array manipulation. With the trio of `map`, `reduce` and `filter`, you can perform practically any type of data manipulation task. Furthermore, if you need to perform a function that these methods don't cover, it's very easy to add your own (e.g., `distinct`).

Collection manipulation is a great way to exercise your functional programming skills, but you can achieve much more with Swift. This section looks at partial application and its somewhat exotic-sounding partner, currying!

Partial application

Create another playground and replace its contents with the following code:

```
import Foundation

let data = "5,7;3,4;55,6"
```

The constant holds some structured data: groups of numbers separated by semicolons, with the numbers in each group separated by commas. This is the kind of data you might expect from a CSV file or perhaps a table formatted in wiki markup or Markdown.

Processing delimited data typically involves a number of "split" steps. Let's see this in action.

Add the following code to the playground:

```
println(data.componentsSeparatedByString(";"))
```

This yields the following output:

```
["5,7", "3,4", "55,6"]
```

(I've added quotes around the strings for clarity.)

`componentsSeparatedByString` is defined on `NSString` and bridged onto the Swift `String` type, which is why you need to import Foundation in this playground. This method splits a string based on the provided delimiter. In your code, it splits on semicolons and thus returns an array containing three strings.

When handling delimited data, you'll often find yourself repeatedly splitting on the same delimiters. Wouldn't it be better to have splitter functions specific to the types of delimiters in your data?

You could create your own semicolon split method, but partial application provides a more generic solution to this problem.

Add the following to your playground:

```
func createSplitter(separator:String) -> (String -> [String]) {
  func split(source:String) -> [String] {
    return source.componentsSeparatedByString(separator)
  }
  return split
}
```

This is a funky looking piece of code! Let's break it down.

`createSplitter` takes a single string argument and has a return type of (`String -> [String]`), a function type that takes a string and returns an array of strings.

Within the body of `createSplitter`, you create an inner-function named `split` that has the required return type. You implement this inner-function via `componentsSeparatedByString`.

Putting these pieces together, `createSplitter` is like a factory for new functions. When invoked with a separator, it will return a function that splits strings based on the given separator.

This makes use of both first-class functions and closures—you capture the value of the `separator` argument in a closure.

It's time to put this to use, so add the following to your playground:

```
let commaSplitter = createSplitter(",")
println(commaSplitter(data))

let semiColonSplitter = createSplitter(";")
println(semiColonSplitter(data))
```

You'll see the following in your console:

```
["5", "7;3", "4;55", "6"]
["5,7", "3,4", "55,6"]
```

(I've added quotes around the strings for clarity.)

The first line of console output shows the string split by commas, and the second shows a split by semicolons. You can, of course, use your comma or semicolon splitter over and over again! (Why not give it a try?)

Your code uses a concept called **partial application**, which is the process of "fixing" one or more arguments of a function to create a new function. In this case, `createSplitter` fixes the separator parameter of `componentsSeparatedByString` to create a new function.

This is quite a simple example, where you partially applied a method that has a single parameter in order to create a function without any parameters. You'll see a more complex example later in this section, but first, it's time to look at currying!

A mild curry

In the current implementation of `createSplitter`, you manually create an inner function that is returned as the result of the outer. Currying does away with the need to manually construct the inner function.

Replace `createSplitter` with the following:

```
func createSplitter(separator:String)(source:String) -> [String]
{
  return source.componentsSeparatedByString(separator)
}
```

To make this compile, update the usage of `createSplitter` as follows:

```
let commaSplitter = createSplitter(",")
println(commaSplitter(source: data))

let semiColonSplitter = createSplitter(";")
println(semiColonSplitter(source: data))
```

The function generated by `createSplitter` requires external parameter names, hence the addition of the `source:` name in the above code. With this updated code, you'll see exactly the same output in the console:

```
["5", "7;3", "4;55", "6"]
["5,7", "3,4", "55,6"]
```

The updated `createSplitter` is more concise, but just how does it work?

You've made a subtle change in the function signature. What before was this:

```
(separator:String) -> (String -> [String])
```

Is now this:

```
(separator:String)(source:String) -> [String]
```

It's a slightly odd-looking function at first sight. All the functions you've seen so far in this book follow the same pattern: a number of parameters within parentheses followed by a return type. The signature above has two sets of parameters in parentheses.

When you invoke this function, `createSplitter(",")` returns a new function with the separator parameter bound to the given value. This is much the same as the earlier example, but frees you from the need to manually construct an inner function.

Curried functions certainly take some getting used to; perhaps a few more examples will help!

A hotter curry

Add the following code to your playground:

```
func addNumbers(one:Int, two:Int, three:Int) -> Int {
    return one + two + three
}

let sum = addNumbers(2, 5, 4)
println(sum) // 11 - duh!
```

This code probably requires little explanation. Well, it defines a function that adds three integers!

Now add the curried equivalent:

```
func curryAddNumbers(one:Int)(two:Int)(three:Int) -> Int {
    return one + two + three
}
```

Again, notice the subtle difference in the signature. To put this function to use, add the following code:

```
let stepOne = curryAddNumbers(2)
let stepTwo = stepOne(two: 5)
let result = stepTwo(three: 4);
println(result) // 11
```

As you can see from the above, to add three numbers you are executing a sequence of functions, each one returning a new function with the provided parameter values being "fixed." The final function returns the result.

You can, of course, execute the sequence of functions without assigning each intermediate step to a variable or constant:

```
let result2 = curryAddNumbers(2)(two: 5)(three: 4)
println(result2) // 11
```

As you can see, curried functions are simply a mechanism for generating new functions where the given parameter values are fixed.

For one final example, add the following to your playground:

```
func curryAddNumbers2(one:Int, two:Int)(three:Int) -> Int {
  return one + two + three
}
let result3 = curryAddNumbers2(2, 5)(three: 4)
println(result3) // 11
```

This demonstrates how you can "fix" more than one parameter at each step of the function sequence.

Practical currying

The previous example was a little contrived—it's unlikely you'll ever want to create a curried function just for adding three numbers! In this section, you'll build something more practical.

Add the following to your playground:

```
let text = "Swift"
let paddedText = text.stringByPaddingToLength(10,
                       withString: ".", startingAtIndex: 0)
println(paddedText)
```

The above code pads the string "Swift" to a length of 10 characters, appending dots to yield the following output:

```
Swift.....
```

`stringByPaddingToLength` is pretty flexible, having a padding string and a parameter specifying the index within the given padding string at which to start. Most of the time, you don't need all this flexibility. Let's use currying to provide a simpler mechanism for padding strings.

Add the following to your playground:

```
func curriedPadding(startingAtIndex: Int, withString: String)
                  (source: String, length: Int) -> String {
  return source.stringByPaddingToLength(length,
      withString: withString, startingAtIndex: startingAtIndex);
}
```

The above curried function takes `startingIndex` and `withString` parameters, returning a function that pads strings where all you need to specify is the length.

To create a padding function, add the following to your playground:

```
let dotPadding = curriedPadding(0, ".")
```

This invokes the curried function, providing a start index and a padding string. The `dotPadding` constant is a function with a signature of `(String, Int) -> String`.

Add the following to test this new function:

```
let dotPadded = dotPadding(source: "Curry!", length: 10)
println(dotPadded)
```

This gives the following output:

```
Curry!....
```

You can, of course, use `dotPadding` again and again.

Why not have a go at creating a new padding function using `curriedPadding`? Or try creating your own curried function?

Where to go from here?

I hope this chapter has given you a taste for functional programming and a desire to use it in your own applications. As mentioned in the introduction, functional programming is by no means mandatory for Swift development. However, once you've mastered the techniques in this chapter, you'll find your applications are more concise, expressive and fun to write.

You'll use functional concepts throughout this book; keep your eyes open and see how many you can spot. For example, in Chapter 4, "Generics" you'll use `reduce` to find the bounding box for a collection of map pins, while in Chapter 9, "Swift vs Objective-C" you'll use functional techniques to implement the visitor pattern.

This chapter is far from exhaustive; you can apply functional concepts in all manner of contexts. Use your imagination and be creative!

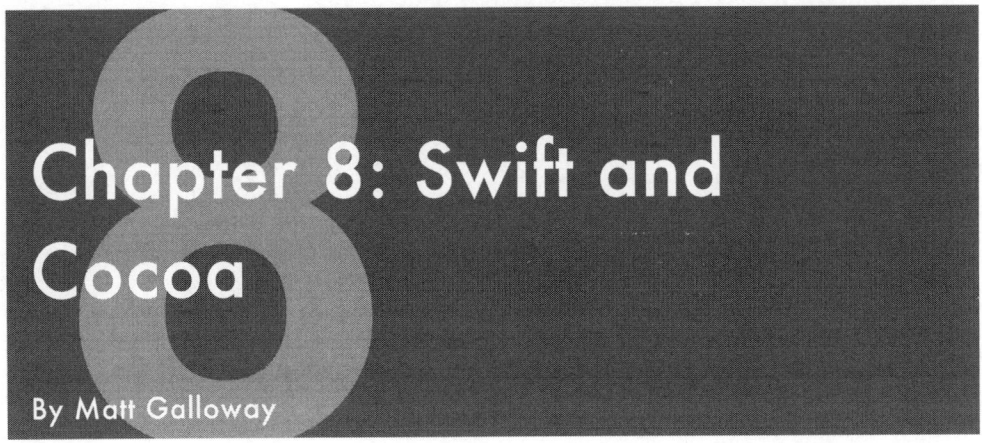

Chapter 8: Swift and Cocoa

By Matt Galloway

Swift may be a shiny new language, but the core of your knowledge when developing iOS applications will remain in the system frameworks collectively known as **Cocoa**. Cocoa includes frameworks such as Foundation and UIKit, both extremely important when writing iOS applications.

In this chapter, you will write an application that explores Swift's interaction with the Cocoa frameworks. You'll cover interoperability as well as take a look at how Cocoa design patterns translate into the Swift world.

The app you're going to build will use the Facebook iOS SDK to log into the Facebook Graph API and fetch a list of cafés around the user's current location. The app will display these cafés on a map view so the user can find their way to their nearest one!

Go grab a coffee (for research purposes only, of course) and then let's dive in!

Getting started

There's a starter project waiting for you in the resources for this chapter, in the **CafeHunter-Starter** folder. Open it and take a look around the project. You'll see three Swift files:

- **AppDelegate.swift**: This is the application delegate, just as you might be familiar with from Objective-C Cocoa development. In Swift, there will be slightly more in the file than you may be used to. Notice the `@UIApplicationMain` at the top. Also notice there is no **main.m** file, which in Objective-C development invokes the `UIApplicationMain`. In Swift, the application delegate class is annotated with

`@UIApplicationMain`, telling Swift to create a UIKit app with that class as the delegate.

- **ViewController.swift**: This is the single view controller at the moment. It doesn't do much right now except ask for permission to use the user's current location, which you'll need to find nearby cafés.

- **JSON.swift**: JSON is quite tricky to parse under Swift due to the compiler wanting to know exactly what type it's dealing with—when you parse JSON, you don't know what each type is until you've parsed it. This helper class makes things a lot easier, as you'll find out later in the chapter.

The other thing you'll see in the project is the Facebook SDK, imported as a framework. Open it and take a look. There is a load of Objective-C headers in there… It's not in Swift!

At the time of writing, the Facebook SDK is Objective-C only. But that's OK; it's an opportunity to learn how to mix and match between Swift and Objective-C. This will be a very handy skill over the coming years: while software slowly migrates to Swift, you may need to use existing Objective-C code in new Swift projects.

> **Note:** Third-party frameworks like the Facebook SDK are really just folders that bundle a static library with headers. This is because until recently, it wasn't possible to create a "true" framework on iOS, as you can when developing for Mac.
>
> That is, until iOS 8 and Xcode 6 came along. Apple has added the ability to create a true framework, which uses a dynamic library and can bundle resources properly.

Build and run the app. You'll see the following screen:

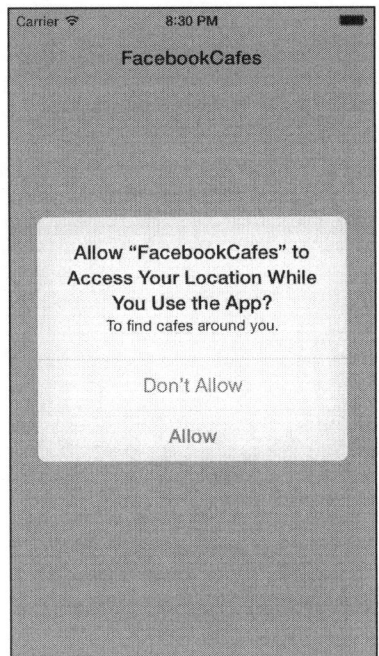

Make sure you allow access to the location—you'll need location permissions later! For now, let's get on with creating the app.

Obtaining a Facebook application ID

The app you're building is going to talk to Facebook. To make that conversation possible, you need to have a Facebook application ID. Follow this link to obtain one:

- https://developers.facebook.com

At the top of the screen, click **Apps**. If it says, "Register as a Developer," then go through that process and come back to the developer home page afterward.

Once you're signed up as a developer, click **Apps\Create a New App**. Choose a display name for the app such as **CafeHunter**. Choose **Food & Drink** for the category and leave everything else as it is. Finally, click **Create App**.

You will land on a screen like the following:

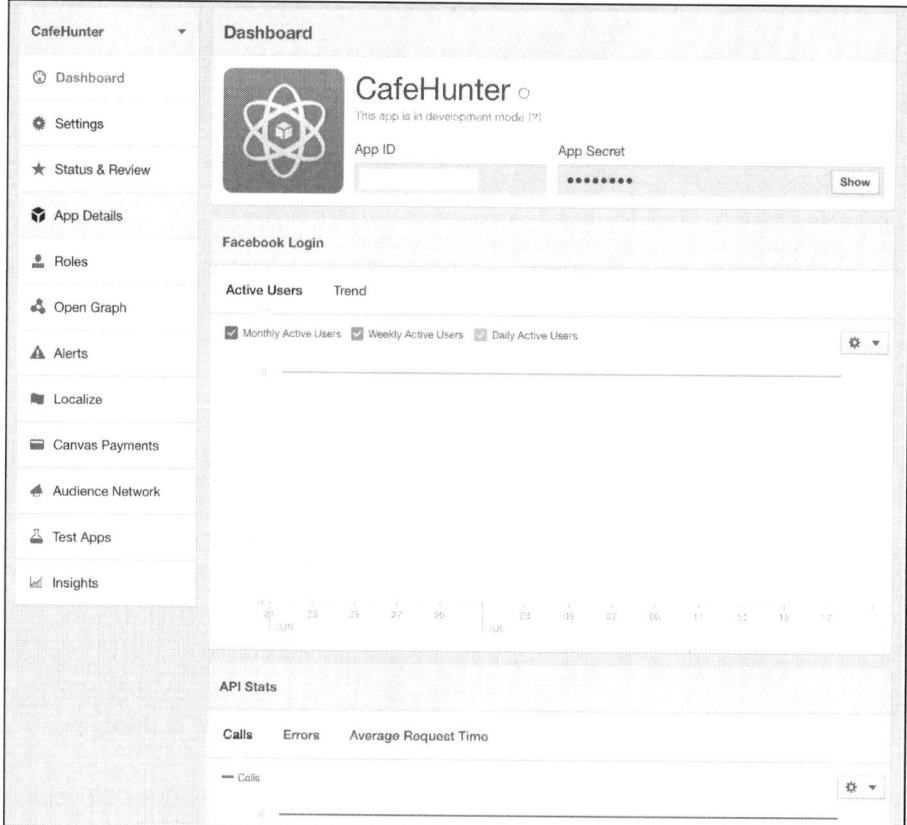

Note the **App ID** (shown blanked out above), as you'll need this later.

> **Note:** For the purposes of this chapter, you could use the app ID of a Facebook application you've already created. You're only going to be developing the app, not releasing it, so instead of polluting your Facebook developer account with another app, you might want to piggyback on one you already have. You also may want to delete your CaféHunter app after you're done with this tutorial.

Now that you have a Facebook app ID, it's time to begin coding!

Bridging Swift and Objective-C

As mentioned earlier, the Facebook SDK included in the starter project is written in Objective-C. But never fear! There is a technique known as **bridging** that enables you to use Objective-C from Swift and vice versa!

Swift bridging header

First, you need to set up the Facebook SDK in your app, so you're going to bridge Objective-C into Swift. You'll do this through the use of a **bridging header**, a standard Objective-C header file that the Swift compiler examines to determine what files it should bridge.

To get started, click **File\New\File...** and then select **iOS\Source\Header File**. Click **Next** and on the following screen, name the file **CafeHunter-ObjCBridging.h** and save it in the same folder as ViewController.swift, AppDelegate.swift and JSON.swift.

Next, click on the project at the top of the project navigator. Select the **Build Settings** tab and search for "bridg". Leave off the "e" so that you pick up bridge and bridging! You'll see the following results:

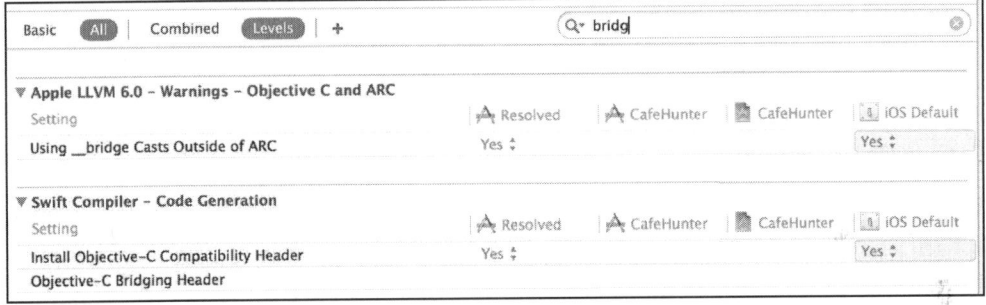

The setting you're interested in now is **Objective-C Bridging Header**. Set the CafeHunter target setting to **CafeHunter/CafeHunter-ObjCBridging.h**. This setting tells the Swift compiler exactly where to find the bridging header. This is why I told you to be careful where you put the file—you did put it where I said, right? :]

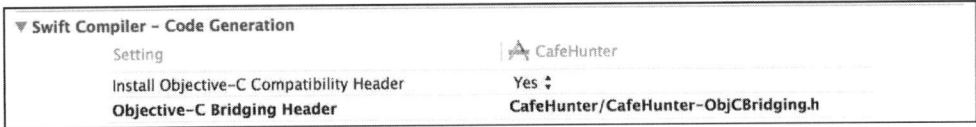

Open **AppDelegate.swift** and add the following to the top of `application(_:didFinishLaunchingWithOptions:)`

```
FBSettings.setDefaultAppID("INSERT_YOUR_FB_APP_ID")
```

Replace **INSERT_YOUR_FB_APP_ID** with the Facebook app ID you created earlier. This code calls the Facebook SDK to set the app ID to use for this iOS app.

Build the app. Ah—you'll notice it doesn't compile! That's because you haven't done anything with the bridging header you installed, so Swift doesn't recognize the Facebook SDK method you've referenced.

Open **CafeHunter-ObjCBridging.h** and add the following to the file, in between the `#define` and `#endif` lines:

```
#import <FacebookSDK/FacebookSDK.h>
```

Build again. This time it works! As if by magic, the Objective-C classes from the Facebook SDK are imported into Swift! The call you added above to `AppDelegate` is actually a call to an Objective-C method, `setDefaultAppId:`, on the Objective-C class `FBSettings`. This is what the declaration looks like inside **FBSettings.h**:

```
+ (void)setDefaultAppID:(NSString *)appID;
```

Talk about magical! In fact, any Objective-C or even C files you import in the bridging header, the compiler will bring over into Swift.

Objective-C compatibility header

As you saw with Swift bridging headers, you can use Objective-C code in your Swift code. What about the other direction—can you use Swift in Objective-C?

Well, remember the **Install Objective-C Compatibility Header** option in the build settings from earlier? That's what it's for. It was already set to **yes**, meaning it's turned on by default. Head to the report navigation and click on the latest **Build** in the left pane. It will be all green and look like this:

Double-click the line that says **Copy CafeHunter-Swift.h** to open that file. You'll see something that looks suspiciously like Objective-C. That's because it is! This is known as the **Objective-C compatibility header**, which does sort of the reverse job of the Swift bridging header.

Go to the bottom of the file and you'll see something like this:

```
SWIFT_CLASS("_TtC10CafeHunter14ViewController")
@interface ViewController : UIViewController
- (void)viewDidLoad;
- (void)viewDidAppear:(BOOL)animated;
- (instancetype)initWithNibName:(NSString *)nibNameOrNil
bundle:(NSBundle *)nibBundleOrNil OBJC_DESIGNATED_INITIALIZER;
- (instancetype)initWithCoder:(NSCoder *)aDecoder
OBJC_DESIGNATED_INITIALIZER;
@end
```

This looks just like a normal view controller interface in Objective-C, except there's a strange-looking `SWIFT_CLASS` macro at the top. Well, it *is* just a normal view controller interface in Objective-C. This is how you can use Swift classes in Objective-C.

The Objective-C compatibility header includes any Swift class in your project that inherits from an Objective-C class, such as `UIViewController` in this example. It also includes Swift classes that don't inherit from Objective-C classes if they are marked with `@objc`. If you were to include CafeHunter-Swift.h in an Objective-C file, then you would be able to use `ViewController` just as though it were an Objective-C class. Neat!

Take a quick look back at **ViewController.swift**. Notice that the `checkLocationAuthorizationStatus` method is missing from the Objective-C interface in the compatibility header. This is because that method is marked as private and therefore is not exposed in the Objective-C interface, even though the method will exist at runtime.

Another thing to notice here is that there is a macro used before the interface. This has what looks like a rather strange reference - `_TtC10CafeHunter14ViewController`.

This is Swift's name mangling in action. Swift implicitly adds namespaces for you, meaning you could have a class called `Foo` in one library and a class called `Foo` in another library and they wouldn't get in each other's way. Swift does this by converting the name of each class, struct, enum or any other symbol into a name that includes the library name along with other information to allow for simple reversion back to the original name. In this case, the library is the app itself, hence the "CafeHunter" in the name.

So `ViewController` class is actually called `_TtC10CafeHunter14ViewController` within the runtime. The `SWIFT_NAME` macro tells the Objective-C compiler that the actual name of the class is the mangled name.

You're here to learn Swift, not Objective-C, so this chapter won't spend any more time on the use of Swift classes in Objective-C. But keep in mind the possibility, in case you need it in the future.

Adding the UI

The app you're building is currently just a white screen with an alert that asks the user for permission to use location services. It's time to spice things up and add the user interface.

Open **Main.storyboard** and find the **CafeHunter** view controller. Add a **MapKit View** and a plain **View** to the view controller's view. Give the plain view a background color of black so you can see it. In the identity inspector, set the plan view's class to **FBLoginView**. Then, arrange the views as shown below:

Set up Auto Layout constraints so that the map view expands horizontally and vertically, and the plain view stays where it is at a width of 200 and a height of 50.

Now open **ViewController.swift** and add the following at the top of the class:

```
@IBOutlet var mapView: MKMapView!
@IBOutlet var loginView: FBLoginView!
```

These are normal property declarations, one for a map view and one for a special Facebook login view that does what it sounds like—it handles login for you!

These properties should look awfully familiar if you're used to Objective-C Cocoa development. `@IBOutlet` does the same thing as the `IBOutlet` modifier you can give to Objective-C class properties: It enables you to hook up a variable in Interface Builder.

The types need to be optional, otherwise the compiler would complain that the variables aren't set in all initializers. Swift doesn't "know" that Interface Builder is supplying the views at run time; therefore it would do its job and raise a build error about the unsupplied values.

However, this does mean you need to be careful when using outlets. Because they are implicitly unwrapped optionals, you may blindly use them without checking for `nil`. If you try to use an outlet before the view controller's view is loaded, the outlet won't be present yet and this will cause a runtime crash! Be careful, my friend.

Also, behind the scenes, the `@IBOutlet` modifier converts the property declaration into a weak property. Therefore, the two properties above actually become the following:

```
weak var mapView: MKMapView!
weak var loginView: FBLoginView!
```

You may be aware from Objective-C Cocoa development that it's common to declare view outlet properties as weak, because the view of the view controller holds strong references to its outlets. Taking an extra strong reference is therefore unnecessary.

Go back to **Main.storyboard** and hook up the map view to the `mapView` outlet and the plain view to the `loginView` outlet. Also, hook up the view controller as the delegate of the map view.

You need to do one more thing to enable Facebook login. The Facebook SDK uses fast app switching to either the Facebook app (if installed) or Safari (as a fallback). After login is complete, the SDK gets back into your app by opening a special URL. This means your app has to handle the special URL scheme.

Click on the project at the top of the project navigator and then on the **Info** tab in the middle pane. Open the **URL Types** box and replace the **fbXXXXX** in the **URL Schemes** box with **fb** followed by the Facebook application ID you created earlier. For example, if your application ID were 12345, you would enter "fb12345".

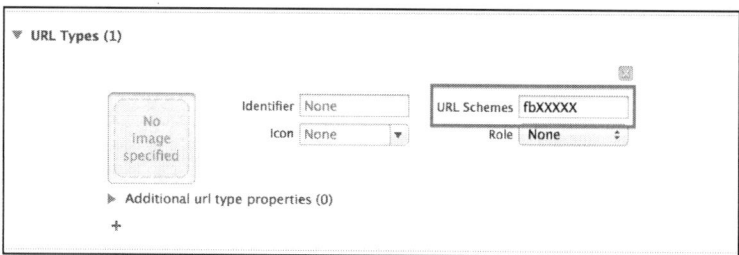

Finally, open **AppDelegate.swift** and add the following method to the class:

```
func application(application: UIApplication!,
                 openURL url: NSURL!,
                 sourceApplication: String!,
                 annotation: AnyObject!) -> Bool
{
    let wasHandled =
        FBAppCall.handleOpenURL(url,
```

```
                sourceApplication: sourceApplication)
    return wasHandled
}
```

This method will be called once the user logs into Facebook and control returns to your app via the special URL. The code simply passes off the URL handling to the Facebook SDK, which will handle the login credentials passed back from Facebook.

Build and run. You'll see your app run with a "Log in with Facebook" button. Tap the button, and the SDK will take you to either the Facebook app or Safari to log in. After you've logged in, you'll come back to the app and see that the button has changed to "Log out".

Congratulations—you're using the Objective-C Facebook SDK to log in from your Swift app! :]

Showing the user's location

Map views can helpfully find the user's location for you. Let's add that now, as well as methods to handle what happens once the app has the location and when the user moves by a significant distance.

Open **ViewController.swift** and add the following variable at the top, just below the `locationManager` variable:

```
private var lastLocation: CLLocation?
```

You'll use this to hold the user's last known location. It's an optional because you might not have a last location—that is, you might not have found the location yet.

Now add the following to the top of the class:

```
let searchDistance: CLLocationDistance = 1000
```

This declares a constant that you'll use to determine how far to search for cafés from the user's current location, as well as how far the user has to move before the app automatically refreshes the cafés. The distance here is in meters.

Next, add the following extension declaration to the bottom of the file, outside the class definition:

```
extension ViewController: MKMapViewDelegate {
}
```

This extension supplies conformance to the map view delegate protocol, which is what the map view will use to tell your view controller about pertinent events, like finding the user's location.

Note: In Swift, it's commonplace to declare conformance to a protocol by using an extension like this. It keeps the protocol methods grouped together, and you can still access other methods and properties as usual. Now, add the following method to the extension you just added:

```
func mapView(mapView: MKMapView!,
            didFailToLocateUserWithError error: NSError!)
{
  println(error)
  let alert =
    UIAlertController(title: "Error",
                      message: "Failed to obtain location!",
                      preferredStyle: .Alert)
```

```
        alert.addAction(UIAlertAction(title: "OK",
                                  style: .Default, handler: nil))
        self.presentViewController(alert,
                              animated: true, completion: nil)
}
```

If the user's location fails to update—for example, because the user is underground and the GPS is not working properly—this method shows an alert to tell the user about the error.

Next, add the following method to the same extension:

```
func mapView(mapView: MKMapView!,
            didUpdateUserLocation userLocation: MKUserLocation!)
{
    // 1
    let newLocation = userLocation.location

    // 2
    let distance =
        self.lastLocation?.distanceFromLocation(newLocation)

    // 3
    if distance == nil || distance! > searchDistance {
        self.lastLocation = newLocation
        self.centerMapOnLocation(newLocation)
        self.fetchCafesAroundLocation(newLocation)
    }
}
```

This method is called when the map view updates the user's location. Here's what it does:

1. You retrieve the new location from the delegate method's `userLocation` parameter.

2. You calculate the distance from the last location. Note the use of the question mark when obtaining the `lastLocation` property value. `lastLocation` is an optional property, meaning its value may be nil. If it is, then this expression returns nil and stops processing. Only if there is a concrete value in `lastLocation` is `distanceFromLocation` called on it. For this reason, the local `distance` variable is also an optional.

3. You want to update the map if there's no previous distance or if the user has moved by a certain amount. Since `distance` is an optional, you can do this check very easily in one `if`-statement. Without optionals, this code would need to be more complex,

because you wouldn't be able to tell the difference between no distance value and a distance value of 0. Optionals FTW! :]

If you do need to update the map, then you set the `lastLocation` property and call two methods to do the work of centering the map and fetching cafés at the user's location.

This method uses two methods you haven't implemented yet. Staying in **ViewController.swift**, add the first new method to the main `ViewController` class definition:

```
private func centerMapOnLocation(location: CLLocation) {
  let coordinateRegion =
    MKCoordinateRegionMakeWithDistance(location.coordinate,
                                       searchDistance,
                                       searchDistance)
  self.mapView.setRegion(coordinateRegion, animated: true)
}
```

This rather simple method takes the passed-in location and centers the map view on that location. You size the region of the map based on the search distance constant, so it will be big enough to show all the cafés once you've fetched them.

Next, add the following method just below the last:

```
private func fetchCafesAroundLocation(location: CLLocation) {
  if !FBSession.activeSession().isOpen {
    let alert =
      UIAlertController(title: "Error",
                      message: "Login first!",
                      preferredStyle: .Alert)
    alert.addAction(UIAlertAction(title: "OK",
                                  style: .Default,
                                  handler: nil))
    self.presentViewController(alert,
                               animated: true,
                               completion: nil)
    return
  }
  
  // TODO
}
```

You'll fetch the cafés shortly. For now, this stub method simply displays an error if the Facebook session isn't open yet. An open session is one in which the user is logged in.

The Facebook graph API requires a user access token, so your user needs to be logged in before the app can fetch the data it needs.

Finally, find `checkLocationAuthorizationStatus` and change it to look like this:

```
func checkLocationAuthorizationStatus() {
  if CLLocationManager.authorizationStatus() ==
      .AuthorizedWhenInUse
  {
    self.mapView.showsUserLocation = true
  } else {
    self.locationManager.requestWhenInUseAuthorization()
  }
}
```

You have added a single line that shows the user's location if the user has authorized the app to do so.

Build and run, and you'll see your location as the usual blue dot.

For testing purposes, you can "teleport" your device to another location by using the "Simulate Location" button in the debugger. You'll find it at the bottom of the text editor pane above the debugger console:

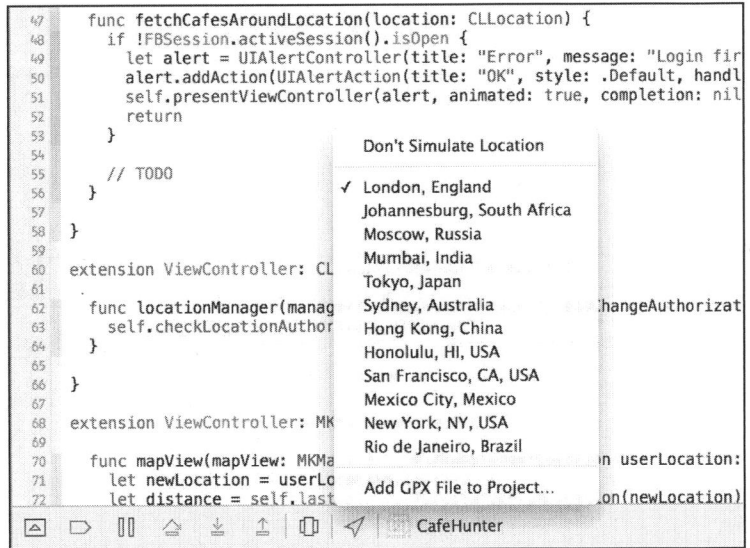

Select **London, England**, and you'll see something like this:

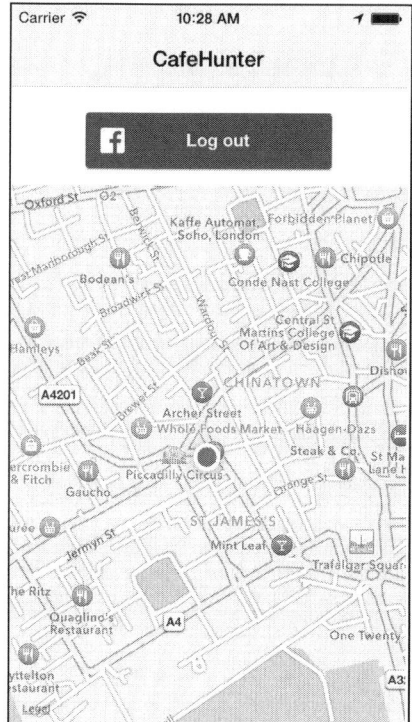

Now it's time to fetch some café data.

Fetching data

The map doesn't yet display any cafes, but that's about to change. First, you'll create the data model. Then, you'll add code to fetch the cafés from Facebook. Finally, you'll parse the café data.

Building the data model

You need a model object to represent each café. In Swift, you have two choices: classes and structs. Since the café object will be pure data, this seems like a job for a struct.

Click **File\New\File…** and select **iOS\Source\Swift File**. Click **Next**, call the file **Cafe** and save it.

Open **Cafe.swift** and add the following code:

```swift
struct Cafe {
  let fbid: String
  let name: String
  let location: CLLocationCoordinate2D
  let street: String
  let city: String
  let zip: String

  init(fbid: String, name: String,
       location: CLLocationCoordinate2D,
       street: String, city: String, zip: String)
  {
    self.fbid = fbid
    self.name = name
    self.location = location
    self.street = street
    self.city = city
    self.zip = zip
  }
}
```

This adds a struct called `Cafe` that has the various properties you get back from the Facebook graph API. There's nothing special here, yet!

You want to show these `Cafe` objects on the map view as annotations. To do that, you need to make the object conform to the `MKAnnotation` protocol. Add the conformance now by adding the following extension at the bottom of the file:

```swift
extension Cafe: MKAnnotation {
  var title: String! {
    return name
  }
  var coordinate: CLLocationCoordinate2D {
    return location
  }
}
```

This simply passes through the `title` and `coordinate` computed properties, which `MKAnnotation` maps to the `name` and `location` properties of the object, respectively.

Oh no! There's a build error:

```
Use of undeclared type 'MKAnnotation'
```

That's easy to fix. The compiler can't find the protocol because you haven't imported MapKit yet.

Go to the top of the file and add the following import:

```
import MapKit
```

But wait... There's *still* a build error! You'll see this:

```
Non-class type 'Cafe' cannot conform to class protocol
'MKAnnotation'
```

This error tells you that `Cafe` must be a class rather than a struct. Why?

`MKAnnotation` objects need to be used by a map view, which is written in Objective-C. The Objective-C bridging described earlier in this chapter does not bridge structs, because there's no support in Objective-C for the type of structs that Swift has. In Swift, structs can have methods, but the only structs in Objective-C are "C" structs, which are pure data objects.

To remove this error, change the declaration of `Cafe` to look like this:

```
class Cafe {
```

Now it's a class. But you'll notice another error:

```
Type 'Cafe' does not conform to protocol 'NSObjectProtocol'
```

`MKAnnotation` inherits from `NSObjectProtocol`, and anything conforming to the former must also conform to the latter.

Once again, it's a simple fix. Change the declaration of `Cafe` to look like this:

```
class Cafe: NSObject {
```

Now that `Cafe` is a class with a super class, the initializer needs to do one more piece of work. Add the following to the bottom of `init`:

```
super.init()
```

This ensures that when a `Cafe` object is initialized, it calls `NSObject`'s initializer too.

> **Note**: If you find the placement of this super call at the end of the method confusing, refer to Chapter 3, "Classes and Structs".

Well, something that could have been a Swift struct has to be a class. You'll find this is a common occurrence when interacting with Cocoa in Swift.

Fetching from Facebook

Open **ViewController.swift**. Add the following property definition to the top of the class, just underneath the `lastLocation` property:

```
private var cafes = [Cafe]()
```

This is going to hold the list of cafés the map is currently displaying.

Now find `fetchCafesAroundLocation` and find the TODO comment. That's what you're going to flesh out now.

Replace the TODO comment with the following code:

```
// 1
var urlString = "https://graph.facebook.com/v2.0/search/"
urlString += "?access_token="
urlString +=
  "\(FBSession.activeSession().accessTokenData.accessToken)"
urlString += "&type=place"
urlString += "&q=cafe"
urlString += "&center=\(location.coordinate.latitude),"
urlString += "\(location.coordinate.longitude)"
urlString += "&distance=\(Int(searchDistance))"

// 2
let url = NSURL(string: urlString)!

println("Requesting from FB with URL: \(url)")

// 3
let request = NSURLRequest(URL: url)
NSURLConnection.sendAsynchronousRequest(
  request,
  queue: NSOperationQueue.mainQueue())
{
  (response: NSURLResponse!, data: NSData!, error: NSError!)
    -> Void in

  // 4
  if error != nil {
    let alert = UIAlertController(
      title: "Oops!",
      message: "An error occured",
```

```
      preferredStyle: .Alert)
    alert.addAction(UIAlertAction(
      title: "OK",
      style: .Default,
      handler: nil))
    self.presentViewController(
      alert, animated: true, completion: nil)
    return
}

// 5
var error: NSError?
let jsonObject: AnyObject! =
  NSJSONSerialization.JSONObjectWithData(
    data, options: NSJSONReadingOptions(0), error: &error)

// 6
if let jsonObject = jsonObject as? [String:AnyObject] {
  if error == nil {
    println("Data returned from FB:\n\(jsonObject)")

    // 7
    if let data =
      JSONValue.fromObject(jsonObject)?["data"]?.array
    {
      // 8
      var cafes: [Cafe] = []
      for cafeJSON in data {
        if let cafeJSON = cafeJSON.object {
          // TODO: Create Cafe and add to array
        }
      }

      // 9
      self.mapView.removeAnnotations(self.cafes)
      self.cafes = cafes
      self.mapView.addAnnotations(cafes)
    }
  }
}
```

That looks like a beast, so let's break it down:

1. First, you construct the URL that you're going to use to ask Facebook for the places around the current location that match the search term "café." Notice that the use of string interpolation makes it simple to build a complex string. This code would be much more complicated to read if it used `NSString`'s `stringWithFormat:`.

2. You then convert the string into an **NSURL**. Even though the parameter to **NSURL**'s initializer is an **NSString**, it still works with a Swift **String** object. This is because **String** and **NSString** are seamlessly bridged. You can use one in place of the other and Swift will handle the conversion for you—rather handy when using Cocoa APIs!

3. Then you make a request using **NSURLConnection**'s **sendAsynchronousRequest**. Since the last parameter is the completion block, you can use trailing closure syntax.

4. If there was an error fetching the data, such as the internet connection is offline, then we show an alert and return.

5. This section of code performs JSON deserialization on the data returned from the Facebook graph API. Existing Objective-C developers will be familiar with the **error** parameter here, which is part of a common pattern in Objective-C Cocoa development: Because methods can't have multiple return values, you pass a pointer to an **NSError** object into the method and then if there's an error, you assign the reference to that error.

   This pattern is no longer necessary in Swift, but it remains because all the Cocoa APIs still use it. Swift handles this pattern neatly by allowing you to pass in a reference to an optional **NSError**, which gets sets in the same way if there's an error.

6. You're expecting the value returned from the JSON deserialization to be a JSON object—that is, a dictionary of strings to other JSON values types such as numbers, strings, arrays, objects and so forth. You know this because, like most APIs, that's what the Facebook graph API returns. This **if**-statement attempts to cast the **jsonObject** variable into a dictionary of **String** to **AnyObject**. If it is successfully downcast and there's no error, then you've successfully retrieved valid data from the API.

   Alert readers will be aware that **NSJSONSerialization** actually returns an **NSDictionary**. This is clever bridging between Cocoa types and Swift types, just as you saw with **NSString** and **String**. **NSDictionary** and **NSArray** are bridged to **[NSObject:AnyObject]** and **[AnyObject]**, respectively.

7. This line uses the **JSONValue** helper defined in the file JSON.swift that I briefly mentioned in the "Getting Started" section of this chapter. You don't know what types are inside a JSON object without looking at it. You could extract each bit of information manually and check its type, but the Swift code for that would be rather nested, with many **if**-statements doing downcast checks. **JSONValue** helps out by parsing the entire JSON structure into an enumeration with a case for each type that JSON supports.

You then use optional chaining to extract the `data` key out of the JSON. If that key exists and its value can be cast to an array, then the `if`-statement passes and you have an array of nearby locations to work with.

8. You create a new array to hold the `Cafe` objects that you'll parse out of the data array. You'll flesh out the innards of this `for`-loop shortly.

9. Finally, you remove the existing cafés from the map and add the new ones.

Phew! That was a bit of a whirlwind, but here are the key points:

- Whether you're writing Swift or Objective-C, error handling in Cocoa is often done through passing a reference to an optional `NSError` variable. The variable is filled upon failure with the relevant error.

- Swift `String` is seamlessly bridged to `NSString` and vice versa.

- Swift `[NSObject:AnyObject]` is seamlessly bridged to `NSDictionary` and vice versa.

- Swift `[AnyObject]` is seamlessly bridged to `NSArray` and vice versa.

- The nature of JSON makes it tricky to deal with in Swift. You can end up with lots of type casting and checks if you're not careful. Using a helper like `JSONValue` (included in this project) makes life much easier.

Build and run the app. Then, look at the console after the app has found the current location. You'll see something like this:

```
Requesting from FB with URL:
https://graph.facebook.com/v2.0/search/?access_token=CAAEn00…&ty
pe=place&q=cafe&center=51.50998,-0.1337&distance=1000
Data returned from FB:
[paging: {
    next =
"https://graph.facebook.com/v2.0/search?type=place&center=51.509
98,-
0.1337&distance=1000&access_token=CAAEn00…&limit=5000&offset=500
0&__after_id=enc_Aez8JAnU-42GS9d-
ffWv1x1cw9sLQy3jvsm7ipg_zDW0Yb9Rqp96AKIhM1CzBuF602DWN7yBabSeyasm
egDQwbJ7";
}, data: (
        {
        category = "Restaurant/cafe";
        "category_list" =            (
                {
                id = 192831537402299;
                name = "Family Style Restaurant";
```

```
        },
                    {
            id = 197871390225897;
            name = Cafe;
        },
                    {
            id = 133436743388217;
            name = "Arts & Entertainment";
        }
    );
    id = 63834778746;
    location =             {
        city = London;
        country = "United Kingdom";
        latitude = "51.510830565071";
        longitude = "-0.13391656332172";
        state = "";
        street = "20-24 Shaftesbury Avenve";
        zip = "W1D 7EU";
    };
    name = "Rainforest Cafe, London";
},
...
```

Now you simply need to finish parsing the JSON by extracting the café data and creating `Cafe` objects for each of them.

Parsing the JSON data

Open **Cafe.swift** and add the following method in the `Cafe` class definition:

```swift
class func fromJSON(json: [String:JSONValue]) -> Cafe? {
  // 1
  let fbid = json["id"]?.string
  let name = json["name"]?.string
  let latitude = json["location"]?["latitude"]?.double
  let longitude = json["location"]?["longitude"]?.double

  // 2
  if fbid != nil && name != nil
    && latitude != nil && longitude != nil {
      // 3
      var street: String
      if let maybeStreet = json["location"]?["street"]?.string {
        street = maybeStreet
      } else {
        street = ""
```

```
    }
    // 4
    var city: String
    if let maybeCity = json["location"]?["city"]?.string {
      city = maybeCity
    } else {
      city = ""
    }

    var zip: String
    if let maybeZip = json["location"]?["zip"]?.string {
      zip = maybeZip
    } else {
      zip = ""
    }

    // 5
    let location =
      CLLocationCoordinate2D(latitude: latitude!,
                             longitude: longitude!)
    return Cafe(fbid: fbid!, name: name!, location: location,
                street: street, city: city, zip: zip)
  }
  // 6
  return nil
}
```

This method's job is to take the data found in the JSON for a single café and return a `Cafe` object if it parses correctly, or nil if it doesn't. Here's what's going on, section by section:

1. First, you pull the required parameters `fbid`, `name`, `latitude` and `longitude` out of the JSON. Notice the use of optional chaining to ensure very simple code. If the JSON doesn't contain a value for the "id" key, then `fbid` will be nil. `fbid` will also be nil if the value it contains isn't a string.

2. If the Facebook ID, name, latitude and longitude were successfully parsed, then you can create a `Cafe`.

3. Here you handle the first of the optional parameters. It's OK if there's no street—you simply use an empty string.

4. The same goes for the city and the zip code – empty strings are OK.

5. Finally, you create the `Cafe` from the data and return it.

6. If you couldn't create the `Cafe` because one of the required parameters was missing, then you return nil to signify an error.

If you're an Objective-C developer, you might wonder why this can't be done in an initializer method. After all, that's likely how you would have done it in Objective-C.

You can't use an initializer method here because in Swift, initializers cannot return nil— they must return a fully-fledged object. If an initializer could return nil, then every variable would need to be optional to handle the nil case. That would mean Swift couldn't have non-optional types that guarantee an object at runtime.

Swing back to **ViewController.swift** and find `fetchCafesAroundLocation`. Replace the TODO you left there with the following code:

```
if let cafe = Cafe.fromJSON(cafeJSON) {
  cafes.append(cafe)
}
```

Here you use the method you just added to `Cafe` to parse the JSON. If it succeeds, then you add the new `Cafe` object to the array.

Build and run the app. You'll now see something like this:

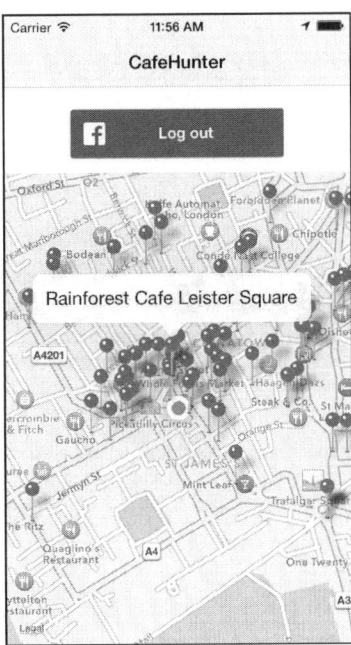

W00t, you're showing data on your map now! And there's so much caffeine out there!

Selectors

The app will automatically refresh the café search when the user moves beyond the search distance. Some impatient users might want to see fresh results sooner than that, so you're going to add a refresh button. Such a button is also worth having in case the user has trouble with her Internet connection and needs to retry.

This section will neatly illustrate another thing you need to know about when interacting with Cocoa APIs: **selectors**.

Objective-C uses dynamic dispatch, which is what makes it possible to execute a method by name at runtime. In this context, an Objective-C method name is called a selector. You could, for example, ask the user to type something into a text box and then call the method with that name on any object! It's powerful, but also potentially dangerous.

Swift has moved away from dynamic dispatch, preferring the compiler to determine if a given method exists. But a few existing Cocoa APIs still require selectors. For example, the target-action pattern of controls requires you to define a target upon which to perform a given selector. Gesture recognizers require you to do the same.

Fortunately, Swift has a handy way to bridge the gap, as you will see.

Open **ViewController.swift** and add the following code to the end of `viewDidLoad`:

```
self.navigationItem.leftBarButtonItem =
  UIBarButtonItem(barButtonSystemItem: .Refresh,
           target: self, action: "refresh:")
```

This is the target-action pattern I just described. The target here is `self`, the `ViewController` instance. The action, though, is a Swift `String`. That seems odd if you look at the definition of the `UIBarButtonItem` initializer:

```
init(image: UIImage!, style: UIBarButtonItemStyle,
    target: AnyObject!, action: Selector)
```

The `action` parameter should be a `Selector`, but you're passing in a `String`! If you look at `Selector`, you'll see it conforms to the `StringLiteralConvertible` protocol, which means it can be converted directly from a string literal. Neat!

The selector you're using here is called `refresh:`, which will look for a method called `refresh` that takes one parameter. This is exactly the same as it would be in Objective-C, because Swift methods follow the same pattern of using named parameters.

Build and run the app. Then tap on the refresh button that will be at the top-left of the screen. You'll see an error in the console that looks like this:

```
Terminating app due to uncaught exception
'NSInvalidArgumentException', reason: '-
[CafeHunter.ViewController refresh:]: unrecognized selector sent
to instance 0x7c230a90'
```

Ah, well this is less than ideal! The error is telling you that `refresh:` hasn't been implemented on the `ViewController` class. Swift's support of selectors is still dynamic in nature and is therefore an area where the compiler can't help you. The compiler itself doesn't know anything about Objective-C selectors, so it can't determine that you haven't implemented the method. After all, it might be implemented at runtime anyway, through Objective-C runtime hackery.

Let's fix the runtime error by implementing `refresh`. Add the following method to the end of the `ViewController` class definition:

```swift
func refresh(sender: UIBarButtonItem) {
  if let location = self.lastLocation {
    self.centerMapOnLocation(location)
    self.fetchCafesAroundLocation(location)
  } else {
    let alert =
      UIAlertController(title: "Error",
                      message: "No location yet!",
                preferredStyle: .Alert)
    alert.addAction(UIAlertAction(title: "OK",
                                  style: .Default,
                                handler: nil))
    self.presentViewController(alert,
                      animated: true,
                    completion: nil)
  }
}
```

The parameter to this method is the `UIBarButtonItem` instance that caused the refresh to fire, which is implicitly passed by UIKit. The target-action pattern usually passes the button or control that caused the action to fire, in case you want to perform specific actions based on it.

The method centers the map and fetches cafés if there is a location. Otherwise, it shows an error that the location hasn't been found yet.

Build and run the app. Then, move the map away from the current location and tap the refresh button. The map should return to the user's current location and reload the cafes.

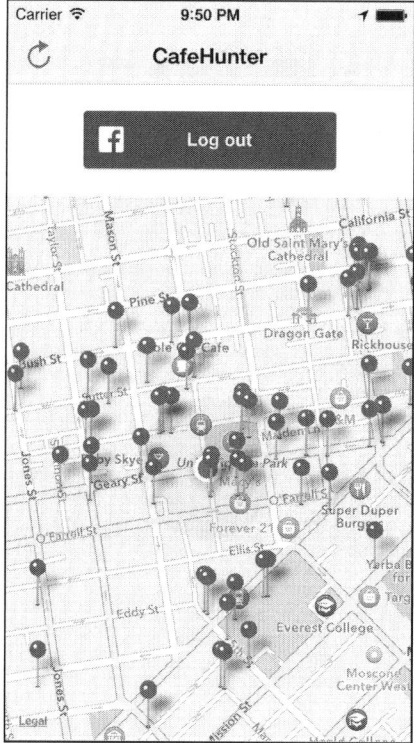

Protocols and delegates

Currently, the app only lets you see the cafes on the map. It would be nice to be able to tap each café and see some information about it. After all, you have the street, city and zip information at hand. And you can obtain a picture for each café through the Facebook graph API, as well.

The next part of the chapter will create a café detail view and wire it up so you can access this new view for each café, directly from the map. You'll also define your own protocol and implement it from a delegate, ensuring the protocol is accessible from Objective-C too.

Creating the detail view

Click **File\New\File…**, select **iOS\Source\Cocoa Touch Class** and click **Next**. Call the class **CafeViewController** and make it a subclass of **UIViewController**. Ensure that the language is **Swift** and that **Also create XIB file** is **unchecked**. Click **Next** and then **Create**.

Open **CafeViewController.swift** and add the following to the top of the class definition:

```
@IBOutlet var imageView: UIImageView!
@IBOutlet var nameLabel: UILabel!
@IBOutlet var streetLabel: UILabel!
@IBOutlet var cityLabel: UILabel!
@IBOutlet var zipLabel: UILabel!
```

These will become the views that you will populate. Once again, they are Interface Builder outlets, so you'll link them with the UI elements in the storyboard.

Next, add the following, again at the top of the class definition:

```
var cafe: Cafe? {
  didSet {
    self.setupWithCafe()
  }
}
```

This defines a variable of type optional-`Cafe`. It will hold the café that the view controller is currently set up to display.

The second part of this declaration sets up a listener for when the variable changes. Variables can have `willSet` and `didSet` closures defined. The former is called just before the variable is set to a new value and the latter just after.

In this case, your `didSet` will be called just after `cafe` is set to a new value so that the view controller can set itself up with the current café.

Before you implement the setup method, you need to add something to the `Cafe` object. In this view you also want to display the picture for the café, which comes from a URL in the Facebook graph API.

Open **Cafe.swift** and add the following code just below the property definitions:

```
var pictureURL: NSURL {
  return NSURL(string:
    "http://graph.facebook.com/place/picture?id=\(self.fbid)" +
```

```
        "&type=large")!
}
```

This defines a computed property of type `NSURL`. The URL points to the large type of picture for the place with the café's Facebook ID. Notice that because the `fbid` property is not an optional, there must be a Facebook ID. This is a good example of Swift's strictness—you don't need to worry about coping with nil values everywhere.

Now implement the view controller's setup method. Open **CafeViewController.swift** again and add the following method to the end of the class definition:

```
private func setupWithCafe() {
  // 1
  if !self.isViewLoaded() {
    return
  }

  // 2
  if let cafe = self.cafe {
    // 3
    self.title = cafe.name

    self.nameLabel.text = cafe.name
    self.streetLabel.text = cafe.street
    self.cityLabel.text = cafe.city
    self.zipLabel.text = cafe.zip

    // 4
    let request = NSURLRequest(URL: cafe.pictureURL)
    NSURLConnection.sendAsynchronousRequest(
      request, queue: NSOperationQueue.mainQueue())
    {
      (response: NSURLResponse!, data: NSData!, error: NSError!)
      -> Void in
      let image = UIImage(data: data)
      self.imageView.image = image
    }
  }
}
```

Here's what this method does:

1. This method is going to use properties that are IB outlets. Recall that these are implicitly unwrapped optionals. They only contain values once the view is loaded, so if this method is called before then, variables such as `nameLabel` and `streetLabel` won't yet be set up. You could check for the existence of each outlet directly, but that

would be a lot of superfluous code. In this case, it's simpler to check if the view is loaded.

2. If there's no café, then there's nothing to set on the views. Only if there's a café do you want to proceed.

3. The next few lines set up the various labels and the title of the view.

4. Finally, you load the picture for the café by using an `NSURLConnection`.

Imagine what would happen if the café is set before the view is loaded. As it stands, the view won't be set up correctly because the various `IBOutlet`s won't be loaded yet. To fix that, find `viewDidLoad` and change it to look like this:

```
override func viewDidLoad() {
  super.viewDidLoad()
  self.setupWithCafe()
}
```

This performs the setup when the view loads, as well. Perfect!

Finally, it's time to design the UI in Interface Builder. Open **Main.storyboard** and drag a view controller onto the scene. Give it a storyboard ID of **CafeView** and set its custom class to **CafeViewController**. Then add an image view, four labels and a button to the view to make it look like this:

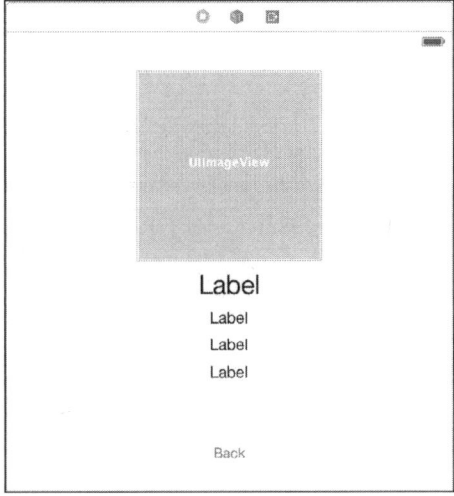

Add Auto Layout constraints to center everything horizontally and make the image view a size of 200x200. Then, connect the outlets to the image view and the four labels. The four labels should be from top to bottom: `nameLabel`, `streetLabel`, `cityLabel` and `zipLabel`.

That's all there is to the café details UI! Now you're going to wire it up.

Wiring up the detail view

Currently, you're letting the map view itself display the pins. You're going to make it so that when the user taps a pin, the callout bubble shown will have a button on it. When the user taps the button, it will present the café detail view for that café.

Open **ViewController.swift**. Find the `MKMapViewDelegate` extension and add the following method to the top of it:

```swift
func mapView(mapView: MKMapView!,
            viewForAnnotation annotation: MKAnnotation!)
    -> MKAnnotationView!
{
  // 1
  if let annotation = annotation as? Cafe {
    let identifier = "pin"
    var view: MKPinAnnotationView

    // 2
    if let dequeuedView =
mapView.dequeueReusableAnnotationViewWithIdentifier(identifier)
as? MKPinAnnotationView
    {
      // 3
      dequeuedView.annotation = annotation
      view = dequeuedView
    } else {
      // 4
      view = MKPinAnnotationView(annotation: annotation,
                                reuseIdentifier: identifier)
      view.canShowCallout = true
      view.calloutOffset = CGPoint(x: -5, y: 5)
      view.rightCalloutAccessoryView =
        UIButton.buttonWithType(.DetailDisclosure) as UIView
    }
    // 5
    return view
  }
  return nil
}
```

This map view delegate method is called when the map view needs a view to display an annotation. It's your job to return a view initialized with the supplied annotation.

Here's what the method does:

1. You only handle `Cafe` annotations in this view controller. Other annotations, such as the user location (blue dot), you want the map view itself to handle. You therefore use a conditional downcast to pick out the annotations that are `Cafe` objects.

2. Map views maintain a reuse queue (similar to `UITableView`) so that you don't need to keep creating annotations as new annotations come into view. Instead, you can attempt to dequeue an existing annotation. If there's one in the reuse queue, then you want to use that. You use another conditional downcast to ensure that the view is of type `MKPinAnnotationView`.

3. If there is a view dequeued, then you only need to set the annotation on the view.

4. If no view could be dequeued, you create a new `MKPinAnnotationView` and set it up to show a button as the callout accessory.

5. Finally, you return the annotation view.

Build and run the app. Tap on a café and you'll see a button in the callout, like so:

You've got the button in the callout, so now you need to add handling for when the user taps the button. Add the following method just underneath the previous method:

```swift
func mapView(mapView: MKMapView!,
             annotationView view: MKAnnotationView!,
             calloutAccessoryControlTapped control: UIControl!)
{
  // 1
  if let viewController =
    self.storyboard!.instantiateViewControllerWithIdentifier(
      "CafeView") as? CafeViewController
  {
    // 2
    if let cafe = view.annotation as? Cafe {
      // 3
      viewController.cafe = cafe
      viewController.delegate = self
      self.presentViewController(viewController,
                                 animated: true,
                                 completion: nil)
    }
  }
}
```

This method is called when the user taps the callout button. Here's what it does:

1. You instantiate a new `CafeViewController` by asking the storyboard to create one from the Storyboard ID you already set. This could fail and return nil, so you employ the usual conditional optional unwrapping.

2. Then, you check the annotation from the tapped view to see if it's a `Cafe` object. You know it is, but the compiler doesn't because the type of the `annotation` property is `MKAnnotation`.

3. Finally, you set up the view controller and present it.

Notice that you've declared the `ViewController` instance as the delegate of the `CafeViewController`. You haven't defined this delegate yet, but you're going to use it to tell the `ViewController` when the user has finished with the `CafeViewController`—that is, when the user has tapped the Back button.

Open **CafeViewController.swift** and add the following at the top of the file, above the class definition:

```
@objc protocol CafeViewControllerDelegate {
  optional func cafeViewControllerDidFinish(
            viewController: CafeViewController)
}
```

This defines a protocol to which objects can conform to be told when the user is finished with the café detail view and it should be dismissed. The `optional` tells the compiler that the method doesn't have to be defined, leaving it up to the implementation class to decide whether it needs the method or not.

If you want optional methods in your protocol, you have to declare the protocol as `@objc`. Marking the protocol as `@objc` enables Swift to put various runtime checks in place to check for conformance to the protocol and to check that various methods exist to support optional functionality.

> **Note**: You can also limit your protocols to be implemented by classes only:
>
> ```
> protocol MyClassOnlyProtocol: class { ... }
> ```
>
> This means only classes may adopt the protocol. Without it, structs may adopt the protocol, as well. Adding the `@objc` modifier as you've done for `CafeViewControllerDelegate` makes it a class-only protocol as well since the runtime checks that `@objc` adds for optional method checking requires the object to be a class.

Now add the following variable to the `CafeViewController` class, just above the IB outlets:

```
weak var delegate: CafeViewControllerDelegate?
```

Here you declare a property called `delegate` as an optional `CafeViewControllerDelegate`. You also mark it as weak, which is standard practice for delegate properties to avoid retain cycles. If an object holds a strong reference to another object, of which it is the delegate, then a strong delegate would cause a retain cycle between these two objects.

Using weak here means the protocol must be class-only, because only classes can have weak references to them. Remember that structs are value types, so it doesn't make sense to have a weak reference to one.

Next, add the following method to the end of the `CafeViewController` class definition:

```
@IBAction private func back(sender: AnyObject) {
  self.delegate?.cafeViewControllerDidFinish?(self)
}
```

The `@IBAction` here means you can hook this up in Interface Builder to the action on a control such as a button.

The method uses optional chaining to call the delegate method to say it has finished. If the `delegate` property is nil, then this expression will do nothing. Similarly, if the delegate is set but doesn't implement `cafeViewControllerDidFinish`, then the expression also does nothing. Optional chaining is brilliant for this sort of thing. In Objective-C, this would have required a separate `if`-statement to check if the delegate implements the given method, and call it if it does.

Now open **Main.storyboard** and hook up the Back button to the new `back` method.

There's one last thing to do! Head back to **ViewController.swift** and add the following code at the bottom of the file:

```
extension ViewController: CafeViewControllerDelegate {
  func cafeViewControllerDidFinish(
       viewController: CafeViewController)
  {
    self.dismissViewControllerAnimated(true, completion: nil)
  }
}
```

This declares conformance to the `CafeViewControllerDelegate` protocol and implements the optional method. You dismiss the view controller when the user has finished with it.

Build and run the app. Select a café pin and then tap the info button in the callout. You will see something like this:

You can also go back to the map by pressing the Back button. Excellent! Your work here is done!

Where to go from here?

In this chapter, you've taken a tour through various ways your apps will interoperate with the Cocoa framework.

First, you learned how Objective-C interoperability works by integrating the Facebook SDK. Understanding this bridging behavior is crucial because so much code out there – including Cocoa itself! – is still in Objective-C.

Then, you built an app that makes use of various standard Cocoa features. You saw automatic bridging of types between Swift and their Objective-C counterparts. You also saw how to use selectors from within Swift. Finally, you made your own delegate, a common pattern in Cocoa development.

Go forth with your new knowledge of how Swift interacts with Cocoa and build great apps!

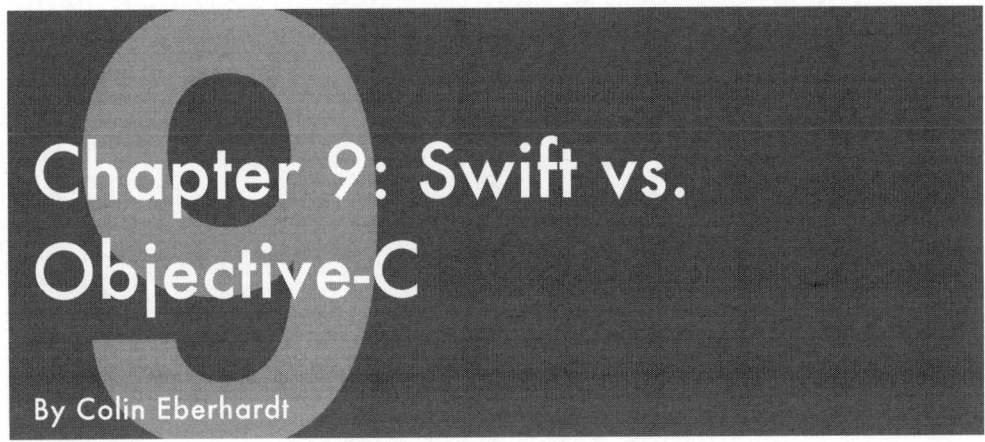

Chapter 9: Swift vs. Objective-C
By Colin Eberhardt

This is the last chapter in *Swift By Tutorials* (**sniff**). I hope you have enjoyed the journey!

By now, you should have a good working knowledge of the Swift programming language and be itching to put it into practice. I'm sure you will agree with both Matt and myself that Swift is a powerful and elegant language lacking some of the quirks of the Objective-C language that it replaces.

In this final chapter, you're going to build an application that touches on many of the Swift topics you've learned so far. You will recreate the popular board game Reversi, where your users can put their skills to the test against a computer player.

This Reversi app has already been implemented in Objective-C and published on raywenderlich.com as a two-part series:

- http://www.raywenderlich.com/29228/how-to-develop-an-ipad-board-game-app-part-12
- http://www.raywenderlich.com/29248/how-to-develop-an-ipad-board-game-app-part-22

The equivalent Swift implementation in this chapter will follow exactly the same build and run steps as its Objective-C counterpart, allowing you to compare the two implementations side-by-side.

Getting started

The game has a number of assets that are included as part of the starter project. Unpack the project, open it with Xcode and then build and run. The following screen will greet you:

Take a little time to familiarize yourself with the structure of this project. The project has a single view controller with the view laid out in **Main.storyboard** and the corresponding code in **ViewController.swift.** The view controller has a few outlets that you'll use later in this tutorial.

Modeling the playing board

In Reversi, the players place what are called **disks** or **counters** white-side or black-side up in each **cell** of a board with an 8x8 grid. The rules of the game are simple, but if you're not familiar with them it's worth popping over to Wikipedia, which has a good summary: http://en.wikipedia.org/wiki/Reversi.

Your first task is to create a model that represents the current state of the board. Each of the 64 cells that comprise the playing board can be black, white or empty. This sounds like a good candidate for a Swift enumeration!

Add a Swift file to the **Model** group and name it **BoardCellState.swift.** Replace the file contents with the following:

```
import Foundation

enum BoardCellState {
  case Empty, Black, White
}
```

The above defines an enumeration with the three required states for each cell on the board.

Much of the logic you will add in subsequent steps deals with navigating from one square on the board to the next. You will represent the location of each square with a pair of integers: the row and column. It's logical to combine these into a single type.

Add a Swift file to the **Model** group, naming it **BoardLocation.swift**, and add the following to the file:

```
import Foundation

struct BoardLocation {
  let row: Int, column: Int

  init(row: Int, column: Int) {
    self.row = row
    self.column = column
  }
}
```

The above defines a simple structure that combines an integer row and column into a single type called `BoardLocation`. You might have contemplated using a tuple for this purpose, such as `let position:(Int, Int)`, but you will find a structure is much more descriptive. Furthermore, structures can implement protocols and have methods, and you'll use these features later in this chapter.

Now it's time to add the board itself. Add a Swift file to the **Model** group, naming it **Board.swift**, and add the following code to the file:

```swift
import Foundation

class Board {
  private var cells: [BoardCellState]
  let boardSize = 8

  init () {
    cells = Array(count: boardSize * boardSize,
                  repeatedValue: BoardCellState.Empty)
  }

  subscript(location: BoardLocation) -> BoardCellState {
    get {
      return cells[location.row * boardSize + location.column]
    }
    set {
      cells[location.row * boardSize + location.column]
        = newValue
    }
  }
}
```

This defines the `Board` class, which contains a constant array of cells and a constant `Int` that indicates the board's size. The initializer creates the `cells` array, populating each element with the `BoardCellState.Empty` value.

The subscript provides a succinct method for getting and setting the value of each cell, as illustrated by the following example:

```swift
var board = Board()
board[BoardLocation(row: 4, column: 5)] = BoardCellState.White
```

However, an even more succinct format is possible. Add the following subscript to the `Board` class:

```swift
subscript(row: Int, column: Int) -> BoardCellState {
  get {
    return self[BoardLocation(row: row, column: column)]
  }
  set {
    self[BoardLocation(row: row, column: column)] = newValue
  }
}
```

The above exposes a subscript that you can use as follows:

```
var board = Board()
board[4, 5] = BoardCellState.White
```

Subscripts allow you to create a very flexible API for your Swift classes. You can define more than one subscript too, which allows you to have multiple ways to access data within the class.

To exercise the code you've just added, you need to build a UI that makes use of this model. However, there is a more direct mechanism available to you immediately… unit tests!

Open **SwiftReversiTests.swift** and add the following method to the `SwiftReversiTests` class:

```
func test_subscript_setWithValidCoords_cellStateIsChanged() {
  let board = Board()

  // set the state of one of the cells
  board[4, 5] = BoardCellState.White

  // verify
  let retrievedState = board[4, 5];
  XCTAssertEqual(BoardCellState.White, retrievedState,
                 "The cell should have been white!");
}
```

This code is for a simple unit test that exercises the subscript implementation by setting and then getting the value of one of the cells. This actually tests both subscript implementations, because one delegates to the other.

Before you build the project, make sure that the Swift files you wish to test have the correct **target membership**. You can view this information via the **File Inspector**. Ensure that each of **BoardCellState.swift**, **BoardLocation.swift** and **Board.swift** are in both the SwiftReversi and SwiftReversiTests targets, or the tests will not compile.

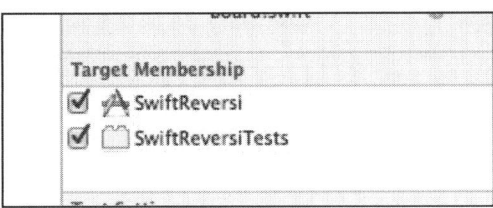

Select **Product\Test** from the Xcode menu (keyboard shortcut ⌘U) to build and run the tests.

A satisfying indication that the tests have passed will greet you:

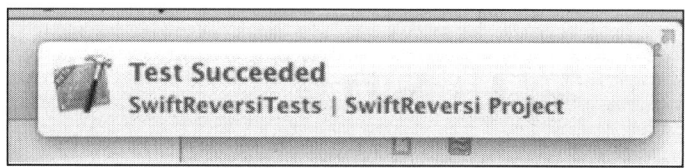

You will also see a report on the tests' progress within the console and small green ticks next to each test case in your code.

```
func test_subscript_setWithValidCoords_cellStateIsChanged() {
    let board = Board()
    
    // set the state of one of the cells
    board[4, 5] = BoardCellState.White
    
    // verify
    let retrievedState = board[4, 5];
    XCTAssertEqual(BoardCellState.White, retrievedState,
        "The cell should have been white!");
}
```

> **NOTE:** The rest of this tutorial excludes unit tests. As you proceed through this tutorial, you might want to add them yourself as a fun exercise.

Exposing the cell locations via a subscript on the `Board` class is quite elegant, but it does have a small weakness at the moment. If the row or column value you supply to the subscript functions is out of bounds, nasty things could happen. It's time to rectify that.

Within the `Board` implementation, add the following method to the bottom of the class:

```
func isWithinBounds(location: BoardLocation) -> Bool {
    return location.row >= 0 && location.row < boardSize &&
        location.column >= 0 && location.column < boardSize
}
```

The above simply ensures that both the row and column properties of the given `BoardLocation` are valid.

Update the subscript implementation (the one that takes a `BoardLocation` argument) to make use of this check:

```swift
subscript(location: BoardLocation) -> BoardCellState {
  get {
    assert(isWithinBounds(location),
                      "row or column index out of bounds")
    return cells[location.row * boardSize + location.column]
  }
  set {
    assert(isWithinBounds(location),
                      "row or column index out of bounds")
    cells[location.row * boardSize + location.column] = newValue
  }
}
```

The above code adds an assertion to the subscript getter and setter. As a result, if the row or column is out of bounds, the application will terminate and you'll be dropped into the debugger if you are in Debug mode.

Swift vs. Objective-C

It's time to pause for a quick comparison of the Swift and Objective-C implementations of Reversi thus far.

There are a few obvious differences in syntax between the two implementations, but syntax aside, here are a few noteworthy differences.

The Swift subscript provides a significant improvement over the Objective-C code, where setting cell values requires a lengthy method call:

```
[board setCellState:BoardCellStateWhitePiece forColumn:4
                                                  andRow:5];
```

The Swift alternative is much simpler:

```
board[4, 5] = .White
```

When it comes to initializing the array of cells, the Objective-C implementation uses `memset` as follows:

```
memset(_board, 0, sizeof(NSUInteger) * 8 * 8);
```

You really shouldn't use C APIs with Swift. Hence, the Swift implementation takes an alternative approach, filling the array with values during initialization:

```
cells = Array(count: boardSize * boardSize,
              repeatedValue: BoardCellState.Empty)
```

> The function and intent of this code is much clearer.
>
> Finally, the Swift application uses a 1-dimensional array to store the cells, whereas the Objective-C implementation uses a 2-dimensional array. There's a very good performance reason for this, which we'll go over later in this chapter, that relates to the use of memset above.
>
> In a later step, you'll add logic that clones the game board. The Objective-C implementation uses the C memcpy function, which you can easily apply to a 2-dimensional array, while the Swift implementation simply makes a copy of the array. Fortunately, the subscript will hide this implementation detail from all the other classes and subclasses in this app.

Additional game state

The current `Board` class is quite generic—you could use it for a range of board games. Next, you're going to add a `Board` subclass with Reversi-specific logic.

Add a Swift file to the **Model** group, naming it **ReversiBoard.swift**, and add the following code:

```
import Foundation

class ReversiBoard: Board {
  private (set) var blackScore = 0, whiteScore = 0

  func setInitialState() {
    super[3,3] = .White
    super[4,4] = .White
    super[3,4] = .Black
    super[4,3] = .Black

    blackScore = 2
    whiteScore = 2
  }
}
```

`ReversiBoard` subclasses `Board`, adding a simple `setInitialState` method that initializes the board with the starting position for the game.

When adding the game logic, there are numerous occasions when you need to navigate over all the cells of the board to apply some logic or operation. Rather than have multiple nested `for` loops (one for rows and an inner loop for columns), it makes sense to centralize this logic.

Open **Board.swift** and add the following method to the bottom of the file:

```swift
func cellVisitor(fn: (BoardLocation) ->()) {
  for column in 0..<boardSize {
    for row in 0..<boardSize {
      let location = BoardLocation(row: row, column: column)
      fn(location)
    }
  }
}
```

The above function iterates over every cell, applying the supplied function to each cell in turn. The easiest way to understand this method is to see it in action.

Within the same file, add a `clearBoard` method:

```swift
func clearBoard() {
  cellVisitor { self[$0] = .Empty }
}
```

The above invokes `cellVisitor`, passing the closure that follows as the method's `fn` argument. `cellVisitor` invokes this function for each cell on the board, with the `$0` argument (using the shorthand notation) being the `BoardLocation` for each iteration. The net result of `clearBoard` is a board with the value of every cell set to `Empty`.

Finally, go back to **ReversiBoard.swift** and add a call to clear the board at the top of `setInitialState()`:

```swift
clearBoard()
```

Now setting the initial state will clear the board before adding the pieces for the starting position.

> **NOTE:** `cellVisitor` is an implementation of a classic "Gang of Four" design pattern: the "Visitor Pattern" (http://en.wikipedia.org/wiki/Visitor_pattern).

Visualizing the board

The starter project includes a background image for the entire playing field. However, you need to create a view to place on top of each board square, which will contain the appropriate image for that square – white piece, black piece, or empty.

Add a Swift file to the **View** group, naming it **BoardSquare.swift**, and add the following code:

```swift
import Foundation
import UIKit

class BoardSquare: UIView {
  private let board: ReversiBoard
  private let location: BoardLocation
  private let blackView: UIImageView
  private let whiteView: UIImageView

  required init(coder aDecoder: NSCoder) {
    fatalError("init(coder:) has not been implemented")
  }

  init(frame: CGRect, location: BoardLocation,
                              board: ReversiBoard) {
    self.board = board
    self.location = location

    let blackImage = UIImage(named: "ReversiBlackPiece.png")
    blackView = UIImageView(image: blackImage)
    blackView.alpha = 0

    let whiteImage = UIImage(named: "ReversiWhitePiece.png")
    whiteView = UIImageView(image: whiteImage)
    whiteView.alpha = 0

    super.init(frame: frame)

    backgroundColor = UIColor.clearColor()

    addSubview(blackView)
    addSubview(whiteView)

    update()
  }

  private func update() {
```

```
    let state = board[location]
    whiteView.alpha = state == BoardCellState.White ? 1.0 : 0.0
    blackView.alpha = state == BoardCellState.Black ? 1.0 : 0.0
  }
}
```

This is a `UIView` subclass that you will use to render an individual board cell. The `init` method stores the various arguments passed to the initializer and creates the required UI elements. The `update` method updates the visibility of the white and black counter images, based on the state of the cell associated with this instance.

Now that you've taken care of a single cell, it's time to build the board.

Views within views

To render your board, you need 8×8 or 64 instances of `BoardSquare` properly positioned onscreen. To keep things organized, you'll set up another view that will hold the 64 squares.

Add a Swift file to the **View** group, naming it **ReversiBoardView.swift**, and add the following code:

```
import Foundation
import UIKit

class ReversiBoardView: UIView {
  required init(coder aDecoder: NSCoder) {
    fatalError("init(coder:) has not been implemented")
  }

  init(frame: CGRect, board: ReversiBoard) {
    super.init(frame: frame)

    let rowHeight = frame.size.height / CGFloat(board.boardSize)
    let columnWidth = frame.size.width /
                                       CGFloat(board.boardSize)

    board.cellVisitor {
      (location: BoardLocation) in
      let left = CGFloat(location.column) * columnWidth
      let top = CGFloat(location.row) * rowHeight
      let squareFrame = CGRect(x: left, y: top,
                      width: columnWidth, height: rowHeight)
      let square = BoardSquare(frame: squareFrame,
```

```
                              location: location, board: board)
      self.addSubview(square)
    }
  }
}
```

The code above computes the width and height of each square using the size of the board in relation to the number of cells. Notice the explicit type conversion required between Swift `Int` constants and `CGFloat`. Following this, the code uses `cellVisitor` to visit each of the cell locations, creating a `BoardSquare` instance for each at the required location.

Just like that, you're already putting your new `cellVisitor` method to good use!

Now that you've set up the view, it's time to put everything within the app's view controller.

Open **ViewController.swift** and add the following code inside the class definition:

```
private let board: ReversiBoard

required init(coder aDecoder: NSCoder) {
  board = ReversiBoard()
  board.setInitialState()

  super.init(coder: aDecoder)
}
```

The above simply creates an instance of the `ReversiBoard` as a constant in the `ViewController` initializer and sets the board to the starting position for the game.

Update the existing `viewDidLoad` as follows:

```
override func viewDidLoad() {
  super.viewDidLoad()

  let boardFrame = CGRect(x: 88, y: 152,
                          width: 600, height: 600)
  let boardView = ReversiBoardView(frame: boardFrame,
                                   board: board)
  view.addSubview(boardView)
}
```

This creates an instance of the `ReversiBoardView`, associates it with the `ReversiBoard` and adds it to the view hierarchy.

Yes, those are magic numbers in there that position the view… and no, I feel no shame! ☺

Build and run to witness the fruits of your labor:

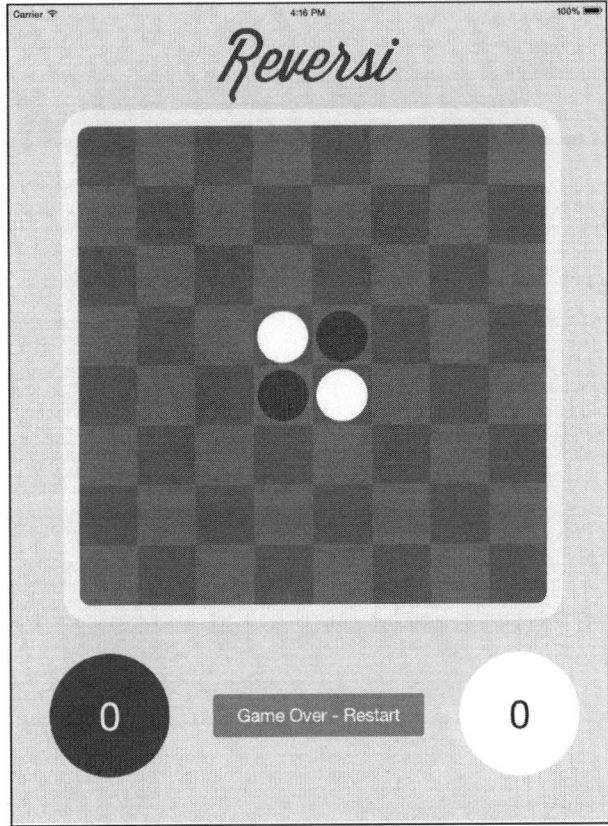

Your app is starting to look like a real game now, but your players will be itching to make their first move. You'll begin to address that in the next section.

> ### Swift vs. Objective-C
>
> The Swift and Objective-C implementations of `ReversiBoardView` and `BoardSquare` are similar. This is no great surprise, because the language has changed but UIKit has not (other than gaining a bunch of great new features with iOS 8!).
>
> One notable difference between the two implementations is the Swift version's `cellVisitor` method, which uses functional programming techniques to implement a visitor pattern. You can apply functional techniques with Objective-C, many of which are entirely possible with the use of blocks. However, the syntax results in something far less elegant. Contrast the use of the Swift `cellVisitor`:
>
> ```
> cellVisitor { self[$0] = .Empty }
> ```
>
> With an Objective-C equivalent:
>
> ```
> [self cellVisitor:^void (struct SHCBoardLocation location) {
>   [self setCellState:BoardCellStateEmpty
>                         forLocation:location];
> }];
> ```
>
> As you've seen throughout this book, Swift can make functional programming much more rewarding!

Adding user interaction

Currently, each of the 64 `BoardSquare` instances is associated with a specific row and column and each sets its initial state accordingly. You will expand this concept to allow the `Board` to notify the individual views of state changes.

Add a Swift file to the **Model** group, naming it **BoardDelegate.swift**, and add the following code:

```swift
import Foundation

protocol BoardDelegate {
  func cellStateChanged(location: BoardLocation)
}
```

You can use this delegate to notify the view when the state of a cell changes.

However, the `Board` has 64 associated `BoardSquare` instances. The standard delegation pattern, where you expose a property of the delegate type, only supports a single subscriber. To use the above delegate within the Reversi app, you need to add multicasting capabilities.

Add a Swift file to the **Model** group, naming it **DelegateMulticast.swift**, and add the following code:

```swift
class DelegateMulticast<T> {

  private var delegates = [T]()

  func addDelegate(delegate: T) {
    delegates.append(delegate)
  }

  func invokeDelegates(invocation: (T) -> ()) {
    for delegate in delegates {
      invocation(delegate)
    }
  }
}
```

The `DelegateMulticast` class contains an array of delegates, using the type parameter `T` to ensure they all conform to the correct protocol. `addDelegate` adds a delegate to the array of observers and `invokeDelegates` invokes the given function for each delegate.

If you have experience with C#, you may recognize the multicasting pattern as a C# "event." If not, you may find it easier to understand how this class works by seeing it in action!

Open **Board.swift** and add the following property:

```
private let boardDelegates = DelegateMulticast<BoardDelegate>()
```

The type parameter ensures that only delegates implementing the `BoardDelegate` protocol can be added to the multicast array.

Further down in the same file, add the following:

```
func addDelegate(delegate: BoardDelegate) {
  boardDelegates.addDelegate(delegate)
}
```

This provides a public method that allows classes to add themselves as delegates to the `Board`. The final step is to inform these delegates when the board state changes.

Within the subscript that has a `BoardLocation` argument type, add the following to the bottom of the setter implementation:

```
boardDelegates.invokeDelegates { $0.cellStateChanged(location) }
```

The above creates a closure that invokes the `cellStateChanged` delegate method on the `BoardDelegate` argument passed into the inline closure. As a result of the `for` loop within `invokeDelegates`, this method is then invoked on every delegate.

Now that you have a mechanism in place for multicasting to multiple delegates, it's time to put it to use.

Open **BoardSquare.swift** and update the class declaration to adopt the `BoardDelegate` protocol:

```
class BoardSquare: UIView, BoardDelegate {
```

Now that the class will conform to the protocol, you can add it as a delegate. Add the following line to the end of `init`:

```
board.addDelegate(self)
```

This will add the square to the multicast delegate so it will be notified when a cell changes state.

Each `BoardSquare` instance is associated with a specific location on the board. It only needs to update its state if the `cellStateChanged` delegate is invoked with the corresponding location.

Add the following delegate method implementation inside the class definition:

```
func cellStateChanged(location: BoardLocation) {
  if self.location == location {
    update()
  }
}
```

This ensures that the view is only updated when its associated cell state is updated. However, you'll find that the above code does not compile because you haven't provided an equality operator for the `BoardLocation` structure.

Open **BoardLocation.swift** and update the struct definition to adopt the `Equatable` protocol:

```
struct BoardLocation: Equatable {
```

This protocol defines a single function, the equals operator ==. Beneath the structure definition, add the implementation:

```
func == (lhs: BoardLocation, rhs: BoardLocation) -> Bool {
  return lhs.row == rhs.row && lhs.column == rhs.column
}
```

The above considers two `BoardLocation` instances equal if they have the same row and column. Note that you have to put this function **outside** the struct definition, right in the global scope!

You've done a fair bit of coding, and the base game models are all set. It's time to add some game logic!

Adding the game logic

Reversi is a turn-based game, meaning that play alternates between the white and black players. To support this, open **BoardCellState.swift** and add the following method to the enumeration:

```
func invert() -> BoardCellState {
  if self == Black {
    return White
  } else if self == White {
    return Black
  }
  
  assert(self != Empty, "cannot invert the empty state")
```

```
    return Empty
}
```

`BoardCellState` keeps track of the current state, and `invert` switches from black to white and vice-versa. It can also be a useful convenience method to swap play from one player to the next. You'll put this to use shortly.

Open **ReversiBoard.swift** and add the following property and methods to the `ReversiBoard` class:

```
private (set) var nextMove = BoardCellState.White

func isValidMove(location: BoardLocation) -> Bool {
  return self[location] == BoardCellState.Empty
}

func makeMove(location: BoardLocation) {
  self[location] = nextMove
  nextMove = nextMove.invert()
}
```

`nextMove` keeps track of whose turn it is. The default game rules are that the player controlling the white pieces moves first.

The first method, `isValidMove`, determines whether a player can make a move to a particular location on the board. For now you're going to let a player move to any empty cell.

The second method, `makeMove`, sets the cell at the given location to the current player's color and then uses `invert` to switch to the other player's turn.

The final step is to handle the user interactions that will execute the above code.

Handling tap gestures

Within **BoardSquare.swift**, add the following to the end of `init`:

```
let tapRecognizer = UITapGestureRecognizer(target: self,
                                           action: "cellTapped")
addGestureRecognizer(tapRecognizer)
```

This adds a tap gesture recognizer that invokes `cellTapped` when the gesture occurs.

Now, within the same class, add the function that handles the tap recognizer:

```
func cellTapped() {
  if board.isValidMove(location) {
    board.makeMove(location)
  }
}
```

When the user taps on a square, the game executes the above code. The code checks whether the move is valid and if it is, performs the move to set that cell's state to either black or white. Let's see this in action!

Build and run the application, and tap on any empty square on the board.

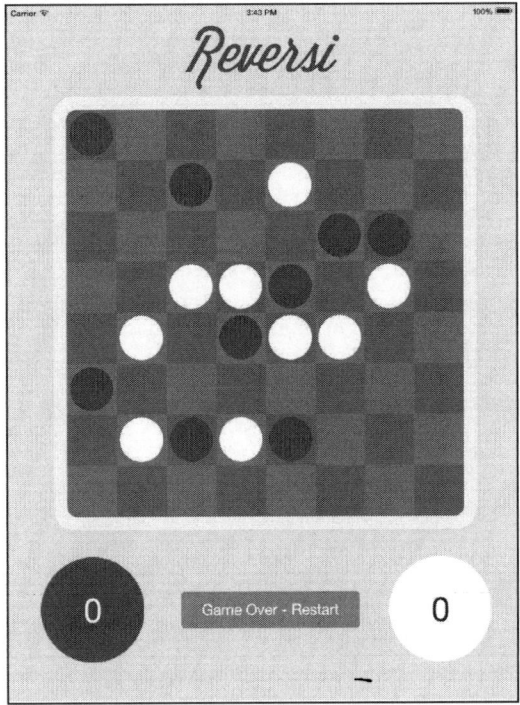

It's not exactly Reversi, but it's progress!

> ### Swift vs. Objective-C
>
> Probably the most significant difference between the Swift and Objective-C implementations of Reversi relates to the multicasting of messages to delegates. The Objective-C version uses message forwarding, which requires quite a few lines of code. In contrast, the Swift version is much simpler.
>
> The Swift `DelegateMulticast` class sidesteps the problem of dynamically invoking delegate methods by passing that responsibility back to the user of this class. Since you initialize the `DelegateMulticast` with a specific type, the compiler handles the type checking.
>
> In this app, you can be sure that all objects added to the multicast implement the `BoardDelegate` protocol. The `ReversiBoard` class is aware of the delegate protocol too and can invoke `cellStateChanged` directly:
>
> ```
> boardDelegates.invokeDelegates
>                    { $0.cellStateChanged(location) }
> ```
>
> As a result, `DelegateMulticast` remains generic and free from complex message forwarding logic.
>
> This code also touches upon Swift's use of protocols. In Chapter One, you saw how classes adopt the `Sequence` protocol to make them usable in `for-each` loops. Here, the `BoardLocation` adopts `Equatable` so you can compare its instances easily with the `==` operator.
>
> There are other protocols within Swift that fulfill a similar purpose. For example, a class can adopt `LogicValue`, allowing you to use it directly as a condition within an `if` statement.

Detailed game logic

In Reversi, when you play a piece, it and another of your pieces must surround one or more of your opponent's pieces in a straight line horizontally, vertically or diagonally.

To illustrate this, consider the playing board, with black set to play next:

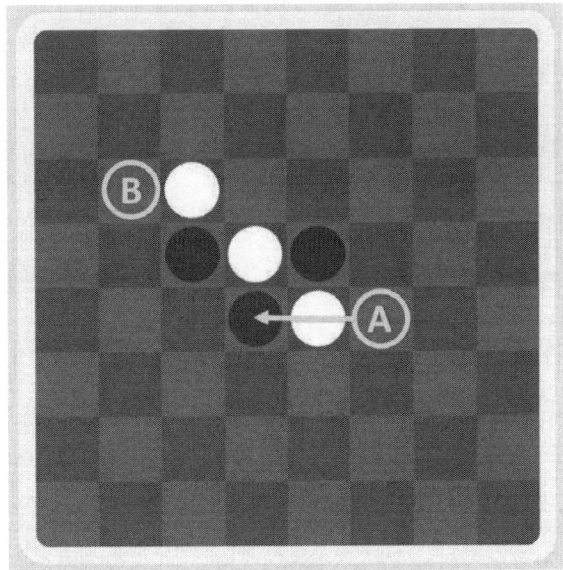

The position marked **A** on the board is a valid move, because it would surround a white piece to the left. However, **B** is not a valid move, as it would not surround any white pieces in a straight line in any direction.

So to determine whether a move is valid, you need to check for surrounded pieces in eight different directions.

While this might sound like a lot of work, the logic applied for all eight directions is exactly the same: one or more pieces must be surrounded. You can use this commonality to come up with a concise validity check.

First, add the generic concept of a "move direction." Add a Swift file to the Model group, naming it **MoveDirection.swift**. Add the following code to the file:

```swift
enum MoveDirection {
  case North, South, East, West,
       NorthEast, NorthWest, SouthEast, SouthWest

  func move(loc: BoardLocation) -> BoardLocation {
    switch self {
    case .North:
      return BoardLocation(row: loc.row-1, column: loc.column)
    case .South:
      return BoardLocation(row: loc.row+1, column: loc.column)
    case .East:
      return BoardLocation(row: loc.row, column: loc.column-1)
```

```
    case .West:
      return BoardLocation(row: loc.row, column: loc.column+1)
    case .NorthEast:
      return BoardLocation(row: loc.row-1, column: loc.column-1)
    case .NorthWest:
      return BoardLocation(row: loc.row-1, column: loc.column+1)
    case .SouthEast:
      return BoardLocation(row: loc.row+1, column: loc.column-1)
    case .SouthWest:
      return BoardLocation(row: loc.row+1, column: loc.column+1)
    }
  }

  static let directions: [MoveDirection] = [
    .North, .South, .East, .West,
    .NorthEast, .NorthWest, .SouthWest, .SouthEast
  ]
}
```

This enumeration defines the directions for the eight adjacent squares from a board location. It also has a convenient `move` method that will calculate the new BoardLocation from an existing location and the current direction.

You need the static `directions` constant containing every direction because Swift currently doesn't have a mechanism for iterating over the values of an enumeration.

Within **ReversiBoard.swift,** add the following method inside the class definition:

```
func moveSurroundsCounters(location: BoardLocation,
    direction: MoveDirection, toState: BoardCellState) -> Bool {
  var index = 1
  var currentLocation = direction.move(location)

  while isWithinBounds(currentLocation) {
    let currentState = self[currentLocation]
    if index == 1 {
      // Immediate neighbors must be the opponent's color
      if currentState != toState.invert() {
        return false
      }
    } else {
      // if the player's color is reached, the move is valid
      if currentState == toState {
        return true
      }

      // if an empty cell is reached give up!
      if currentState == BoardCellState.Empty {
```

```
      return false
    }
  }

  index++

  // move to the next cell
  currentLocation = direction.move(currentLocation)
}

return false
}
```

This method determines whether a move to a specific location on the board would surround one or more of the opponent's pieces. Within the `while` loop, the code checks the required conditions:

- The neighboring cell must be occupied by a piece of the opposing color,

  and

- The following cell is the opposing color, in which case the while loop continues,

  or

- The following cell is the player's color, which means a group is surrounded.

Finally, you need to update the logic within `isValidMove`. At the moment, it only checks whether the given location is an empty cell.

Replace `isValidMove` with the following methods:

```
func isValidMove(location: BoardLocation) -> Bool {
  return isValidMove(location, toState: nextMove)
}

private func isValidMove(location: BoardLocation,
                         toState: BoardCellState) -> Bool {
  // check the cell is empty
  if self[location] != BoardCellState.Empty {
    return false
  }

  // test whether the move surrounds any of the opponents pieces
  for direction in MoveDirection.directions {
    if moveSurroundsCounters(location,
                  direction: direction, toState: toState) {
      return true
```

```
      }
    }
    return false
}
```

As you can see, the above code splits the `isValidMove` method into two, and you'll find out why shortly. The original check that the cell at the given location is empty is still in place, but you have added a second condition, using the `MoveDirections.directions` array to iterate over all the possible directions in which this move could surround some of the opponent's pieces. As soon as the method finds a direction that matches this condition, it returns true—there is no point in checking further.

Build and run the application to see this code in action:

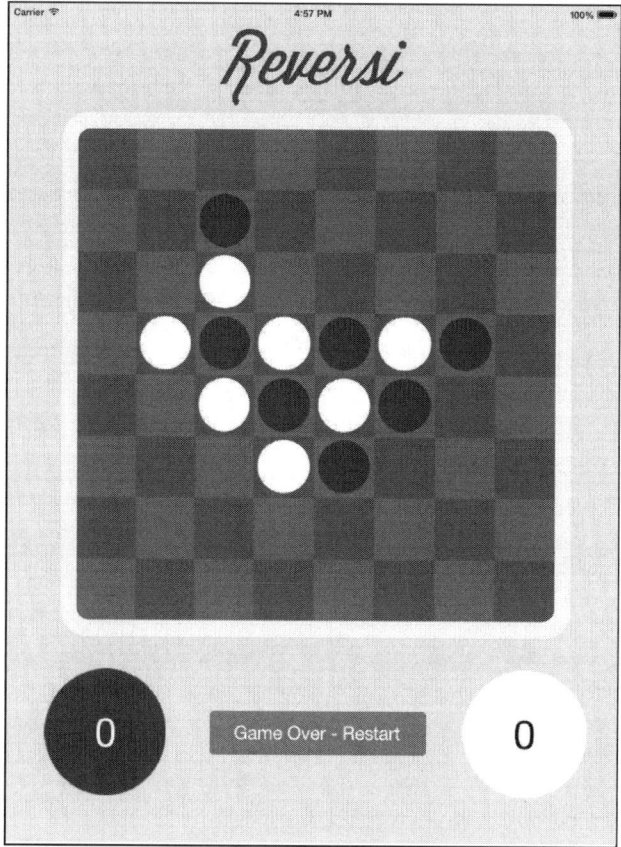

You will now find that you are much more restricted in terms of where you can place pieces on the board.

But it is *still* not quite Reversi!

It's a key rule of Reversi that you must flip any pieces surrounded by pieces of the opposite color. All reversed pieces then show the opposite color and the player controlling that color can use them in later moves. Let's put this rule into action.

Add the following method to the `ReversiBoard` class:

```
private func flipOpponentsCounters(location: BoardLocation,
    direction: MoveDirection, toState: BoardCellState) {
  // is this a valid move?
  if !moveSurroundsCounters(location,
                direction: direction, toState: toState) {
    return
  }

  let opponentsState = toState.invert()
  var currentState = BoardCellState.Empty
  var currentLocation = location

  // flip counters until the edge of the board is reached or
  // a piece with the current state is reached
  do {
    currentLocation = direction.move(currentLocation)
    currentState = self[currentLocation]
    self[currentLocation] = toState
  } while (isWithinBounds(currentLocation) &&
         currentState == opponentsState)
}
```

The above method makes further use of the `MoveDirection` enumeration; after checking whether the move will surround any pieces in the given direction, a short `do-while` loop goes about the business of flipping the opponent's pieces.

To put this method to use, update `makeMove` as follows:

```
func makeMove(location: BoardLocation) {
  self[location] = nextMove

  for direction in MoveDirection.directions {
    flipOpponentsCounters(location,
                direction: direction, toState: nextMove)
  }

  nextMove = nextMove.invert()
}
```

Now the method flips any pieces that are surrounded in any of the eight directions.

Build, run and rejoice!

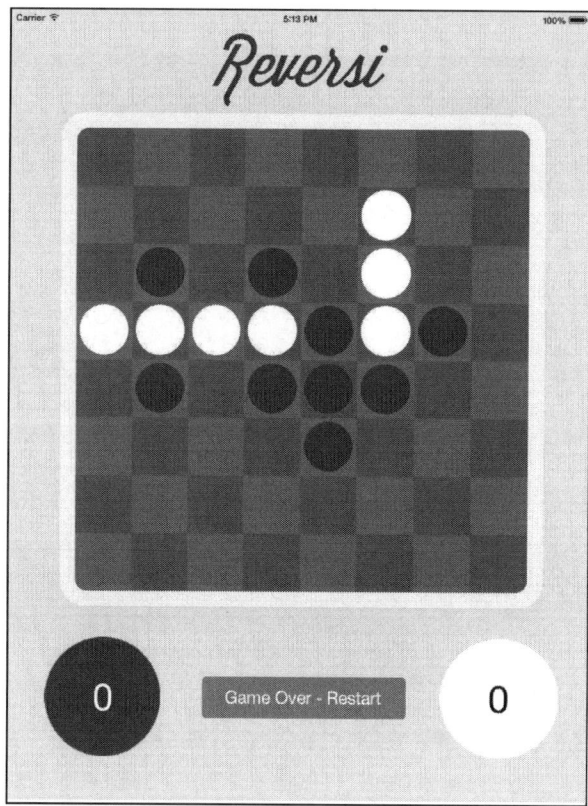

That's much more like a game of Reversi!

But who's winning? Next, you'll tally the score.

> ## Swift vs. Objective-C
>
> Both the Swift and Objective-C versions of Reversi separate the act of navigating the board from the logic that determines whether counters are surrounded. However, the implementations are quite different.
>
> The Objective-C code uses a number of blocks that mutate the values of the row and column integers that are passed by reference.
>
> ```
> BoardNavigationFunction BoardNavigationFunctionRight =
>                   ^(NSInteger* c, NSInteger* r) {
> ```

```
        (*c)++;
    };
```

The Swift implementation, which represents the directions as an enumeration that is able to perform the navigation itself, is much clearer and provides better encapsulation.

Keeping score

Reversi is a competitive game, so your app version definitely needs a scoring mechanism. Each player's score is simply the number of pieces that player has on the board. The `Board` class already has a neat cell visitor concept that you can put to good use computing the scores.

Open **Board.swift** and add the following method to the class:

```swift
func countMatches(fn: (BoardLocation) -> Bool) -> Int {
    var count = 0
    cellVisitor { if fn($0) { count++ } }
    return count
}
```

The method counts the number of cells that match the supplied condition.

Open **ReversiBoard.swift** and add the following to the end of `makeMove`:

```swift
whiteScore = countMatches { self[$0] == BoardCellState.White }
blackScore = countMatches { self[$0] == BoardCellState.Black }
```

The app will now execute the above each time a player makes a move. You use `countMatches` to count the number of cells that contain a black or white disk. That was easy!

The next task is to inform the view that the state has changed so that it can update the UI to reflect the current score.

Add a Swift file to the **Model** group, naming it **ReversiBoardDelegate.swift**, and add the following code to it:

```swift
import Foundation

protocol ReversiBoardDelegate {
```

```
  func boardStateChanged()
}
```

This defines a protocol that you're going to use to implement the delegation pattern.

Open **ReversiBoard.swift** and add the following to the top of the class, with the other variables and constants:

```
private let reversiBoardDelegates =
                DelegateMulticast<ReversiBoardDelegate>()
```

This uses exactly the same delegate multicasting mechanism you saw previously.

Further down the same file, add the following method:

```
func addDelegate(delegate: ReversiBoardDelegate) {
  reversiBoardDelegates.addDelegate(delegate)
}
```

This provides a mechanism for adding delegates that you will inform of state changes.

Within the same file, add the following to the bottom of `makeMove`:

```
reversiBoardDelegates.invokeDelegates { $0.boardStateChanged() }
```

At this point, you've updated the board state and scores so it makes sense to inform any delegates. As a reminder, the above code invokes `boardStateChanged` on every delegate you've added.

You now have a board that updates the current scores and informs delegates, but you haven't added any delegates. It's time to rectify this!

Open **ViewController.swift** and update the class definition to adopt this newly added protocol:

```
class ViewController: UIViewController, ReversiBoardDelegate {
```

Within the body of `ViewController`, add an implementation of the protocol:

```
func boardStateChanged() {
  blackScore.text = "\(board.blackScore)"
  whiteScore.text = "\(board.whiteScore)"
}
```

This simply updates the text of the two `UILabel`s to reflect the current score.

Add the following to the end of `init`:

```
board.addDelegate(self)
```

This adds the view controller as a delegate so as to invoke the method you just added.

The final step is to ensure that the UI reflects the initial state when a user launches the application. Within the same file, add the following to the end of viewDidLoad:

```
boardStateChanged()
```

Since each player gets 2 pieces on the board to start, this will start the UI with a score of 2 for each player.

Build, run and have a go:

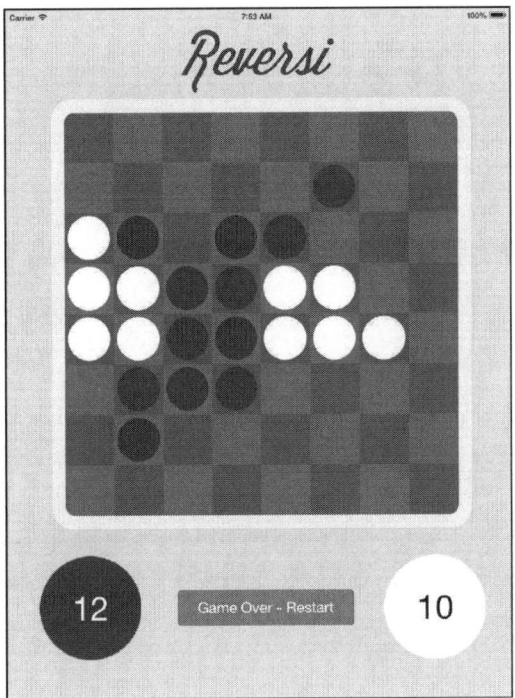

The game is almost complete! :]

Swift vs. Objective-C

Once again, your use of closures and functional programming within your Swift implementation of Reversi has resulted in elegant and concise code. The use of `countMatches` to determine the score for each player is a joy to behold!

However, the little things can also make a big difference.

Here is the Objective-C code for formatting the score:

```
_whiteScore.text = [NSString stringWithFormat:@"%d",
                                    _board.whiteScore];
_blackScore.text = [NSString stringWithFormat:@"%d",
                                    _board.blackScore];
```

And here is the same code in Swift:

```
blackScore.text = "\(board.blackScore)"
whiteScore.text = "\(board.whiteScore)"
```

I know which I prefer!

Adding UI flair

You're going to take a break from game logic to add a bit of UI flair.

Open **BoardSquare.swift** and change `update()` as follows:

```
private func update() {
  let state = board[location]

  UIView.animateWithDuration(0.2, animations: {
    switch state {
    case .White:
      self.whiteView.alpha = 1.0
      self.blackView.alpha = 0.0
      self.whiteView.transform = CGAffineTransformIdentity
      self.blackView.transform =
                    CGAffineTransformMakeTranslation(0, 20)
    case .Black:
      self.whiteView.alpha = 0.0
      self.blackView.alpha = 1.0
      self.whiteView.transform =
                    CGAffineTransformMakeTranslation(0, -20)
      self.blackView.transform = CGAffineTransformIdentity
    case .Empty:
      self.whiteView.alpha = 0.0
```

```
            self.blackView.alpha = 0.0
        }
    })
}
```

Previously, this method set the `alpha` property of the black and white image views directly. The updated form above uses a brief (0.2-second) animation to set the alpha and also apply a small transition.

Build and run to see this action:

There is now a subtle but pleasing transition as cells change color. The above picture really doesn't do it justice!

This is a simple effect, but makes a big difference. I'm sure you can come up with some more funky variations.

Now, back to business! The final step is to determine when one or the other player has won the game.

Handling the end-game

Well, there's good news—and bad news—about the end-game condition.

First, the bad news: In Reversi, determining the end-game condition is not as simple as checking whether or not the board is full of pieces. The game really ends when neither player can play a piece that would surround and flip one or more of their opponent's pieces.

Now, the good news: This is a very easy condition to check!

Open **Board.swift** and add the following method to the class:

```swift
func anyCellsMatchCondition(fn: (BoardLocation)->Bool) -> Bool {
  for column in 0..<boardSize {
    for row in 0..<boardSize {
      if fn(BoardLocation(row: row, column: column)) {
        return true
      }
    }
  }
  return false
}
```

The above iterates over every cell until the supplied function evaluates to true. If this happens, `anyCellsMatchCondition` exits immediately—there is no point in checking further!

Open **ReversiBoard.swift** and add the following variable to the top of the class:

```swift
private (set) var gameHasFinished = false
```

Further down the same file, add the following within `makeMove`, just before `whiteScore` and `blackScore` are re-calculated:

```swift
gameHasFinished = checkIfGameHasFinished()
```

Each time a player takes a turn, the above uses `anyCellsMatchCondition` to check whether the game meets the end condition and updates the variable you just added. All you have to do is add the required logic!

Next, add the following methods to the `ReversiBoard` class implementation:

```swift
private func checkIfGameHasFinished() -> Bool {
  return !canPlayerMakeMove(BoardCellState.Black) &&
    !canPlayerMakeMove(BoardCellState.White)
```

```
}

private func canPlayerMakeMove(toState:BoardCellState) -> Bool {
  return anyCellsMatchCondition
                  { self.isValidMove($0, toState: toState) }
}
```

The first method tests whether black or white can make a move. If neither is able to, the game is over. The second method determines whether a given player has any valid moves to make on any location on the board. `anyCellsMatchCondition` makes it easy to implement the end-game logic!

There's one small wrinkle in the game logic: it's possible for one play to run out of moves but the game can still continue. For example, if black takes a turn and white has no legal moves, white has to pass and it becomes black's turn again.

Add the following method to the `ReversiBoard` class to handle switching turns:

```
func switchTurns() {
  var intendedNextMove = nextMove.invert()

  // only switch turns if the player can make a move
  if canPlayerMakeMove(intendedNextMove) {
    nextMove = intendedNextMove
  }
}
```

Before changing `nextMove` to the next player, this method checks that the player has a valid move to make.

Now you need to call this method. In `makeMove`, replace the line that calls `nextMove.invert()` directly with the following:

```
switchTurns()
```

This will call the new method to handle the turn-switching logic.

It remains only to update the UI. Open **ViewController.swift** and add the following to the end of `boardStateChanged`:

```
restartButton.hidden = !board.gameHasFinished
```

This displays the restart button when the game ends.

Build and run your app. You can play a complete game, although you'll still have to play against yourself if you don't have a willing friend nearby:

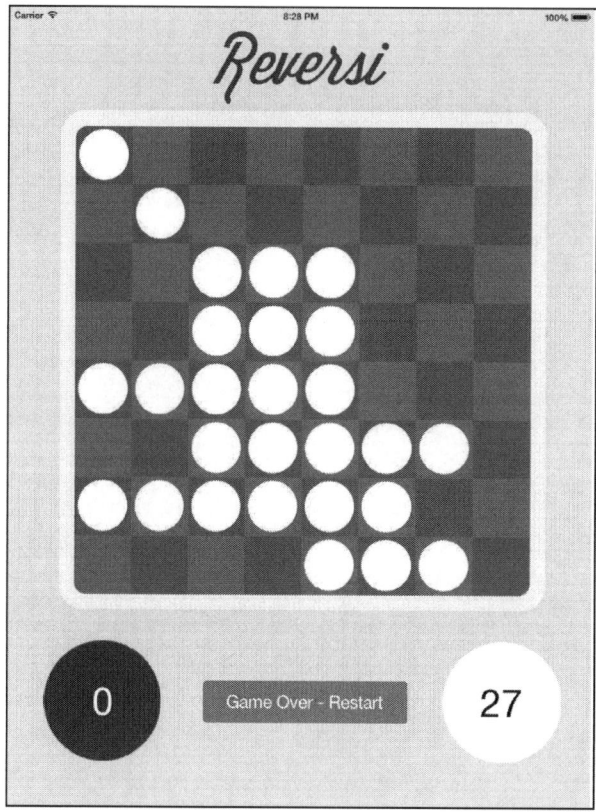

In the screenshot above, black has had a very poor game, with white taking every piece. You can see that the app has correctly determined the end-game state and is displaying the restart button.

The button indicates that tapping on it will restart the game. You'll now add code to deliver on that promise.

Within **ViewController.swift,** add the following to the end of `viewDidLoad`:

```
restartButton.addTarget(self, action: "restartTapped",
  forControlEvents: UIControlEvents.TouchUpInside)
```

Then further down the same file, add the following:

```
func restartTapped() {
  if board.gameHasFinished {
    board.setInitialState()
    boardStateChanged()
  }
}
```

You can now play over and over and over again to your heart's content!

After a few games, it's apparent that playing against yourself always guarantees a win. If you're losing against yourself, then you've got bigger issues at hand! :]

In the next and last section of this tutorial, you're going to use Swift to create a computer opponent that employs a simple algorithm to make its move.

Adding a computer opponent

Your computer player will rely on a "brute force" strategy that evaluates all of the possible moves and chooses the one that results in the highest score. To support this, you'll add code that clones the current board state so you can test the different scenarios without affecting the state of the principal board.

Open **Board.swift** and add the following initializer:

```
init(board: Board) {
  cells = board.cells;
}
```

This initializer gives you the option of providing a starting state for a board. Remember that Swift arrays are structures, which means that the newly created board will now have a copy of the `cells` array from an existing board.

> **NOTE:** Swift uses copy-on-write for structures, which means that the cells array will not be copied within the initializer. Instead a copy will be made when either array is mutated. This is a very powerful performance optimization!

Next, open **ReversiBoard.swift** and add the following initializers:

```
override init() {
  super.init()
}

init(board: ReversiBoard) {
  super.init(board: board)
  nextMove = board.nextMove
  blackScore = board.blackScore
  whiteScore = board.whiteScore
}
```

The first initializer with no parameters just calls through to Board's initializer. This creates a blank board as usual.

The second initializer delegates to the `Board` superclass to copy the cells, and then copies the `ReversiBoard`-specific properties.

It's time to add the computer opponent!

Add a new Swift file to the **Model** group, naming it **ComputerOpponent.swift**, and add the following code to the file:

```
import Foundation

class ComputerOpponent : ReversiBoardDelegate {
  private let board: ReversiBoard
  private let color: BoardCellState

  init(board: ReversiBoard, color: BoardCellState) {
    self.board = board
    self.color = color

    board.addDelegate(self)
  }
}
```

You give the computer player a color that indicates whether it plays on the black or the white turn. The computer player also adds itself as a delegate to the `ReversiBoard` so it can determine when to make its move.

Next, add the following global utility function just above the class declaration:

```
func delay(delay: Double, closure: ()->()) {
  let time = dispatch_time(
    DISPATCH_TIME_NOW,
    Int64(delay * Double(NSEC_PER_SEC))
  )
  dispatch_after(time, dispatch_get_main_queue(), closure)
}
```

This provides an elegant mechanism for wrapping up the Grand Central Dispatch API to run the code passed in as a closure expression after some number of seconds.

Within the body of the `ComputerOpponent` class add the following method:

```
func boardStateChanged() {
  if board.nextMove == color {
    delay(1.0) {
      self.makeNextMove()
    }
  }
}
```

The `ReversiBoard` invokes the above, via the `ReversiBoardDelegate` protocol, each time a player takes their turn. If the next move belongs to the computer's color, you use your `delay` function to pause before the computer takes its turn. This pause is purely cosmetic—it makes it appear that the computer is thinking! Little tricks like this really add polish to your app.

Finally, add the following methods:

```
private func makeNextMove() {
  var bestScore = Int.min
  var bestLocation: BoardLocation?

  board.cellVisitor {
    (location: BoardLocation) in
    if self.board.isValidMove(location) {
      let score = self.scoreForMove(location)
      if (score > bestScore) {
        bestScore = score
        bestLocation = location
      }
    }
  }

  if bestScore > Int.min {
```

```
      board.makeMove(bestLocation!)
    }
}

private func scoreForMove(location:BoardLocation) -> Int {
  let testBoard = ReversiBoard(board: board)

  testBoard.makeMove(location)
  let score = color == BoardCellState.White ?
    testBoard.whiteScore - testBoard.blackScore :
    testBoard.blackScore - testBoard.whiteScore;

  return score
}
```

The first method uses `cellVisitor` to iterate over all of the cells. At each location, it determines the score that would result from making that move, keeping track of which move gives the best score. Once it's visited all the cells, the method makes the best move.

For Reversi, finding the "best" move out of all possible moves is fairly simple. The goal of the game is to occupy as many cells on the board as possible, so the "best" move is (usually) the one that leaves the board in a state with as many of the player's pieces as possible.

The second method above computes the score for a particular move. It does this by cloning the board, making the move and then determining the difference in score between the white and black player.

Now put the computer into action. Open **ViewController.swift** and add the following property:

```
private let computer: ComputerOpponent
```

Within `init`, add the following just before the call to `super.init`:

```
computer = ComputerOpponent(board: board,
                    color: BoardCellState.Black)
```

That's your computer opponent—all ready to play.

Build and run, and see how you fare against the computer!

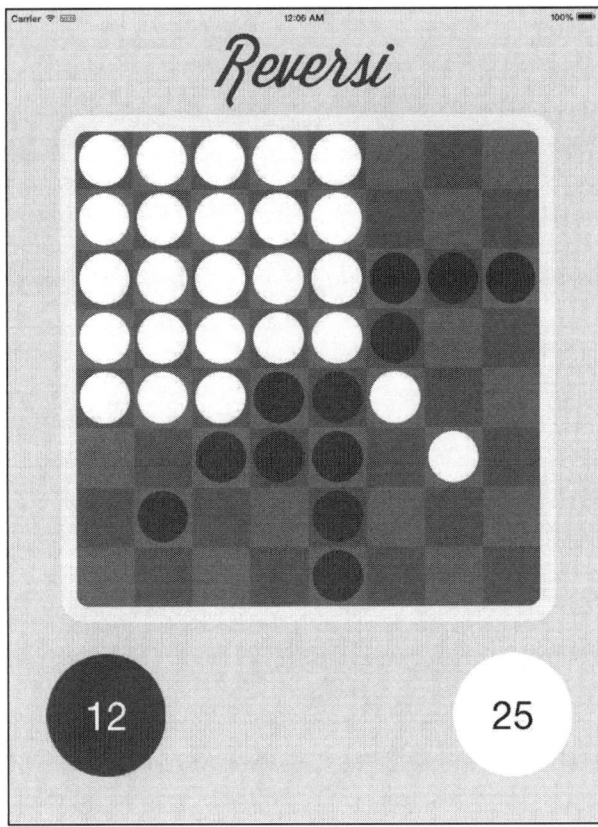

A quick tip to beat the computer: The edges and corners of the board are the most valuable squares to occupy, as they are harder for your opponent to surround. With a good corner fortress, you'll have a great chance of beating the computer!

> ### Swift vs. Objective-C
>
> The board-cloning code in the Objective-C implementation uses the `memcpy` function as follows:
>
> ```
> SHCBoard* board = [[[self class] allocWithZone:zone] init];
> memcpy(board->_board, _board, sizeof(NSUInteger) * 8 * 8);
> ```
>
> That's a bit ugly! The Swift equivalent is much cleaner:
>
> ```
> cells = board.cells;
> ```
>
> The above code is the reason why the Swift implementation uses a 1-dimensional array of cells rather than a 2-dimenisional array. The computer opponent repeatedly clones the board to determine the score of each potential move, so the performance of the copy operation is critical. Copying a 2-dimensional array requires copying an array of arrays, which is much slower.

Challenge

I hope you've enjoyed this last tutorial where you have re-implemented an Objective-C application with Swift. Along the way, you've witnessed many diflferences in the two languages and seen for yourself how the Swift implementation is more elegant and easier to understand.

It's time for one final comparison. Have you noticed that the Swift implementation of Reversi has far fewer lines of code than its Objective-C counterpart? Fewer lines of code means less code for you to write and faster app development. Good times!

Are you ready for your final challenge? The Objective-C version of Reversi has a more advanced computer player that uses the minimax algorithm (https://en.wikipedia.org/wiki/Minimax) to search ahead over multiple turns. Why not finish off the Swift implementation by adding this to your code?

Check out part 2 of the original post (http://www.raywenderlich.com/29248/how-to-develop-an-ipad-board-game-app-part-22) for more details on the Objective-C implementation.

Chapter 10: Swift Language Quick Reference

By Colin Eberhardt

This final chapter is a simple one. It is intended as a quick reference if you find yourself struggling to recall the syntax of a particular language feature.

In the following pages, you'll find a section and accompanying code for each of the major Swift features. You'll see examples of basic language features, control structures and data structures. You can paste the code from any section into a playground to observe how the feature works.

Language basics

```swift
// variables can be updated
var variableNumber: Int = 1
variableNumber = variableNumber + 1

// constants cannot be updated
let constNumber: Int = 1
// constNumber = constNumber + 1 <- error!

// inferred type
let inferredInt = 1

// Swift types
let int: Int = 20
let double: Double = 3.5
let float: Float = 4.5
let bool: Bool = false
let str: String = "Hello, Swift!"

// explicit type conversion
let pi = 3.1415
let multiplier = 2
let twoPi = pi * Double(multiplier)
```

Tips:

- You should define values as constants with `let` wherever possible. This will help make your code more robust and easier to follow for humans, as well as allow for more compiler optimizations.

- Swift is strongly typed, so be prepared to do more explicit type conversions than you may be used to in other languages.

Basic control structures

```swift
for index in 1..<3 {
  // loops with index taking values 1,2
}

for index in 1...3 {
  // loops with index taking values 1,2,3
}

for index in stride(from: 10, through: 20, by: 2){
  // loops from 10 to 20 (inclusive) in steps of 2
}

var index = 0
while index < 5 {
  // loops 5 times
  index++
}

index = 0
do {
  // loops 5 times
  index++
} while index < 5

// if/else
let temperature = 45
if temperature > 60 {
  println("It's hot!")
} else if temperature > 40 {
  println("It's warm.")
} else {
  println("It's chilly.")
}
```

Tuples

```
let tuple = (1, 3, 5)    // inferred type (Int, Int, Int)
let tuple2 = (1, 5.0)    // inferred type (Int, Double)
let tuple3: (Double, Double) = (5, 6)

// indexing a tuple
println(tuple.0)
println(tuple.1)
println(tuple.2)

// a tuple with named elements
let product = (id: 24, name: "Swift Book")
println(product.name)

// decomposing a tuple
let (x, y, z) = tuple
println("\(x), \(y), \(z)") // "1, 3, 5"
```

Tip: Tuples are great for creating quick and easy composite types. In many cases, a struct is a better choice with stronger type safety and more functionality.

Arrays

```swift
// empty array creation
let empty1 = [String]()
let empty2 = Array<String>()
let empty3: [String] = []

// a constant array with inferred type
let animals = ["cat", "dog", "chicken"]
// animals.append("cow")   <- error!
// animals[2] = "fish"     <- error!

// a variable array with explicit type
var mutableAnimals: [String] = ["cat", "dog", "chicken"]
mutableAnimals.append("cow")
mutableAnimals[2] = "fish"

// iteration
for animal in animals {
  println(animal)
}

// array API
animals[0]                          // "cat"
animals[1..<3]                      // "dog", "chicken"
animals.count                       // "3"
contains(animals, "cat")            // true
mutableAnimals.removeAtIndex(0)     // "cat"

// functional API
animals.map { $0.uppercaseString }    // "CAT", "DOG", ...
animals.filter { $0.hasPrefix("c") }  // "cat", "chicken"
animals.sorted { $0 < $1 }            // "cat", "chicken", ...

// bridged NSArray API
let nsArray = animals as NSArray
nsArray.objectAtIndex(2)            // "chicken"
```

Tip: Remember, arrays use value semantics and are passed by value into methods and functions.

Dictionaries

```swift
// empty dictionary creation
let empty1 = [Int:String]()
let empty2 = Dictionary<Int, String>()
let empty3: [Int:String] = [:]

// a constant dictionary with inferred type
let animals = [24 : "cat", 36 : "dog"]
// animals[88] = "fish"    <- error!

// a variable dictionary with explicit type
var mutableAnimals: [Int:String] = [24 : "cat", 36 : "dog"]
mutableAnimals[55] = "fish"
mutableAnimals[24] = "chicken"

// dictionary API
animals[24]                // "cat"
animals[1]                 // nil
animals.count              // "2"
mutableAnimals.removeValueForKey(24) // "chicken"

// dictionary values are returned as optionals
animals[24]!.hasPrefix("c") // true

// iteration
for (key, value) in animals {
  println(key)
  println(value)
}
```

Tip: Remember, dictionaries use value semantics and are passed by value into methods and functions.

Optionals

```swift
// an optional variable
var maybeString: String?   // defaults to nil
maybeString = nil          // can be assigned a nil value
maybeString = "fish"       // can be assigned a value

// unwrapping an optional
if let unwrappedString = maybeString {
  // unwrappedString is a String rather than an optional String
  println(unwrappedString.hasPrefix("f")) // "true"
} else {
  println("maybeString is nil")
}

// forced unwrapping - fails at runtime if the optional is nil
if maybeString!.hasPrefix("f") {
  println("maybeString starts with 'f'")
}

// optional chaining, returning an optional with the
// result of hasPrefix, which is then unwrapped
if let hasPrefix = maybeString?.hasPrefix("f") {
  if hasPrefix {
    println("maybeString starts with 'f'")
  }
}

// nil coalescing
var anOptional: Int?
var coalesced = anOptional ?? 3 // nil value coalesced to 3
```

Implicitly unwrapped optionals

```
// an implicitly unwrapped optional variable
var maybeString: String!
maybeString = nil
maybeString = "fish"

// methods invoked directly, failing at runtime
// if the optional is nil
if maybeString.hasPrefix("f") {
  println("maybeString starts with 'f'")
}else {
  println("maybeString does not start with an 'f'")
}
```

Tips:
- Implicitly unwrapped optionals are useful in classes and structs where you won't have a property's value available in the initializer, but will have a value later before it is used.

- Remember, implicitly unwrapped optionals are still optionals – use with them with care since they remove a bit of safety around nil values!

Switch

```swift
let bit = Bit.Zero

// a simple switch statement on an enum
switch bit {
case .Zero:
  println("zero")
case .One:
  println("one")
}

// interval matching
let time = 45
switch time {
case 0..<60:
  println("A few seconds ago")
case 60..<(60 * 4):
  println("A few minutes ago")
default:                   // default required in order
  println("Ages ago!")     // to be exhaustive
}

// tuples and value bindings
let boardLocation = (2, 5)
switch boardLocation {
case (3, 4), (3, 3), (4, 3), (4, 4):
  println("central location")
case (let x, let y):
  println("\(x), \(y) is not in the center")
}
```

Tip: Remember, switch cases in Swift must be exhaustive and cover all possible cases.

Enums

```swift
// enum declaration
enum Direction {
  case North, South, East, West
}

// assignment
var direction = Direction.North
direction = .South    // enum type inferred

// switching on enums
switch direction {
case .North:
  println("Going North")
default:
  println("Going someplace else!")
}

// advanced enumerations - using generics
enum Result<T> {
  case Failure
  // enumeration member with associated value
  case Success(T)
}

// creating an instance - where the type T is an Int
var result = Result.Success(22)

// switching and extracting the associated value
switch result {
case .Failure:
  println("Operation failed")
case .Success(let value):
  println("Operation returned value \(value)")
}
```

Functions

```swift
// a simple function
func voidFunc(message: String) {
  println(message);
}
voidFunc("Hello, Swift!")

// a function that returns a value
func multiply(arg1: Double, arg2: Double) -> Double {
  return arg1 * arg2
}
let result = multiply(20.0, 35.2)

// external and default parameters names
func multiplyTwo(#first: Double,
    andSecond second: Double) -> Double {
  return first * second
}
let result2 = multiplyTwo(first: 20.0, andSecond: 35.2)

// in-out parameters
func square(inout number: Double) {
  number *= number
}
var number = 4.0
square(&number) // number = 16

// function types
let myFunc: (Double, Double) -> Double = multiplyTwo

// a generic function
func areEqual<T: Equatable>(op1: T, op2: T) -> Bool {
  return op1 == op2
}
```

Closures

```swift
let animals = ["fish", "cat", "chicken", "dog"]

animals.sorted({
  (one: String, two: String) -> Bool in
  return one > two
})

animals.sorted({
  (one, two) -> Bool in    // inferred argument types
  return one > two
})

animals.sorted({
  (one, two) in            // inferred return type
  return one > two
})

animals.sorted({
  // no brackets around parameters
  one, two in return one > two
})

animals.sorted({
  // no return keyword
  one, two in one > two
})

// shorthand arguments
animals.sorted({ $0 > $1 })

// trailing closure
animals.sorted() { $0 > $1 }
animals.sorted { $0 > $1 }
```

Classes and protocols

```swift
public class BaseClass {
  private let id: Int            // private constant property

  init(id: Int) {
    self.id = id
  }
}

protocol NamedType {
  var name: String { get }       // a property with a getter
}

public class Animal: BaseClass, NamedType {
  private(set) var name: String  // variable with public getter
                                 // and private setter
  var size: Double = 45.0        // implicit internal property
  public let fullName: String    // public constant property

  init(id: Int, name: String, fullName: String) {
    // all properties initialized before base init invoked
    self.name = name;
    self.fullName = fullName;

    // super initializer invoked
    super.init(id: id)

    // methods on self can now be called
  }
}

// creating an instance
var animal = Animal(id: 24, name: "cat",
                    fullName: "Felis catus")
```

Conclusion

We hope this book has helped you get up-to-speed with Swift! You now know everything you need to know to begin coding iOS apps in Swift, so we encourage you give it a try.

If you have any questions or comments as you continue to use Swift, please stop by our forums at http://www.raywenderlich.com/forums.

Thank you again for purchasing this book. Your continued support is what makes the tutorials, books, videos and other things we do at raywenderlich.com possible—we truly appreciate it!

Best of luck with your Swift adventures,

> - Matt, Colin, Erik, Bradley and Greg
>
> The *Swift by Tutorials* team

Made in the USA
San Bernardino, CA
03 April 2015